African American Female
Speech Communities

African American Female Speech Communities

Varieties of Talk

Barbara Hill Hudson

BERGIN & GARVEY
Westport, Connecticut • London

Library of Congress Cataloging-in-Publication Data

Hudson, Barbara Hill, 1940–
    African American female speech communities : varieties of talk / Barbara Hill Hudson.
        p.   cm.
    Includes bibliographical references and index.
    ISBN 0–89789–506–1 (alk. paper)
    1. Afro-American women—Languages.   2. English language—Spoken English—United
States.   3. English language—Social aspects—United States.   4. English language—
Variation—United States.   5. Afro-American women—Social life and customs.
6. Language and culture—United States.   7. Black English—United States.   8. Afro-
Americans—Languages.   9. Americanisms.   I. Title.
    PE3102.N44 H84   2001
    306.44′082′0973—dc21   00–048603

British Library Cataloguing in Publication Data is available.

Library of Congress Catalog Card Number: 00–048603
ISBN: 0–89789–506–1

First published in 2001

Bergin & Garvey, 88 Post Road West, Westport, CT 06881
An imprint of Greenwood Publishing Group, Inc.
www.greenwood.com

Printed in the United States of America

The paper used in this book complies with the
Permanent Paper Standard issued by the National
Information Standards Organization (Z39.48–1984).

10 9 8 7 6 5 4 3 2

This book is dedicated
to my sister Antonette (Toni) Abernathy (1944–1999)

Contents

Acknowledgments

First I wish to gratefully acknowledge all of the African American female writers whose works were used in this book. Many colleagues and friends and family members helped and supported me while I worked on this project. Among those that I would especially like to thank are: Grace C. Cooper, Anne H. Jenkins, Janet R. Moore, Wilma King, Vivian L. Fuller, Shirley Ruh, Imogene Moyer, Frank Corbett, Jr., Joyce Fritsch, Deborah Goodwin, Laurie Means, Shelly Orr Hauer, Gail Okawa, Bill Thelin, Nourou Yakoubou, Gwen Severin, Beverly Johnson, Donald Pardlow, Joyce Stavick, Linda Miller, Jack Shuler, Delores James, Cathy Renwick, and Jackie Huggins. Finally I want to thank my husband Bill Hudson for all of his help, advice, encouragement, and unfailing good humor.

1

Introduction

The speech of African American females is often imitated, parodied, or stereo-typed. Generally these stereotypes allow for only a limited range of expressions, familiar to most who have seen or read material that contained images of strong mothers, chastising and advising; sassy young females, using popular slang; and no nonsense older women making salty comments on life. As with most stereo-types, these images capture some of the truth about the language use of some Afri-can American female talk, but only a small number of types of talk present in African American speech communities.

There is a lot of interest in the way these females use language, but in the area of language research few have conducted comprehensive studies that have investi-gated the language use from a number of different perspectives. Part of the prob-lem might be getting access to the various speech communities; another problem might be the small number of African American female linguists who have an in-terest in this limited area of study. One challenge is that the researcher must have an interest in researching not only language and gender, but must also be prepared to discuss language and other social contexts such as ethnic group, region, and so-cial class.

Despite the difficulties involved in this type of research, I have found one source of varied female language use that has proven to be a valuable resource for this book: the written works of African American female writers. These females have consistently represented African American female speech in a variety of social contexts. Therefore, in this book I describe how African American female writers portray African American female characters using language to reflect their mem-bership in various speech communities. I also analyze how the language use re-flects the norms, values, and beliefs present in their communities. To conduct this research, I collected and analyzed a variety of materials written in different genres and across a time span of over 100 years. In each piece of written material I looked for examples of dialogues, monologues, and personal narratives. These examples often represent the African American female writers' perceptions and beliefs about how language was used in various speech communities. I used these perceptions as my initial data for conducting a folklinguistic study of African American female language use.

FOLKLINGUISTIC RESEARCH

In the past three to four decades, sociolinguists, anthropologists, and other social scientists have investigated the various relationships that obtain between language and society. One area of interest is the role that language plays in maintaining and promoting social stereotypes (Fischer 1964; Giles & Powesland 1975). The term that I'm using for these types of studies is folklinguistics. According to Kramer (1974), this terms refers to popular beliefs about how people talk. Folklinguistic research forms an important area of study within the field of sociolinguistics. Researchers have investigated language use or attitudes about language use in etiquette books (Eble 1975), magazine advertisements (Courtney & Lockeretz 1971), cartoons (Kramer 1976; Meyer et al. 1980), dramas (Doty 1984), television situation comedies (Hudson 1984), television miniseries (Anderson et al. 1983), television commercials (Courtney & Whipple 1974), children's books (Nilsen 1977), short stories (Hudson 1993), and novels (Meyers 1983; Sewell 1984; Cohane 1984; Hudson 1986).

Many African American writers, both male and female have stereotyped the speech of members of various speech communities. Some, like their white counterparts, make use of the conventional African American speech stereotypes, but others have attempted to include more of the varieties of language present in the African American speech communities. In this regard, African American women writers seem uniquely qualified to serve as folklinguists for the African American female speech communities since many of them use the everyday social interactions of the community as a vivid backdrop for their works. Indeed, critical assessment of some of these writers often includes a discussion of how they are able to portray realistic language use.

While beliefs and perceptions do not always represent actual behavior, they have an importance in their own right. Erlich (1973) writes that these beliefs or stereotypes are transmitted across generations as components of the accumulated knowledge of a society and are thus considered "true" in a sense. Kramer (1975), who also used the term folklinguistics to describe popular beliefs about women's speech, writes that "these beliefs are not always articulated beliefs, but from a reading of etiquette manuals, speech books, cartoons and novels, a stereotype of women as having particular characteristics of speech will emerge" (47).

For more than a century, African American female writers have often made use of varieties of African American English dialect to tell their stories. Some of them, like Hurston and Walker, make use of southern dialects; others, like Fauset, Morrison, and Naylor, use some form of northern dialect. All of the writers in this study made use of language as an important tool of characterization, and the use of dialect in both dialogues and narration helped to point out various attitudes about language use in the African American community. The examples that I analyze show the African American female's use reflecting her social class, ethnic group, or gender.

LANGUAGE AND SOCIAL CLASS

Labov (1972), Trudgill (1983), and others have shown that it is often possible to assign members of a community to one or another social class based, in part, on the kinds and varieties of language that they use. There are discernible differences, for example, in the way that a poor, unskilled laborer speaks and the way that a university-educated lawyer speaks. These differences are a matter of degree, so that while it is possible that a highly educated, middle-class speaker might use some non-Standard forms, it is less likely that the speaker will use the same number of them or more than a speaker from a lower social class. In the examples of speech stereotypes that I collected, I found females who used highly stigmatized, Vernacular forms of English and those who used Standard English exclusively. The majority of speakers, however, style-shifted along a continuum between the two extremes.

The term "style-shifting" deserves a closer examination before we proceed since it will be used extensively throughout the text. I informally define it as a mixture of Standard and non-Standard Vernaculars in the speech of a single individual. Baugh (1983), under a section called "Code Switching versus Style-shifting," writes:

Several influential studies have referred to code switching in black English, as well as in other bidialectal communities. In my opinion this stretches the terminology too far, especially for black street speech. Code switching has typically been used to refer to true bilingual situations, as with Spanish and English in the United States. Style shifting is not a bilingual process, the linguistic adjustments take place among intelligible dialects of a single language. . . . In order to maintain this critical distinction, I will refer to street speech alternations as linguistic style shifts, which do not cross language boundaries. The term "code switching," on the other hand, should be reserved for truly bilingual cases. (58–59)

I have adopted Baugh's definition of this alternation between Standard and non-Standard forms, but I do not call the speech that these females use, "black street speech." In fact from my observations, many African American females regularly use these alternations for many different reasons. Often females may style-shift to signal a change in social context or situation. Many of those who regularly style-shift are Standard speakers.

LANGUAGE AND ETHNIC GROUPS

In 1974 Orlando Taylor offered this discussion of black language:

Black language consists of the totality of language used in the black community. It contains many varieties, with differences occurring as a function of such variables as geography, social class, age, sex, and the amount of education. Some forms are standard and others are nonstandard. Further, differences emerge as a function of the social situations in which the language is produced. Thus an accurate view of the complete language system is best seen as a continuum of features which vary according to the above mentioned variable. While there are differences in the various types of black language, there is nonetheless a common core of features across all types of phonology, syntax, vocabulary, and suprasegmental aspects.

Black language is not totally different from what we might call "American language." Likewise, since it is deeply rooted in Southern linguistics, it probably has many overlaps with "Southern language"—both standard and nonstandard. At the same time, it overlaps with the regional varieties of American language spoken in the geographical areas where African American currently reside. . . .

In other words, the various Black languages (BL) in the United States intersect with both American language (AL) and one or more regional languages (RL), especially Southern language. However, there is a core of linguistic features in African American language which are found in none of the other language systems, for example, the use of the continuative "be" and certain intonational contours which, though presently undefined, are sufficient to make most African American speakers ethnically identifiable. (154–155)

Researchers in the area of African American language have investigated both its form and its use in conversational interactions. Investigators have also discovered that there is a diversity of language styles present in the African American community (e.g., see Daniel 1974; R. Wright 1974; Matthews 1977). It also became clear that in the African American culture speech is often seen as performance—it is not only *what* is said, but also *how* it said. In this book I show that a rich diversity of linguistic and paralinguistic expression is often captured in many of the works of African American female writers.

Though many early studies on African American English focused on language used by males, a complete picture of its use does not emerge because the majority of informants were Vernacular-speaking adolescents. African American female language use has been even more neglected. With the exception of a few articles that focused on aspects of the African American female's conversational interaction (e.g., Mitchell-Kernan 1972; Stoelje 1973; Abrahams 1975), there has been little research conducted on how the African American female is perceived to speak.

LANGUAGE AND GENDER

Research findings on female language use indicate that women's language use varies from that of men's in a number of ways. Women are said to make more use

of expressive language, to use more conservative forms such as softened expletives and polite language, and to prefer to use indirect, rather than direct speech,
forms. On the other hand, they are said to be more willing to engage in self-
disclosure.

There have been many theories about why and, indeed, if males and females use
language differently. Lakoff's claim (1975) that males and females speak different
languages has been largely discounted since there has been little empirical evidence to substantiate such a claim. But interestingly, there is evidence to support
the claim that males and females under certain circumstances and in some contexts
do, indeed, use language differently. Further, it does seem that these differences in
language result from social attitudes about the expected behavior of men and
women.

Many linguists, after investigating one or another feature that has been said to be
used differently by the sexes, have concluded that, though it may be useful to finally list a set of actual differences, it also may be interesting to investigate society's perceptions about these differences since in many cases social groups are
judged not on objective observations of their behavior but on subjective responses
to perceived behavior.

Much of the research on female speech stereotypes reflect what Thorne and
Henley (1975) and Key (1975) admit to be "a white middle class bias." To date,
few linguistics studies have focused specifically on the interaction of language,
sex, and other social variables such as ethnicity, age, geographical location, or social class. This book helps to bridge the gap between existing research on African
American English, which focuses mainly on the language used by African American speakers of Vernacular English (mostly young males), and research on
women's language, which mainly focuses on the language used by white, middle-class females.

WORKS BY AFRICAN AMERICAN FEMALES

For this research I examined many works written by African American females:
slave narratives, novels, short stories, diaries, plays, and autobiographies. The period that I cover ranges from the 1880s to the present.

LINGUISTIC AND PARALINGUISTIC FEATURES

As might be imagined, there were any number of ways that I could have ap-
proached this study. After some consideration I decided to investigate some of the
stereotypes that I had looked at in an earlier research project that analyzed African
American male/female speech stereotypes on television comedies (Hudson 1984).
During the course of setting up the research, I modified some of these forms and
added others. I eventually arrived at the following categories.

Phonological Structures

Chapter 2 describes a variety of phonological structures that have been associated with African American language use. This chapter is divided into four main sections: Non-Standard English (NSE) Features—Consonants, NSE Vowels, African American Vernacular English (AAVE) Consonants, and AAVE Features—Vowels.

Grammatical Structures (Standard and Non-Standard)

I divide this category into three chapters. Chapter 3, "Vernacular Structures—AAVE," describes the use of such verb forms as *be*, *do*, and auxiliary *come*. It also describes the use of irregular pronouns. Chapter 4, "Vernacular Structures—NSE," discusses non-Standard English (NSE) Vernacular structures other than those discussed in Chapter 3. It describes non-Standard use of subject-verb agreement, verb forms, pronouns, and other grammatical structures. Chapter 5, "Standard Structures," discusses the use of modal constructions and other verb forms as well as various forms of pronouns.

Adjectives

Chapter 6, "Adjectives," describes patterns of adjective use, gender-based adjectives, Vernacular adjectives, AAVE adjectives, other NSE Adjectives, and individual adjective use.

Adverbs

Chapter 7, "Adverbs," describes the use of adverbs of time, manner, and degree. It also describes the use of the intensifiers *so* and *such*, female adjectives, Vernacular adjectives, adverb phrases, and transitional adverbs.

Forms of Address

Chapter 8, "Forms of Address," describes the use of names, titles, kinship terms, nicknames, terms of endearment, and labels.

Word Choice and Wordplay

Chapter 9, "Word Choice and Wordplay," describes how the female characters use these two areas to reflect their membership in various speech communities.

Expressive Behavior

Chapter 10, "Expressive Behavior," describes the use of expressive language such as exclamations, interjections, expletives, clichés, and commonplace expressions. It also describes the use of nonverbal communication such as kinesics and paralinguistic behaviors.

Bad Language

Chapter 11, "Bad Language," describes the use of rough talk, taboo words, swearwords, and name-calling. The chapter also discusses social restrictions on the use of bad language and various aspects of the grammar of swearing.

Language Use

Chapter 12, "Language Use," describes the way that female characters talk about using language and comment on language use. It also describes the use of metalanguage, and the final section, "Using Language," describes various ways that the characters studied use language to show either power or solidarity.

2

Phonological Structures

I found most of the phonological structures in earlier works that described Vernacular speakers. Of course, there are probably very good reasons that this should be so. For one thing, the descriptions of language use in early times reflected an almost perfectly dichotomous situation; the Vernacular speakers often spoke a highly stigmatized form of English, and the Standard speakers often used a dialect indistinguishable from that of white, Standard-speaking females.

This situation of deep gulfs between the speakers probably reflects a social stratification in the African American community since the characters depicted represent very different social groups. I hesitate to use the term "class" for those times since, in many cases, both the Vernacular speakers and the Standard speakers were slaves or ex-slaves. Indeed, in the earliest work (mid- and late nineteenth century) most of the females who wrote and spoke in the most acceptable form of English were described as lighter-skinned female slaves who were treated with some favor in the slaveholder's household. During the early part of the 1900s, the light-skinned female was again identified as a speaker of Standard English, but she was no longer a slave or ex-slave; these females represent the modern equivalent of the "middle" and "upper classes" in that they were prosperous and highly educated; they are joined by other African American women whose complexions might be darker but whose backgrounds were very similar to those of the others.

Early works include extensive use of stigmatized Vernacular phonological forms. It is important to remember that most of the passages from these sources were being produced by writers who were describing Vernacular speakers who were living during the time that the words were being produced. This means that though the perceptions of Vernacular speech may be stereotypical, it is still likely that the writers would have had either direct knowledge of, or direct contact with, Vernacular speakers. Furthermore, because the writers and speakers lived in approximately the same time period, it is more likely that these writers would have had access to information about a wider variety of forms. Finally, some of the information about Vernacular speakers comes from slave narratives that are supposed to represent the language used by the slaves and ex-slaves who tell their stories.

The Vernacular speakers of the early twentieth century are represented along a continuum from the speaker with the most highly stigmatized forms (usually older, rural speakers), to those speakers whose language is a mix of Standard and Vernacular forms. This mixture is still evident in works from the latter part of the twentieth century, although in these works fewer females use the more highly stigmatized forms; and the range of variation is much wider, with some females using a small number of Vernacular forms and others using much more. A further division among Vernacular speakers is that between the use of AAVE and the use of other non-Standard forms, including regional and ethnic varieties. Many sociolinguists supply descriptions of some of the variations that are possible in phonological structures; for example, Wardhaugh (1986) defined a linguistic variable as a "linguistic item which has identifiable variants. For example, words like *singing* and *finding* are sometimes pronounced *singin'* and *findin'*. The final sound in these words may be called the linguistic variable (ŋ) with its two variants [ŋ] in *singing* and [n] in *singin'* " (135). He points out that linguists have used a number of linguistic variables. He writes:

The (ŋ) variable has been widely used. So has the (r) variable. Others are the (h) variable in words like *house* and *hospital*, i.e., (h): [h] or ⌀; the (t) variable in *bet* and *better*, i.e., (t): [t] or [ʔ]; the (θ) and (ð) variables in *thin* and *then*, i.e., (θ): [θ] or [t] or and (ð): [ð] or [d]; the [l] variable in the French *il*, i.e. (1): [l] or Ø; and consonant variables like the final (t) and (d) in words like *test* and *told*; i.e., their presence or absence. Vocalic variables used have included the vowel (ɛ) in words like *pen* and *men*; the (a) or (ɔ) in *dog, caught* and *coffee*; the (ɛ) in *beg*; the (æ) in *back, bag, bad,* and *half*; and the (ʊ) in *pull*. (135–136)

NSE FEATURES—CONSONANTS

Several of the NSE features were used in both early and later works. In fact, the forms most commonly used in the earlier works were those that continued to be used in later works. Those forms that were marked for a particular time period (i.e., slavery, 1920s, 1960s) generally disappeared from literature after that period had passed. Exceptions include those words that were adopted into the general dialect of the Vernacular speaker or those that were used metaphorically by Standard speakers. Some of the non-Standard consonant forms are discussed next.

Simplifying Final Consonant Clusters

I found examples of this feature in both early and later works. All of the following females are Vernacular speakers:

1. When yuh git long dere by de cotton gin, *ast* somebody and dey'll tell yuh mo' exact. (Hurston, *Jonah's* 15)

2. When somebody talked mah husband intuh comin' down heah tuh open up uh eatin' place Ah never dreamt so many different kins uh black folks could *colleck* in one place. (Hurston, *Eyes* 209)

3. What you mean? he *ast*. (Walker, *Purple* 32)

Substituting *f* for *p* and *v*

I discuss the substitution of *f* for *th* in the phonological section of Chapter 4. But I also found occasions when *f* substituted for *p* or *v*. These substitutions are listed here since they were not explicitly identified as AAVE, but they are obviously non-Standard. The following examples come from early works. The speaker in the first passage is an adult speaker who substitutes *f* for *p*. She also pronounces *permanent* as *firmamen'*. In the second example, an old ex-slave substitutes *f* for *v*.

1. Don't talk to me 'bout yer *suferstition.* (Hopkins, "Hagar's" 172)

2. Some ob dem ole *Firginians* do so lub to rule a woman. (Harper 155)

Substituting *Gwine* for *Going to*

I am not really sure that this form should be listed with the AAVE forms, but it appears with such regularity in the earlier works that include language used in and around the time of slavery that I am including it in this section. One older female in an early work, Aunt Henny, produces the following sentence:

1. What's I *gwine* ter do wid him? (Hopkins, "Hagar's" 46)

Her daughter Marthy, also an adult, produces this example:

2. Tain't a soul *gwine* tech her. (173)

But Marthy also says:

3. I hope you ain't *goin' ter* have sof'n o' the brain. (178)

Other females living just after slavery produce the following:

4. Linda, is you *gwine* all alone? (Brent 99)

5. She am *gwine* at $500. (Rose 435)

Final Cluster Reduction

Wolfram (1991) writes that both voiced and voiceless final clusters can be reduced under certain conditions. This reduction may occur in clusters that are part of the base word (*find* and *act*) as well as clusters that are made from the past tense suffix *-ed* (*guessed* and *liked*) (278–279). This feature was used extensively in the early works. Vernacular speakers of all ages were represented. As in other exam-

ples, some young adult speakers alternated between pronouncing and not pronouncing the feature.

The following two passages show this feature being used by an older speaker
(example 1) and by a younger speaker (example 2).

1. Dis ain't no time foh all dat *kin'* of fiddle-de roll. (Larsen, "Sanctuary" 321)

2. Haley, where mah hair comb you borried from me *las'* Sunday? Ah wuz nice enough
   tuh *len'* it tuh yuh, but you ain't got manners 'nough tuh fetch it back. (Hurston, *Jonah's* 24)

The following passage, from the speech of Venus, the granddaughter of Aunt
Henny, the ex-slave in Hopkins' "Hagar's Daughter" is an interesting mixture of
Vernacular and Standard pronunciation of this form:

3. Yes, sir; I won't keep you long, but you see Miss Jewel's been my good angel *and* I
   jus' had to come here *and* unburden my *mind* to you or *burst.* (224)

In later works, there were very few instances of this feature. The most common
form used was *ol'*. For example:

4. this lil *ol'* heifer. (Shange, *Betsey* 186)

h Sounds

The sound *h* is added to some words (*hits* for *its*) and lost in others (*'er* for *her*).
In discussing the retention of *h*, Wolfram (1991) writes that this feature is still
common in some of the Vernacular varieties, such as Appalachian English, that retain older forms (281).

I found examples of each of these uses in the early works. The speakers are older
females:

1. Take dis bed heah if *hits* good 'nough fuh yuh. (Hurston, *Jonah's* 18)

2. *Hain't* it these arms done nussed ev'ry Livinston? (Hopkins, "Blood" 604)

Some of the females leave the *h* off the pronouns *her* and *him*, and some substitute a *y* for *h* in the words *here* and *hear*. The following examples come from early
works, and the speakers are older females:

3. 'twas only yisterday dat I was a gal wurkin' right *yere* in dis same ol' kitchen.
   (Hopkins, "Hagar's" 47)

4. Well, I *yered* [heared] so. (Harper 10)

Nasals

Labov and other sociolinguists have identified *g* dropping in words that end in
-ing one of the socially diagnostic features, in that its use signals either informal
Standard speech or Vernacular speech. It is generally conceded that when this

form regularly co-occurs with other stigmatized forms, it marks the speaker as a Vernacular speaker.

Early works included many examples of this feature: *washin', lookin', bein', comin', quiverin', larnin', doin', thinkin', larffin', steppin', ketchin', studyin', cookin'.*

In some speakers, no instances of using *-ing* were found. Here are a few passages that demonstrate the use of this form.

1. When we'uns gits te de *tradin'* block. (Rose 435)

2. I dreamt I was carried up to glory *settin'* on a cloud an' *playin'* on a golden harp. (Hopkins, "Hagar's" 173)

The preceding two sentences are produced by older, less educated females. In the next sentence, a young female with more education alternates between using *-in'* and *-ing*:

3. when I peeked in through the window and saw Miss Jewel an' gran *sitting* there *talkin'*, I was plum crazy for a minute. (Hopkins, "Hagar's" 240)

This style-shifting may be used to characterize the speaker as one who is upwardly mobile, and though it is not possible to determine whether the author used this alternation deliberately, it seems that this behavior is shown consistently in a number of other early works. In Hurston's *Their Eyes Were Watching God*, Janie Starks produces this passage:

4. Naw, 'tain't nothin' lak you might think. So 'tain't no use in me *telling* you *somethin'* unless Ah give you de *understandin'* to go 'long wid it. (Hurston 19)

Janie's friend Pheoby also alternates between the two forms. In some passages she uses words like *puttin'* and *nothin'*, but at other places she is shown using forms like *taking*. Even Nanny, Janie's grandmother, has a few instances of alternation, but her use of *-in'* is much more consistent than that of the two younger women.

In later works the patterns just discussed emerge again. Older Vernacular speakers use the form more often than younger speakers. Both sets of speakers alternate the use of *-in'* and *-ing*, but younger speakers alternate more often.

The following two examples show older females using *-in'*. In example 5, the speaker uses the form in all of the possible instances; in 6, the older woman shifts between the Standard and the non-Standard forms:

5. Oh, *nothin'* special. *Nothin'* worth *botherin'* about. (Hunter 24)

6. If you wants the bus depot, you *walkin'* in the wrong direction, 'cause nobody in their right mind would be *trying* to walk to the train station. (Naylor, *The Women* 30)

The next two passages show adult women talking to their friends in an informal style. Example 7 represents a woman raised in the South, who is now living in the North. Example 8 represents a woman born in the West Indies, but who now lives in Brooklyn, New York. Both characters use both forms:

7. Just bring your *blasphemin'* self on downstairs. I done already missed *morning* services *waiting* on you today. (Naylor, *The Women* 62)

8. *Somethin'* 'bout a house and *thing*. (Marshall, *Brown Girl* 44)

Absence of *r*

Wolfram (1991) writes that in some contexts the liquids *r* and *l* may be lost or reduced to "a vowel-like vestige." He notes that this *r*-lessness may be found in some parts of the South (280). The loss or the absence of *l* is found in the words *he'p* and *fo'ks*.

Examples that show loss or absence of *r* include *cullud* [colored], *Co't* [Court], *fust* [first], *mussy* [mercy], *po'* [poor], *puffick* [perfect], *sah* [sir], *sho'* [sure], *cawn* [corn], *hawses* [horses], *Lawd* [Lord].

Examples of the *r* sound being reduced to a vowel-like vestige include *heah* [hear], *hyah* [here], *fuh* [for], *nevah* [never].

The following passages represent some of the ways that Vernacular speakers are portrayed using the feature. The first passage comes from a book set in the 1860s:

1. I hern tell from Aunt Di, who *nussed* [nursed] Missee Enson. (Hopkins, "Hagar's" 63)

The next passage comes from the narrative of an ex-slave:

2. Two other men am biddin' 'gainst each other and I *sho'* has de worryment. (Rose 435)

Other early writers also use this feature in their works:

3. Naw! he didn't buy it *sho* nuff? (Hurston, *Eyes* 62)

4. If you want any tea for your poor wite trash you'll have to fix it *yo'self!* (Fauset, *Comedy* 305)

The speaker in example 4 doesn't delete the *r* on the words *for, your*, and *poor*. This feature also shows up in a later work by Rosa Guy that is set in the 1920s and 1930s:

5. You *sho* is right. (Guy, *Measure* 3)

The next example comes from later works; the speaker is an older female who lives in a small town in the South:

6. That girl *sho'* do favor you, George. (Campbell 48)

Insertion of *r*

Sometimes instead of leaving out an *r*, a speaker will insert one at the end of a syllable or a word. Wolfram, describing this phenomenon, writes, "There are occasional instances in which an intrusive *r* may occur, so that items such as *wash* may be pronounced *warsh* and *idea* as *idear*. For the most part, these are limited to particular lexical items and are regionally restricted" (281).

The practice of using the intrusive *r*, which occurs in many of the early works that feature Vernacular speakers, is very similar to the use of this form in some British and, possibly by extension, Appalachian dialects. Another possible explanation for this use may be the fact that the speaker is being shown using hypercorrect diction. In the latter case, the speaker would be overcompensating for the perceived absence of postvocalic *r* in cases where there actually should *be* no post vocalic *r*. An example of this would be pronouncing *toe* like *tore*. Examples of this feature include *ter* [to], *yer* [you], *inter* [into], *persition* [position], *ergin* [again], *dorg* [dog], *orful* [awful].

In passage 1, the speaker's use of this structure appears to signal the fact that she is being hypercorrect:

1. Then de Presidun' an' lots of other gemman made a big *furze* [fuss] over me. (Hopkins, "Hagar's" 253–254)

Other examples show females using the forms in a manner that probably reflects regional variation, especially for that time period:

2. I specs' fore dem Yankees gits froo you'll be *larffin* tother side ob your mouf'. (Harper 10)

3. *Marster* did not care. (Albert 5)

th Sounds

Wolfram (1991) writes that *th* is affected by many different processes. For example, at the beginning of the word, *th* is sometimes pronounced *d* (*dey* for *they*), and sometimes pronounced *t* (*tink* for *think*). He points out that the use of *t* for *th* is common in many Anglo- and second-language-influence varieties. The use of *d* for *th* is used in a large number of different varieties.

I found a few examples of *t* substituting for *th*. In Brent's *Incidents*, an older slave uses the expression, "do as you *tink* best" (114), and in Hopkins' "Hagar's Daughter," which features three generations of Vernacular speakers, only Marthy, the daughter of an ex-slave and the mother of Venus, a Standard English speaker, uses this form. It was probably used to indicate a style of speech. Her husband uses this form also. Hopkins has Marthy alternate between substituting the *t* sometimes and producing the *th* at other times:

1. How you *tink* it come so, Mammy? (Hopkins, "Hagar's" 63)

2. Do hish! Ef I didn't kno' yer age, Issac Johnson, I'd *think* you gone dotty. (178)

Whether this style-shifting is done deliberately or not, the author's portrayal of this usage is consistent with information that we know about this behavior.

The substitution of *d* for *th* also appears regularly in the early works. Examples include *de* [the], *den* [then], *dere* [there], *dem* [them], *widout* [without], *oder* [other], *fedder* [feather].

Speakers are shown to produce this feature in initial, intervocalic, and final position. The following passages contain representative examples:

3. When *dey* finds you is gone, *dey* won't want *de* plague ob *de* chillern; but where is you going to hide? *Dey* knows ebery inch ob *dis* house. (Brent 98)

4. What's I *gwine* ter do *wid* him?" (Hopkins, "Hagar's" 46)

5. Massa Black has a big plantation but he has more niggers *dan* he need for work on *dat* place, 'cause he am a nigger trader. (Rose 435)

6. Don't set dere *wid* yo' head hung down. (Hurston, *Eyes* 27)

The following passage was written in 1982, but the story is set in the 1930s:

7. Who *dis* woman, say Squeak, in this teenouncy voice. (Walker, *Purple* 83)

In the final example, an older woman in the play *Paper Dolls* reminisces with her friend:

8. Had me goin' shoppin' *wid'* you. (Jackson 355)

Initial *w* Reduction

Wolfram (1991) writes that in some southern-based Vernaculars the initial *w* may be lost. One of his examples is the pronunciation of *young'uns* for *young ones* (281). I found examples of the loss of the initial *w* in several early works. In the first two examples, the initial *w* is lost after a consonant sound but is retained after vowels. In examples 1 and 2, the speakers are older females:

1. You isn't a white *'ooman.* (Hopkins, "Blood" 604)

2. Dem *young uns* vill kill you dead. (Brent 98)

The next two examples also come from an ex-slave. Her language featured some of the most stigmatized forms, and in her speech the initial *w* is lost after vowel sounds:

3. *We'uns* have to work in de field everyday. (Rose 435)

4. De massa wants *you-uns* to bring forth portly chillen. (Rose 436)

This form also shows up in later works, generally with the word *young*. The next two examples come from older speakers:

5. Ah, that *young'un* can't sit still long 'nough to write no letter. (Taylor, *Circle* 95)

6. leapin' 'round that little old room playing' with *youngins* with three beets to my name. (Morrison, *Sula* 68)

Unstressed Initial Syllable Loss

In casual speech all speakers, including Standard speakers, may delete unstressed initial syllables, but Wolfram (1991) notes that this practice is "extended in Vernacular varieties so that a wider range of word classes (e.g., verbs such as *'member* for *remember*; nouns such as *taters* for *potatoes*) and word-initial forms (e.g., *re-, po-, to-, sus*, and so on) are affected by this rule" (281).

This form is used in a number of the early works. Examples include: *'bout* [about], *'cause* [because], *'way* [away], *'cept* [except], *'scuse* [excuse], *'nother* [another], *'speck* [expect], *'change* [exchange], *'membrance* [remembrance], *'buke* [rebuke], *'count* [account], *'thout* [without], *'stead* [instead], *'lasses* [molasses], *'bused* [abused], *'ducement* [inducement], *'nuff* [enough], *'ticement* [enticement].

The following passages show how speakers use this form. The first three examples are from early works; the speakers are older females. Examples 4 and 5 come from later works. The fifth speaker is an older woman:

1. You is de mos' *'quis'tive* [inquisitive] gal on dis plantation. (Hopkins, "Hagar's" 58)

2. You got to quit dat house *mejuntly* [immediately]. (Hopkins, "Blood" 606)

3. Eat dis heah *tater* pone. (Hurston, *Jonah's* 19)

4. I can *'member* Grandma Dee without the quilts. (Walker, "Everyday Use" 2373)

5. we went shoppin' in downtown Boley . . . *'member* . . . (Jackson 55)

Other Non-Standard Consonant Sounds

There is a wide variety of non-Standard consonant sounds. Some are recognizable regional or social class features; a few seem to result from individual style choices. Early examples include: *atter* [after], *bress* [bless], *carridge* [carriage], *clo's* [clothes], *creeter* [creature], *drefful* [dreadful], *fambly* [family], *gownd* [gown], *he'p* [help], *highsterics* [hysterics], *lem me* [let me], *les* [let's], *li'l* [little], *licker* [liquor], *nachally* [naturally], *mizzable* [miserable], *sogers* [soldiers], *suddent* [sudden], *suddintly* [suddenly], *vill* [will], *villyun* [villain], *wuss* [worst].

Several have more than one pronunciation: *ast, arst, asted* [ask]; *chillun, chillen, chillern* [children]; *handksher, hankercher* [handkerchief]; *gemmen, gemplemen* [gentlemen].

There are only a few examples in later works. Many of these examples come from older speakers and from West Indian Vernacular speakers: *awready* [already], *a-tall* [at all], *ast* [ask], *bed' not* [better not], *chirren* [children], *I'ma* [I am going to], *oughta* [ought to], *mussa* [must of], *sposed* [supposed], *tha's* [that's], *'ere* [there], *wha'* [what], *wun* [won't].

Summary

In early works, NSE phonology is also used extensively to signal different dialects and individual styles. It appears that some writers prefer to reflect dialect differences using one set of phonological features; others prefer other sets. Even given these facts, it is still easy to see that some of these forms are used by most of the writers at one time or another. The absence of the postvocalic *r* and the substitution of *d* for *th* and the substitution of *-in* for *-ing* are features that appear regularly in most of the works and in fact, it seems that their presence in the speech of the characters is one of the strongest indications that the speaker uses non-Standard Vernacular. It appears to be the case that differences in consonant use can strongly signal information about the age, social class, and ethnicity of the speakers as well the time period in which they lived or the region from which they came.

NSE VOWELS

Wolfram (1991) writes that different vowel patterns play important roles in distinguishing many English dialects. The majority of these patterns are used to distinguish regional, rather than social, varieties (282). In this section are some of the patterns that I found. The phonetic symbols that I am using are taken from Wolfram's table of phonetic symbols in his *Dialects and American English* (ix).

There are many examples of non-Standard vowels used in the early works. In the following section I describe a sample of some vowels that are used most often.

Older Females

Older females were responsible for most of the non-Standard vowels used in the early works. These females are often described as slaves or ex-slaves, and many lived or had lived in rural areas. In general, their speech contains the most stigmatized forms of both syntax and phonology. Some of the non-Standard vowels used by these speakers are described.

Substituting [a] for [ɛ] (e.g., *fotch* for *fetch*)

1. You make Ike *fotch* [fetch] out de res'. (Hopkins, "Hagar's" 173–175)
2. Now I wants ter hab a good talk 'bout our feller-*sarvants*. (Harper 157)

Other examples include *larnin'*, *sartin*, *sartinly*.

Substituting [ɛ] for [ɪ] (e.g., *ef* for *if*)

In example 1, *ef* is substituted for *if*; in example 2, *et* is substituted for *it*:

1. I think it would gib me de hysterics *ef* I war to try to get book larnin' froo my pore ole head? (Harper 156)
2. An' w'at am you lookin' foh me to do 'bout *et*? (Larsen, "Sanctuary" 321)

I also found *tell* [till].

Substituting [æ] for [i] (e.g., *clar* for *clear*)

1. I *rarely* [really] think ole Miss war fon' ob yer. (Harper 176)
2. Jes' ask her ef Miss Jewel's summer wrapper is to be *clar* [clear]-starched or biled-starched. (Hopkins, "Hagar's" 175–179)

Substituting [a] for [ɛ] (e.g., *whar* for *where*)

1. I specs yer's got a nice little wife up *dar whar* yer comes from. (Harper 154)

2. de oberseer was in de barn an he *'clar'* [declared] dat ober in the de corner he say de lightnin' play, an' while he looked he see hell wid all its torments an' de debbil *dar* too. (Hopkins, "Hagar's" 64)

Substituting [*I*] for [ʌ] (e.g., *kivver* for *cover*)

1. You better git dat *kivver* [cover] offa dat youngun and dat quick! (Hurston, *Eyes* 32–34)

2. Neber 'spected ter see *sich* good times in all my born days. (Harper 156)

I also found *jis'* [just].

Adult Females

In early works, adult females also use non-Standard forms, but they are more likely to vary quite a bit along a continuum of use of both the syntax and phonology. In many of the following examples, the syntax is Standard or nearly Standard, but the vowels are nonstandard. Most of these women lived in towns or cities.

Substituting [ɛ] for [æ] (e.g., *ketch* for *catch*)

1. De booger man might *ketch* yuh. (Hurston, *Eyes* 13)

2. When Missee Hagar git *married* to Marse Ellis. (Hopkins, "Hagar's" 63)

Other examples include *ez* [as], *ketch* [catch], and *chesstize* [chastise].

Substituting [a*I*] for [o*I*] (e.g., *biled* for *boiled*)

1. Jes' ask her ef Miss Jewel's summer wrapper is to be clar-starched or *biled* [boiled]-starched. (Hopkins, "Hagar's" 175–179)

2. wid a pissle *pinted* plum at me. (Hopkins, "Hagar's" 48)

3. Maybe Ah kin *pint* yuh war some work is. (Hurston, *Jonah's* 11)

Other examples include *pizened* [poisoned], *jined* [joined].

Substituting [*I*] for [ae] (e.g., *skeer* for *scare*)

1. Ole Miss jis' tryin' to *skeer* [scare] a body. (Harper 11)

2. Don't *keer* [care] what it was. (Hurston, *Eyes* 12)

I also found *keering* [carrying].

More Than One Age Group

The next set contains a few examples of vowels used by at least two different age groups.

Substituting [e] for [ɛ] (e.g., *haid* for *head*)

The first speaker is a young girl; the last two speakers are older females:

1. Ah ain't got no boogers in mah *haid.* (Hurston, *Jonah's* 24)
2. Git yo'se'f in dat dere feather *baid.* (Larsen, "Sanctuary" 321)
3. de bes' *laigs* I'll eber hab in dis wurl. (Hopkins, "Hagar's" 175)

I also found *aigs* [eggs].

Substituting [ɛ] for [ʌ] (e.g., *teched* for *touched*)

The first example comes from an adult female, the other two are from older adults:

1. Ah change *jes* ez many words ez Ah durn please! (Hurston, *Jonah's* 3)
2. You's *teched* in de head. (Rose 435–436)
3. Yas, massa *jedge.* (Hopkins, "Hagar's" 256)

I also found *sech* [such].

Substituting [a] for [aɪ] (e.g., *mah* for *my*)

The first example comes from an older woman; the second, from an adult:

1. Ah done kep' *mahself* outen trubble all *mah* life. (Larsen, "Sanctuary" 323)
2. *Ah* ain't brought home a thing but *mahself.* (Hurston, *Eyes* 14)

Substituting [ɔ] for [ai]

Mought and *mout* for *might* was used by a character, Amy, who appears in Hurston's novel *Jonah's Gourd Vine.* This form is sometimes used by some people from Florida. My family is from central Florida, very near where Hurston was born and raised, and I've heard older members of the family use both of these words.

Substituting More Than One Non-Standard Vowel

Sometimes more than one non-Standard vowel is used to substitute for the Standard one. For example, *just* is pronounced *jis* and *jes*; *such* is pronounced *sich* and *sech*. *Pretty* is another example of such a word. In the first example an older female ex-slave is singing a song:

1. Dem *pooty* angels I shall see. (Hopkins, "Hagar's" 65)

Example 2 also comes from an old ex-slave, and example 3 comes from an adult female who appears in a work set in the 1930s, though it was written in the 1980s:

2. De quarters am *purty* good. (Rose, 435–436)
3. Ain't it *purty*? (Guy, *Measure* 109)

Some non-Standard vowels are used in both early and later works.

Substituting [æ] for [aI] (e.g., *lak/lack* for *like*)

The first two examples come from early works. Example 1 comes from an older speaker, and example 2 from an adult female:

1. It 'pears *lack* 'twas only yisterday dat I was a gal wurking right yere in dis same ol kitchen. (Hopkins, "Hagar's" 47)

2. Youse always uh runnin' and uh rippin' an *clambin* trees. (Hurston, *Jonah's* 11)

In a scene from the play *Paper Dolls*, an older woman sings the lyrics of an old song:

3. An it looks *lak* my cotton dress
   Dyed wid copperse an' oak bark. (Jackson 356)

Substituting [aU] for [o] (e.g., *naw* for *no*]

The word most commonly used to represent the substitution of [aU] for [o] is *naw*. The first example comes from an early work and the speaker is a young girl:

1. Aw *naw* yuh don't Clary. (Hurston, *Jonah's* 15)

The following examples come from later works. Example 2 comes from an older female. The other examples come from adult females:

2. *Naw*, it makes my layers too moist. (Naylor, *Mama Day* 45)

3. *Naw,* she ain't got no boyfriend. (Jones, *Eva* 85)

4. Well, *naw* she aint. (Morrison, *Bluest* 24)

Other examples of the substitution of [aU] for [o] include *dawg* and *hawg*.

Substituting [e] for [æ] (e.g., *cain't* for *can't*)

The first example comes from an early work, and the other two come from later works; all of the speakers are older females:

1. *Cain't* see w'at foh, mahse'f . (Larsen, "Sanctuary" 321)

2. *Caint* even go pee without them having something to say about you. (Jones, "Jevata" 133)

3. Gointa check on the chirren, though I *cain't* say I heah 'em. (Shange, *Betsey* 178)

Substituting [ɚ] or [ə] for [o] (e.g., *swaller* for *swallow*; *fella* for *fellow*)

The first two examples are from early works; the third example comes from a work set in the 1930s but written in the 1980s. The last example comes from a later work, and the speaker is an older female who style-shifts regularly:

1. you am gwine take and take offa 'em and *swaller* all his filth. (Hurston, *Jonah's* 11)

2. I wants ter hab a good talk 'bout our *feller*-sarvants. (Harper 157)

3. that high *yeller*, smoochy-eyed bitch. (Guy, *Measure* 110)

4. to meet some nice hardworking *fella*. (Shange, *Betsey* 77)

Substituting [ə] for *to* or *of* (e.g., *gointa* for *going to*; *kinda* for *kinda*)

The substitution of [ə] for either *to* or *of* is found in both early and later works. The first two examples are taken from an earlier work; the speaker is an adult female:

1. Ahm *kinda* glad fuh yuh tuh be 'way from 'round 'im. (Hurston, *Jonah's* 11)

The next two examples come from later works, and the speakers are older females:

2. Getting *kinda* quick at the mouth, Miss C. (Naylor, *Mama Day* 52)

3. She was *gointa* stay in St. Louis, no matter what. (Shange, *Betsey* 12)

The final example comes from a later work, and it shows that the [a] replaces *of* in the expression *out of* the same way it does in example 1. Once again, the speaker is an older female:

4. coax my heart to come up *outta* my knees. (Jackson 357)

Other examples include *sorta, useta, gotta, wanta, outta.*

Substituting [ɚ] for *to* (e.g., *gointer* for *going to*)

I found several examples of [ɚ] substituting for *to* in early works. The following example is typical. The speaker is an adult female: "Ned Crittenden, you raise dat wood at mah boy, and you *gointer* make a bad nigger *outa* me" (Hurston, *Jonah's* 2). Other examples include *sorter* and *useter.*

I found very few non-Standard vowels in later works. The following are some that appear with some regularity.

Substituting [o] for [a] (e.g., *wont* for *want*)

An adult female produces the following: "And Sweet man said he didn't *wont* to be no old man raising no babies" (Jones, *Eva* 86).

Substituting [ae] for [I] (e.g., *thang* for *thing*)

The first two examples come from adult females; the third comes from an older female:

1. I'm going to cut his *stanking guts* out! (Walker, *Third* 32)

2. if he didn't have sex regular his *thang* would shrink. (DeVeaux, "Tapestry" 171)

3. Pearl was shittin' worms and I was supposed to play *rang*-around-rosie? (Morrison, *Sula* 69)

Sometimes the non-Standard sounds may come about as the result of individual speech patterns. For example, an older woman in Hopkins, "Hagar's Daughter," pronounces *professor* as *prefesser* and *particularly* as *preticularly*. Another female in Walker's *The Color Purple* pronounces *tuberculosis* as *tewberkolosis.*

Each author in each time period chose to focus on various non-Standard vowel sounds. Many were "eye dialect" or close approximations of Standard sounds: *turrible* [terrible], *wuz* [was], *whut* [what], *yuh* [you], *tuh* [to], *naw* [no], and *nuh* [now]. Others seem to be the result of using non-Standard verb forms: *clom* [climbed].

Summary

Non-Standard sounds used to portray individual speaking styles are not used very often. With the exception of a few speakers in slavery times and one or two examples in later works, the speakers seem to represent *types* rather than individuals. We will see later that individuality is more often portrayed in the use of syntactic features and expressive styles.

In all, the African American females who write about non-Standard features rely on a small group of forms to consistently portray various groups. As we see in the following chapters, some groups are more likely than others to be shown using these forms. They include very old speakers, very young speakers, speakers from lower social classes, speakers from rural areas, speakers from urban areas, and speakers from the West Indies.

In an appendix labeled "A Selective Inventory of Socially Diagnostic Structures," Wolfram (1991) also discusses variants of some phonological structures that are generally identified as being part of AAVE. Next I describe some of those features that I found in the works that I examined.

AAVE CONSONANTS

Most of the following descriptions are taken from either Dillard (1972) or Wolfram (1991).

Absence of -*d* or -*t* at the End of Past Tense Verbs

Dillard (1972) describes an early controversy over whether African American speakers have a past tense category in their dialect. Those linguists who feel that these speakers don't have such a feature reported overhearing such sentences as, "That man *stare* at me and I ain' know him" (50). Others feel that it was more likely that in some cases this category may be optional for some speakers. The absence of the -*d* and -*t* sounds is evident in several works. For example, I found it in the speech of Rose, the ex-slave. In this passage below she is quoting a man at the auction block:

1. What am I *offer* for dis portly, strong young wench. (Rose 435)

She also uses the feature herself:

2. and he *whip* de cullud folks. (Rose 435)

In her book *The Color Purple*, Walker has Celie quote Mr.____'s father as saying:

 3. It all just too trifling and *confuse*. (59)

Celie also says:

 4. She *look* surprise. (38)

In Marshall's *Brown Girl, Brownstones*, Silla says to her husband, who shows her a letter saying that he has inherited land:

 5. It can't be true. This is all some *forge* up something. (25)

Example 6 comes from an adult Vernacular speaker; example 7 is from an adult Standard speaker who has been shown to style-shift.

 6. Cause you *spose to* go in your closet and do stuff like that. (Jones, "Jevata" 147)

 7. Here the three of us *suppose to* be traveling together and she just ups and leaves, ruining the rest of the trip for the two of us. (Marshall, *Praisesong* 27)

I found the appearance of this feature in literature interesting for two reasons: First, it is a structure that might easily be overlooked since many speakers may leave this form off in rapid speech, yet it does appear in some passages. Second, it appears only under a very few circumstances. It appears as part of some Vernacular dialects. The characters Rose (example 2) in an early work and Celie (examples 4 and 5) in a later work use it as part of their everyday speech. In two examples (1 and 3), females are quoting males. Third, the characters in examples 6 and 7 use it to show either aggravation or annoyance. Fourth, in two examples (6 and 8) the speaker is a West Indian female. Finally, the form with the final *-d* alternates with the form without the final *-d* in some passages. For example, the following adult female speaker pronounces *supposed* with and without the *-d* in the course of a long soliloquy of fussing:

 8. I don't know what I'm *suppose* to be running here, a charity ward, I guess . . . I guess I ain't *supposed* to have nothing. I'm *supposed* to end up in the poor house. (Morrison, *Bluest* 23)

Substituting *f* for *th*

Wolfram (1991) writes that in Vernacular Black English *th* may be pronounced as *v* between vowels (*efer* for *ether*; *brover* for *brother*) or at the end of a word (*smoov* for *smooth*) (280).

The following form appears in many of the works that I examined. Examples include *nuffin'* [nothing], *def* [death], *munfs* [months], *bof* [both], *mouf'* [mouth], *Norf* [North], *froo* [through]. Larsen (1989) uses this form in her short story "Sanctuary," which seems to be set sometime after slavery; the speaker is an older woman, an ex-slave:

 1. Ah shuah don' see *nuffin'* in you but a heap o' dirt. (Larsen 321)

In later works Walker shows speakers substituting *f* for *th*:

2. Her mouth open showing all her *teef* and don't nothing seem to be troubling the mind. (Walker, *Purple* 33)

As in many other examples showing style-shifting, this speaker substitutes *f* for *th* in only one of three possible instances. She does not substitute in the words *mouth* and *nothing*. Guy also uses this form to stereotype a female character who is identified in her novel as a loud, cheerful person from "the country," the kind whose behavior embarrasses more urban and sophisticated African American people:

3. Hee-hee, now ain't that the *truf*? (Guy, *Measure* 3)

In both the Walker and the Guy examples, the novels are set in the 1930s and 1940s, and characters are from rural areas, so their use of the form is perhaps not so surprising. I didn't find any examples in novels of the 1950s and beyond except in those cases when the form is used to metaphorically style-shift. In Morrison's novel *Tar Baby*, Jadine, a Standard speaker, makes a sarcastic commentary on Son's (a Vernacular speaker) lack of ambition by singing a song in a way meant to mock the stereotypical "do-nothing nigger":

4. Ah got duh sun in duh mawnin' and duh moon at night. . . . Oooooo, Ah got plenty of *nuffin* and *nuffin's* plenty for meeeeee. (Morrison, *Tar* 171)

Substituting *b* for *v*

Wolfram (1991) discusses the substitution of *b* for *v* under the heading of "Nasals" because, "[b]efore nasals *th* participates in a rule in which fricatives including *z*, *th*, and *v* may also become stops." One of his examples includes the use of *sebm* for *seven* (280).

In the very earliest works, this form appears regularly, especially in the speech of older females, many of whom are slaves or ex-slaves.

Examples include *nable* [navel], *gib* [give], *ebenin'* [evening], *oberseer* [overseer], *hebbenly* [heavenly], *eberything* [everything], *hab* [have]. The following passages are examples of how this form is used:

1. an' dat *bery* night de *debbil* 'pear to ole Miss, an' Unc' Ned *neber* was whopped tell de day he died, *neber*. (Hopkins, "Hagar's" 64)

2. Ef de Lawd had *gib* you a white face 'stead o' dat dere black one, Ah shuah would turn you out. (Larsen, "Sanctuary" 321)

3. Yo' *nable* string is buried under dat air chanyberry tree. (Hurston, *Jonah's* 19)

Possibly related to this substitution is the substitution of *b* for *f* in words like *of*, which is often pronounced *ov*. The word *ob* is used to represent the word *of* in many of the works. The following example comes from an early work, and the speaker is an older female:

4. Dey knows *ebery* inch *ob* dis house. (Brent 98)

Substituting *w* for *v*

Sometimes the females substitute a *w* for a *v*. Dillard (1972) writes that "a phonological characteristic of Plantation Creole, found still in Gullah and sporadically in other forms of Black English is the voiced bilabial fricative written [β] by phoneticians" (311). He notes that dialect fiction writers variously render this sound. When it replaces the *v*, it is sometimes rendered as a *b*, as in *heaby*, and sometimes as a *w*, as in *heawy* [heavy].

I found a few examples of the use of a *w* for a *v*. They all appear in early works. These two examples are from older females who are ex-slaves:

  1. You's a selling yore *wote* [vote]. (Harper 178)

  2. Ol' Miss jes' went into *conwulsions*. (Hopkins, "Hagar's" 63)

AAVE FEATURES—VOWELS

Only a few vowel sounds or glides might be said to be associated with AAVE features. The one that appears most often is the [aI] sound of the word *gwine* [going to].

SUMMARY

It would seem that the authors of the works examined use a similar set of features to identify the female characters as members of African American speech communities. Within the communities themselves, however, there are some differences in the way that the language is used.

We saw examples of older, stigmatized forms used by people born during or just after slavery. We saw examples of rural speech and speech used by West Indians. In addition, we saw at least two examples of speakers who shifted styles.

As I have noted, there are not very many of these forms in later works unless they are used metaphorically, but those writers who choose to set their works in earlier times rely on these features to characterize the people and the times.

3

Vernacular Structures—AAVE

Trudgill (1983) describes a pyramid with Standard dialects at the top and non-Standard dialects making up the rest of the structure. He notes, "Speakers of the highest social class employ the dialect we call Standard English which . . . is only slightly different in different parts of the country" (40). On the other hand, he points out that at the other end of the pyramid there is a great deal of variation.

In my research on African American female speakers, I also found a great deal of variation in Vernacular speakers. In this chapter I describe some of the Vernacular structures that appear regularly in the works. As is true with other sections that I've already discussed, these female characters produce language that varies along a continuum from the almost Standard to highly stigmatized forms of Vernacular. In addition, sometimes the same individual style-shifts along some parts of this continuum. The first set of features has generally been identified as part of African American Vernacular English (AAVE). Many of the descriptions are taken from Dillard (1972) or Wolfram (1991).

COMPLETIVE *DONE*

Completive *done* has been identified as being part of both AAVE and NSE. Wolfram (1991) writes that in Southern white and black Vernaculars the form *done* may function in a number of different ways. He writes that *done* may "mark a completed action or event in a way somewhat different from simple past . . . *I done forgot what you wanted*." Or it may "add intensification to the activity, as in *I done told you not to mess around*" (287).

The following examples come from African American females who appear in works that I examined. This structure is used extensively in both early and later works.

Early examples include the following; all of the speakers are older females:

1. Then de Presidun' an' lots of other gemman made a big furze over me, an' dey *done* gib me my job fer life. (Hopkins, "Hagar's" 253–254)

2. Ah *done done* it. (Hurston, *Jonah's* 6)

3. Ah *done* kep' mahse'f outen trubble all mah life. (Larsen, "Sanctuary" 321)

Done as an auxiliary is used in all of the preceding sentences. Normally it appears with the past participle form of the verb. A few structures combine a form of the verb *to have* with *done* + past participle. In Hopkins's "Hagar's Daughter," Aunt Henny uses the expression, *"had*n't *don lef"* (47), and in Hurston's *Their Eyes Were Watching God*, Nanny uses the expressions *"had* done *been kilt"* (32) and "I *had done managed"* (33). Aunt Henny's daughter, Marthy, uses another interesting construction that consists of a future tense + *done* + a past participle: *"we'll done lose* this place" (177). Those who are familiar with a form that some call future completive (e.g., *I'll be done knocked him out*) will notice that this form is quite similar to it, with the exception of the absence of the verb *be*. Another structure containing *done* is the combination of *done* + *come* + an adverb. Marthy at one point says, "The mor'gage money *done come due* in June" (177), and her mother, Aunt Henny says, "when Marse St. Cla'r *done comed* home" (63).

Done is used with the past participle form in later works also. All of these speakers are adults:

4. I *done* already *missed* morning services. (Naylor, *The Women* 62)

5. Me, I *done got* all fat. (Jones, *Eva* 84)

6. I *done worked* round the clock, did more work in twenty-four hours than these good-timing niggers out here on Fulton Street done for the year. (Marshall, *Brown Girl* 29)

The females in the next set of examples are older women. The speaker in example 7 style-shifts regularly.

7. Oh, you *done forgot* that, huh? (Jackson 355)

The same speaker in example 7 also says, "You've *done* that" (384).

8. You *done* undone months of care. (Naylor, *Mama Day* 76)

Of the later writers who set their works in earlier times, both Guy and Walker use this form extensively. In other later works writers Naylor, Jackson, and Hansberry all show older females using most of these forms. In Marshall's works, the form is often used by adult West Indian females, but the females would not be described as "old." I did find a few interesting structures in these later works. In Guy's *A Measure of Time*, Dorine Davis, herself a Vernacular speaker, parodies a more highly stigmatized form of the dialect by asking herself, "is you *done* took leave of your senses!" (5).

As with the early works, later writers also used the construction of the verb *have* + *done* + past participle. In Naylor's *Mama Day*, an older woman, speaking about a health condition says, "It's [It has] *done* pussed up" (76).

The construction of *done* + *come* also appears in later works. In one form *done* + *come* is combined with an adverb. In McMillan's *Mama* one woman tells another woman, "He *done come* back to me and his daughter after all this time" (22).

Another construction using *done* + *come* includes a present participle. In the next example *done* + *come* and *done* + *come* + *-ing* appear in the same passage:

9. Yes—death *done come* in this here house. . . . *Done come walking* in my house. (Hansberry 105)

Other examples of the use of *done* + present participle include *done give*, *done wiggle*, and *done run off.*

There were other examples of *done* used in combination with other forms. One example comes from Cooper's *Homemade Love*. In this work an adult female narrates the story of her life, and in one passage she uses *done* with past forms of *have*, *be*, and the present participle form of *work*:

10. She *had done been working* hard to support herself for years. (1–2)

In one example from Clair's *Rattlebone*, a speaker combines the past tense form of *have* and *be*:

11. She'*d done been* down at the teachers' college. (72)

In another example, a speaker combines past tense forms of *have* and *be* and *marry*:

12. We *hadn't done been married* a year when I up and got pregnant. (72)

In this section, I've supplied a sampling of the forms of completive *done* that appear in the literature that I examined. I believe that I can make a strong case for completive *done*'s being placed into that small group of words that have been used consistently in the African American speech community from earliest times to the present. It survives today as a strong marker of African American Vernacular speech (especially in older speakers and in ethnic groups like those West Indians who speak an English-based creole). Completive *done* is also used as a definite marker of metaphoric style-shifting, as with Dorine Davis' self-mocking statement to herself "Is you *done* took leave of your senses!" (Guy, *Measure* 5).

Finally, another interesting aspect of the way that completive *done* is used is that it appears in a wide range of environments—from the highly stigmatized "an' dey *done* gib me my job fer life" (Hopkins, "Hagar's" 253–254), to sentences in which *done* is the only marker of Vernacular use: "You *done* met a few promising ones along the way, Etta" (Naylor, *The Women* 61).

BLACK ENGLISH VERBS

Remote-Time *Been* [bín]

Wolfram (1991) writes that remote-time *been* can be used to indicate that an event or activity took place in the distant past. He notes that the use of the form is often associated with Black English (BE). He points out that although the use is dying out in some areas, it is still prominent in those varieties that have strong creole associations (287–288). In this section I place [bín] next to the conventionally spelled *been* to let readers know that this word, when spoken often, carries a very heavy stress.

So far I've discovered only a few instances of this form in the literature. The first example comes from Hurston's *Mules and Men*, an early work:

1. Ah *been* [bin] knowin' dat ole tale. (Hurston, *Mules* 30)

The next example comes from a later work, and the speaker is a young girl in Guy's *The Friends*; she is explaining to another young girl why she acted disrespectfully toward a teacher:

2. What was so awful about it? She ask for it, ain't she? She *been* [bin] asking for it. (Guy, *Friends* 44)

Another example comes from a short story by Ansa, the female is a young, adult Vernacular speaker who is responding to a woman who asks her if she is still living with an aunt:

3. Naw, girl, I *been* [bín] moved out of my aunt's. (Ansa, "Willie" 15)

Substituting *Been* for *Was/Were*

Dillard (1972) describes the use of *been* for *was* or *were* this way: "In the Aspect category (the one which is negated by *ain'*) is the verb structure which differs most obviously from Standard English" (46). He supplies several examples, including the following: "I *been* cook for heap of these white folk" and "We *been* bother" (46).

The two examples that I found are located in works that are set in or around slavery time. Example 1 is uttered by an old ex-slave who is discussing her legs:

1. but I got a heap 'o hope [help] outen dem whilst dey *ben* limber. (Hopkins, "Hagar's" 175)

Example 2 is spoken by a young girl:

2. Folks whut wuz borned in slavery time go 'round callin' dese white folks Marse but we *been* born since freedom. We calls 'em Mister. (Hurston, *Jonah's* 14)

Is for *Have*

Dillard (1972) notes that in some African American English Vernaculars some of the auxiliary functions of *have* in Standard English are filled by Black English *is* (48). Examples from early use include the following sentences spoken by Marthy, an adult female. In both examples she is in an agitated state:

1. *Is* you gone crazy? (Hopkins, "Hagar's" 178)
2. I*'se* seed a ghos'! Lawd, my days is done. (178)

This speaker also style-shifts regularly, and another time she says, "I*'ve* had my trials" (172). Another early example shows an older ex-slave saying:

3. I*'s* never tasted white flour. (Rose 436)

Though this is a highly stigmatized form, it has turned up in later works. Usually, either the speaker is an older woman, or the work is set in an earlier time. In example 4, an older woman is addressing a younger woman:

4. Your resistance *is* always been low. (Naylor, *Mama Day* 48)

Example 5 comes from Celie, an adult female who appears in Walker's *The Color Purple*, which is set in the 1930s and 1940s:

5. My little sister Nettie *is* got a boyfriend. (14)

Absence of *Be* Forms

This feature is quite common in the speech of African American and white speakers in the South. I found it in a large number of the works. In the earlier ones, all age groups—adult females, older females, and young girls—use it. The first two examples come from an adult female who sometimes leaves the *be* form out (example 1) and sometimes includes it (example 2):

1. You, Isaac, *wha'* in the lan' *you talkin'* 'bout? (Hopkins, "Hagar's" 178)
2. *Is* you gone crazy? Them remarks o' yourn *is* suttingly cur'ous. (178)

Example 2 comes from a young girl:

3. *Whut you* doin' over heah. (Hurston, *Jonah's* 14)

Most linguists describe the absence of *be* forms as occurring in the present tense, but I also found several examples of the absence occurring in the past tense. Rose, an ex-slave, produces these statements when narrating the story of her life:

4. Mammy and pappy *powerful* glad to git sold. (Rose 435)
5. Now, I don't like dat Rufus, 'cause *he a bully*. (436)
6. Dat nigger jump up and *he mad*. (436)

In another early work the absence of a *be* form is evident in a narration produced by an older woman:

7. *Unc' Ned conjure* man. (Hopkins,"Hagar's" 64)

This woman also alternates between leaving out the *be* form and including it; in the next example, she includes it:

8. Las' time he *was* here ol' Marse he bus' a blud vessel in his head. (63)

Here is an example from a young girl:

9. Haley, *where mah* hair comb you borried from me las' Sunday? (Hurston, *Jonah's* 24)

All of the preceding examples reflect only one of the possible structures that the speakers have available. Even the oldest speakers shift between using and not using the *be* form. When looking at later works, I found many examples of the absence of *be* forms in those works that were set in earlier times. For example, the following is taken from Childress's "Wedding Band":

10. Oh, Miss Julia, I'm glad *you my neighbor*. (84)

Note that in the last example, the copula is present after "I."
Other later works include the following examples:

11. *They different people*, you know. (Morrison, *Sula* 56)

12. You know, *you getting too big* for this. (Naylor, *Linden* 220)

13. Mothers are something ain't they? *They mostly the one person* you can count on! (Cooper, *Homemade* 1)

Note that in the preceding example, the first *be* form, *are*, is present in the first sentence.

Am Used with Other than First Person

The use of this structure, like the use of the word *gwine,* is one of the strongest indications that the speaker was born in or near slavery. It appears only in early works. In the first two examples, an ex-slave recounts events from her life:

1. *Massa Black am* awful cruel. (Rose 435)

2. Dat gal *am* a likely lookin' nigger, she *am* portly and strong, but three *am* more dan I wants, I guesses. [Describing what a prospective slave buyer said.] (435)

The next two speakers are also older females:

3. You *am* gwine take and take offa 'im and swaller all his filth lak you been doin' here of late. (Hurston, *Jonah's* 11)

4. An' w'at *am* you lookin' foh me to do 'bout et? (Larsen, "Sanctuary" 321)

Habitual *Be*

Trudgill (1983) writes, "Perhaps the most important characteristic of AAVE is called 'invariant be': the use of the form *be* as a finite verb" (55).

Following is an early example of the use of this form; the speaker is Venus, a young adult female who often style-shifts. In this passage she is quoting her father:

1. You *be waitin'* by the front door, an' I'll have 'm out in a jiffy. (Hopkins, "Hagar's" 240)

In Walker's *The Color Purple*, set in earlier times, Celie, the main character and an adult female, makes the following statements:

2. She *be tagging* long hind a lady. (22)

Celie also talks about a habitual action using *be* + participial form *-ed* (pronounced without the *-d*):

3. She *be dress* to kill. (16)

Later examples from other works show that this form is used by both adult and younger speakers. The first example comes from a work set in an earlier time but written at a later date; the speaker is an adult female:

4. You *be renting* him out to pay for me way after I'm gone to Glory. (Morrison, *Beloved* 146)

The next example, also from a later work, comes from an adult female:

5. Don't *be standing* there talking about no daddys. (Naylor, *Mama Day* 46)

The last two examples come from later works, and the speakers are young girls:

6. That's some stuff Daddy *be taking* off the base. (Bolton 83)

7. You *be thinking* you're having the horriblest dream. (Tate 37)

It was surprising to me that, although this form is so often cited as one of the prime examples of AAVE, it does not show up more often in my examination of the early works, and the one example that I did find is a quote from a male. But there are several examples from later works, including some from young females. In the preceding second example from Walker, the speaker uses a form of *be* + a past participial form *-ed* (*be dress*[*ed*]) to show habitual action. The *be* form alone has also been used to show the same type of action. Examples 8 and 9 come from adult females; example 10, from a young girl:

8. By time I git back from the well, the water *be* warm. By time I git the tray ready the food *be* cold. By the time I git all the children ready for school it *be* dinner time. (Walker, *Purple* 12)

9. Most mothers *be* your friend and love you no matter what you do! (Cooper, *Home-made* 1)

10. I bet you and him *be* in the dark. (Marshall, *Brown Girl* 19)

The use of this form reflects an interesting pattern. I found no very old speakers who use it. The fact that I didn't find many examples of this form in early works coupled with the fact that no very old speakers are shown to use it in later works leads me to suspect that either the writers of these early works weren't aware of the presence of this feature in the African American speech community or, and this may be more likely, at the time that they wrote the form was not used to represent the way African American female Vernacular speakers spoke.

The appearance of this form in the later works may signal either that the writers were portraying members of a particular speech community or that the form might be used more often by African American female Vernacular speakers in later years. The former possibility does not seem to be the best explanation since the speakers whom I listed come from a variety of speech communities, including ones in the rural South during the 1930s and ones in West Indian communities in New York during the 1950s.

Auxiliary *Come*

Baugh (1983) identifies this form as one that is used regularly by Vernacular speakers. Wolfram (1991) says that its use "conveys a special sense of speaker indignation" (288). Examples from early works include:

1. It was de cool of de evenin' when Mistis *come walkin'* in mah door. (Hurston, *Eyes* 33)

In the same passage, the speaker also said:

2. She *come stood* over me in de bed. (33)

Example 2 is interesting in that most of the *come* auxiliaries that act the way that Wolfram describes them have the form of *come* + verb participial form. Its use may be similar to the use of *come* + verb discussed in Chapter 4.

Auxiliary *come* is also present in later works. The first example comes from an adult female; the other two come from older females:

3. Pot Limit'll *come bamming* on the door. (Bambara, "Medley" 104)

4. [I] know she gonna *come dragging* in here puny as the law allows. (Naylor, *Mama Day* 37)

5. Oh, wasn't you smart, *come fixing* my hair and Oh Miss Lydia ain't we prettying me, sewing them short dresses so you can get that man away from his wife. (Clair 84)

Another use of this feature occurs in the conversation of a West Indian woman talking about her friend's pregnancy:

6. You's a disgrace to *come tumbling big* so soon after the last one. (Marshall, *Brown Girl* 30)

A final example of this form shows it combined with the *done* auxiliary. Mama in Hansberry's *A Raisin in the Sun* speaks of death this way:

7. *Done come walking* in my house. (105)

Ain't Used as a Correspondence for *Do* + *Not*

Wolfram (1991) notes that when *ain't* is used as a correspondence for *be* + *not* or *have* + *not*, the use is considered non-Standard, but when it is used as a correspondence for *do* + *not*, the usage is considered Vernacular Black English (293).

I found examples of this use in both early and later works. The first example is taken from an early work. Instances of this form's use also appear in second example, which was written in the 1980s, but was set in the 1930s and 1940s; the speaker in both examples is an adult female:

1. you *ain't tried* tuh chesstize 'im nothing uh de kind. (Hurston, *Jonah's* 3)

2. I *ain't* sneaked. (Guy, *Measure* 194)

In the following examples, all from later works, the speakers represent different age groups. The first two examples come from young girls:

3. What was so awful about it? She ask for it, *ain't* she? (Guy, *Friends* 44)

4. See? Daddy *ain't* do nothing to me. (Bolton 77)

In examples 5 and 6 the speaker is an adult female; in example 7, an older woman.

5. I *ain't* say I not looking for someone suitable. (Rahman 215)

6. it'll be a cold day in hell 'fore someone 'cuse me of being in love with Lisa 'cause my mama *aint* raised no dykes! (Woodson 171)

7. Why *ain't* nobody known Bernice is pregnant? (Naylor, *Mama Day* 71)

Multiple Negation—Strings of Three or More

Although I discuss multiple negation in Chapter 4, I include this particular structure here since it seems to me that the stringing together of three or more negatives in a single utterance represents a particular style that can be found frequently in AAVE speech communities. I believe that, more than showing negation, the speaker is using the multiple forms to indicate very strong feelings. The first three examples come from early works. All of the speakers are adult females. Example 2 shows this form used as part of creative wordplay:

1. Tea Cake *ain't wasted up no* money of mine, and he *ain't left* me for *no* young gal, *neither.* (Hurston, *Eyes*, 18)

2. and *no* black gal *ain't never* been up tuh de big house and dragged Marse *Nobody* out. (Hurston, *Jonah's*, 9–10)

3. she *ain't* seen *notin'*, *nor* hearn *notin'.* (Brent 114)

There are several examples of this type of multiple negation in later works also. Examples 4 and 5 come from adult females; example 6, from an older female:

4. I ain't no intell—whatever you call it *neither.* (Guy, *Measure* 107)

5. *Ain't nothing* but a fool that *ain't* got *nothing* to do in this here world. (Cooper, *Homemade* 1)

6. but *ain't nobody* in my family *never* let *nobody* pay 'em *no* money that was a way of telling us we *wasn't* fit to walk the earth. We *ain't never* been that poor. . . . We *ain't never* been that dead inside. (Hansberry 104)

Standard speakers sometimes use multiple negation in the same way that they use completed *done*—to metaphorically style-shift. In the following passage one of the Delany sisters, Bessie, a well-educated, middle-class professional woman, indignantly threatens to write to David Duke, a white supremacist: "David Duke *doesn't* think there are Negroes like me and Sadie, colored folks who have *never done nothin'* except *contribute* to America. Well, I'm just as good an American as he *is—better!*" [her italics] (Delany et al. 231).

Irregular Pronouns

Female speakers in the AAVE speech community are shown to use irregular pronouns in both early and later works. Most are discussed in Chapter 4, but a few forms have been identified by Wolfram as being "quite rare in most current Vernaculars except those still closely related to a prior creole state" (295). One structure that is used by both Hurston in an early work and Walker in a work set in earlier times but written in the 1980s is the substitution of the objective *us* for the subjective *we*. All of the speakers are adult females:

1. 'Nother thing, Ah hates tuh see folks lak me and you mixed up wid 'em. *Us* oughta class off. (Hurston, *Eyes* 210)
2. What *us* needs tuh do is git offa dis place. *Us* been heah too long. (Hurston, *Jonah's* 6)
3. *Us* sit looking at all the folks that's come to town. (Walker, *Purple* 23)

I also found examples of the objective used as a possessive in the speech of the slave Rose, who refers to "*us* washin' " [our washing] and "*Him* name Hawkins" (Rose 435). There are also several examples of the subjective form used as a possessive. Example 4 comes from Rose, who says:

4. Massa Hawkins am good to *he* niggers. (436)

Other early examples include the following; both of the speakers are adult females:

5. neber been whopped in all *he* life. (Hopkins, "Hagar's" 64)
6. And Ah reckon they got me up in *they* mouth now. (Hurston, *Eyes* 16)

In later works, a construction in the speech of West Indian speakers has the subjective form serving as the objective. All of these examples come from Marshall's *Brown Girl, Brownstones*; the speakers are adult females:

7. But look at *she*! (19)
8. Wha' land? . . . Deighton? Who give *he*? (31)
9. One call *sheself* getting married. (306)

Another example of irregular pronoun use is what Wolfram (1991) calls "regularization of the pronoun *mines* on the basis of analogy with *yours, his*" (34). He points out that this particular use of possessives is typical of Black English Vernaculars (295). I found very few examples, but the reason might be that this form, like *gwine* and completed *done*, is highly stigmatized. The first example from Walker's *The Color Purple*, shows an adult female quoting a male:

10. No wife of *mines*. . . . He go on and on. (74)

The second example comes from Ansa's *Baby of the Family*. The speaker is a ghost of an old slave woman:

11. Look at *mines*, my whole body, so covered with scabs and scars and whelps. (162)

SUMMARY

Dillard (1972) writes: "In the system of its verbs, Black English reveals the greatest difference from white American dialects—as from British dialects—and the closest resemblance to its pidgin and creole ancestors and relatives" (40). In my analysis I found a few features that are used by most Vernacular speakers, but many expected features do not appear in the language of any of the women in the works that I examined. Perhaps this absence can be accounted for by the fact that, although the females are shown using Vernacular structures, they, like some females in other speech communities, may signal their social position by avoiding some of the most heavily stigmatized forms. I know from my own experience with these texts that the males are often shown using more stigmatized forms and using them more frequently.

The use of syntactical features is similar to that in the phonological section, but there are some differences. One problem that I encountered is that often a form would appear that could not be easily placed within the framework of this study. That is, it would look similar to a form described by the literature AAVE, but it would be slightly different. Some examples from the completed *done* section include the phrases *hadn't done left* and *we'll done lose*. These phrases raise the interesting question of whether the author is reflecting a knowledge of individual (idiosyncratic) use or whether she is simply mistaken in her understanding of how this form is typically used by Vernacular speakers. If the latter is the case, these forms may be labeled fictional stereotypical language as opposed to fictional accounts of actual language use. In general, this chapter exposes some of the conventions used to show the kind of Vernacular used by female characters that indicate that the authors want readers to know that the speakers are African American. In the next chapter, I discuss other types of Vernacular structures used by these females.

4

Vernacular Structures—NSE

Chapter 3 focuses on AAVE Vernacular features and how they are used by African American female characters to reflect their membership in the some segments of the African American speech community. The non-Standard English (NSE) Vernacular structures discussed in this section cover a wider range of social contexts.

Many of the features that I discuss in this chapter take their labels and at least partial descriptions from Wolfram's *Dialects and American English*; others come from descriptions in linguistic books or from my own observations.

LACK OF SUBJECT-VERB AGREEMENT

This feature is commonly used to portray non-Standard speakers. There are many instances of its use among the early works. Rose, an ex-slave, produces the following sentences. In example 3 she is quoting a white slave trader:

1. *I has* de correct mem'randum of when de war start. (Rose 435)
2. When *we'uns gits* te de tradin' block. (435)
3. But three am more dan *I wants, I guesses.* (435)

In a novel written in 1893, another ex-slave produces the following:

4. an' when *she war* done she jis' set down and sniffled and cried, an' *I war* so glad I didn't know what to do. (Harper 11)

Hurston's characters use this form regularly. The following sentences are produced by Janie, the main character in *Their Eyes Were Watching God*:

5. Well then, we can set right where *we is* and talk. (19)
6. To start off wid, *people* like dem *wastes* up too much time puttin' they mouf on things they don't know nothin' about. (17)

Note that in this utterance Janie also says *they don't* instead of *they doesn't*, using Standard subject-verb agreement.

Annie Poole, an old lady in Larsen's "Sanctuary," utters the following:

7. You ain't in no hurry, *is you*, Jim Hammer? (320)

Sally, a slave in Brent's work, says:

8. When dey finds *you is* gone. (98)

Other examples in early works include:

I:	*Ah aims, I's, I goes, I does, Ah takes, I feels, Ah sees*
we:	*we gets, we calls*
us:	*us gets*
you:	*you looks, you shows, you's, you knows, you switches, you has*
he:	*he were, he do, he love*
she:	*she feel*
they:	*dey was, dey does, they wants*
other:	*no-one neber goes, men isn't, you and your sister was, Jack say, folk is*

The same set of speakers also include Standard subject-verb agreement in many of their other utterances. Early examples include:

9. Your *grandmother is* all bowed down wid trouble now. (Brent 98)

10. It 'pears lack 'twas only yisterday dat *I was* a gal wurkin' right yere. (Hopkins, "Hagar's" 47)

11. *Obadiah's* right fond of you. (Larsen, "Sanctuary" 321)

Lack of subject-verb agreement appears in later works also, but not with the same frequency. All of the following speakers are older females:

12. If *you wants* the bus depot. (Naylor, *The Women* 30)

13. Oh, *I does* all right for an old woman, but I ain't had me much school learning. (Taylor, *Circle* 96)

14. Why they ain't got no Great-Aunt cups? *There is* great aunts, ya know—even in Atlanta. (Naylor, *Mama Day* 35)

In example 15, the speaker is an adult female born in the West Indies:

15. But be-Jesus-Christ, what kind of man *is you*, nuh? (Marshall, *Brown Girl* 24)

As with certain other AAVE features, this form is often used as a "token" to signal that the speaker is either speaking in a non-Standard manner or metaphorically shifting to another style for some reason. In the next passage, a Standard speaker parodies the form by placing it within a very formal structure:

16. One never knows, *do one*, what's hidden away in the backwoods of Connecticut? [The author wrote: "she rolled her eyes like Mantan Moreland in the movies."] (Marshall, *Daughters* 27)

BEING USED AS AN ADVERB

I noticed that this construction appears in one of the earliest works. It is used by an ex-slave in example 1 and by her daughter in example 2:

1. Some new Yankee fashion cookin' chicken, I reckon, *bein'* Mis' Johnson's from out Bos'n way. (Hopkins, "Hagar's" 172)

2. Ef you don' fin' your granny, stop at yer pa's an' *bein'* as the Gin'ral's away yer pester him to try an' hunt her up. (174)

A-PREFIXING

A-prefixing is often associated with rural areas such as Appalachia. Its use shows up in several of the early works. Most of the speakers are older women who live or lived in rural areas. The first two speakers, Aunt Henny, (example 1) and Annie Poole (example 2) were born during slavery:

1. I'm *a gwine* to keep *a climbin'* high. (Hopkins, "Hagar's" 65)

Aunt Henny also says, "*a struttin'* " and "*a poundin'*."

2. Ah'm *a-gwine* hide you dis one time. (Larsen, "Sanctuary" 321)

Annie also says, "*a tellin'*."

The next example comes from a speaker who is an adult female with a rural background but who may not have been an ex-slave:

3. Youse always *uh runnin'* and *uh rippin'* and clambin' trees and rocks and jumpin', flingin' rocks in creeks and sich like. (Hurston, *Jonah's* 11)

An example of this form also appears in a later work. An old lady in Naylor's *Mama Day* produces the following passage:

4. Just *a poking* me in my back, poking in my left hip. (37)

IRREGULAR VERBS

Wolfram (1991) identifies five categories of irregular verb patterns. In the works that I examined there are examples of each.

Using Past Form as Participle

The first example of this form is from an ex-slave, an older woman:

1. 'Pears like folks *is took* up wid makin' money an' politics. (Harper 62)

The first two of the next examples come from a later autobiographical work, called *Gal*, written by Ruth Bolton. The third example also comes from a later work; the female is an older female Vernacular speaker:

2. Somehow she must *have knew* I was up to something. (149)

3. I figure I *had gave* him the wrong number. (127)

4. I want this *took care of* tonight. (Monroe 507)

Using Participle as Past Form

Two verbs stand out as being used most often. They are forms of the verb *done* and *seen*.

Done

As with several other features, the use of this form generally signals a Vernacular speaker. Early examples include the following two; both are from older females:

1. What he *done* am force me to live with dat nigger, Rufus, 'gainst my wants. (Rose 436)

2. And, Janie, maybe it wasn't much, but Ah *done* de best Ah kin by you. (Hurston, *Eyes* 37)

In later works this form is used by both adult females (example 3) and older females examples (4 and 5):

3. Naw. *Done* it. You know, with a man. (Jones, *Eva* 89)

4. what he been through and what it *done* to him. (Hansberry 106)

5. did more work in twenty-four hours than these good-timing niggers out here on Fulton Street *done* for the year. (Marshall, *Brown Girl* 29)

Seen

Older females supply these examples. The first two come from early works:

1. but they don't know—they never *seen* good dancing. (Larison 60)

2. At de bery time ole Miss *seen* de debbil in de summer house. (Hopkins, "Hagar's" 64)

3. I *seen* a secondhand bureau over on Maxwell Street. (Hansberry 102)

4. I never *seen* nobody take it out of the mailbox. (Hunter 24)

The past participle form for the verb *take* is sometimes used this way also: "You better make haste and tell 'em 'bout you and Tea Cake gittin' married, and if he *taken* all yo' money and went off wid some young gal" (Hurston, *Eyes* 17).

Bare Root as Past or Present Form

In my examination of various works by African American females, I found the bare root of *be* used as a past form. Generally, this feature is used by older females. Here is an early example of its use:

1. Dey neber *be* easy goin' 'gin, fuh sho'. (Hopkins, "Hagar's" 175)

Walker's *The Color Purple*, set in earlier times, has several characters who used this form:

2. It *be* more then a notion taking care of children ain't even yourn. (14)

3. I know she *be* big. (15)

Other verbs are used this way also. The next two examples come from early works; the first from an ex-slave:

4. He *talk* to pappy and pappy *talk* to him and *say*, "Dem my woman and chiles." (Rose 435)

5. She *begin* tuh slap mah jaws ever which a'way. (Hurston, *Eyes* 34)

Older females in later works produce the following examples:

6. Well, he *run* off with that trifling Peggy—from Elyria. (Morrison, *Bluest* 15)

7. You *give* him up for me? (Hansberry 106)

The final example comes from a later work set in an earlier time; the speaker is a young adult female:

8. He *come* home with a girl from round Gray. (Walker, *Purple* 14)

In later works adult females used the bare root of *be* as a present form:

9. Go on now, Sterling, and get dressed before we *be* late. (Meriwether 61)

10. Cain't nobody hardly understand him lessen you came from wherever he *be* from. (Bambara, "Playin" 74)

Regularization

Regularizing irregular verbs is something that female speakers do in many of the works that I examined. The following two sentences are examples of this practice. The first one comes from an early work; the second one comes from a later work:

1. The worst thing Ah ever *knowed* her to do was taking a few years offa her age. (Hurston, *Eyes* 13)

2. I *would have sweared* it was a joke. (Jones 35)

Other examples of regularization include *throwed, seed, comed, tored, drawed,* and *borned.*

Other Irregular Past Forms

I made an unexpected discovery while researching for this section; it has to do with the word *tooken,* the form that some speakers use for the past participle of *take.* For example, I found the following sentence in an early work:

1. but we'uns am never *tooken* to church and has no books for larnin'. (Rose 436)

When I first listed the verb *tooken*, I assumed that it represented an archaic form similar to that of a verb like *gwine*. I was therefore quite surprised to find the following use of *tooken* in a contemporary autobiographical work about a young woman called *Gal*:

> 2. Aunt Beezy would always drive us to the fields, and we never had *tooken* any food with us. (Bolton 33–34)

Other irregular forms appear in the works. Some examples are *het* [heated], *kilt* [killed], *wropped* [wrapped], *hern* [heard], *skint* [skinned], *helt* [held], and *asted* [asked].

For the foregoing examples, it appears that the use of non-Standard irregular verbs is just another means of characterizing Vernacular speakers. Writers show these forms being used in nearly all of the works that contain Vernacular speakers. They are used by old, young, urban, and rural speakers.

OTHER NON-STANDARD VERB FORMS

I include in this section other kinds of examples that represent non-Standard use of one kind or another. Some of the examples represent recognized Vernacular forms; some may represent individual style.

Verb Subclass Shifts

Wolfram (1991), in discussing different types of verb patterns, describes one in which the speaker makes shifts among various subclasses. One of these subclass shifts is called "the formation of verb complement structures (i.e., the structures of items that occur with the verb)" (286). His example is: "The students *started to messing* around." The example I found comes from an adult, Vernacular-speaking female in a later work: "I *started acted* mean and evil" (Bolton 185).

Verb + *for* + Infinitive

This is an older form that seems to be associated with southern or rural use. It appears in the spiritual "Swing Low Sweet Chariot" (e.g., *Coming for to carry* me home). The following examples are produced by older women who are ex-slaves:

> 1. De massa *wants* you-uns *fer to bring* forth portly chillen. (Rose 436)
>
> 2. An Ah don' spec' dey'll *go for to do* dat. (Larsen, "Sanctuary" 321)

Absence of Expected Infinitives

These examples come from an early work; the speaker is an adult female:

> 1. You ain't *gwine put* no chile uh mine under no Mimms. (Hurston, *Jonah's* 7)
>
> 2. John, promise me yuh *goin' quit* dat. (11)

Come and + Verb

There are several appearances of this form. The first three examples come from early works. Examples 1 and 2 are produced by adults; example 3 comes from a young girl:

1. After I's in, dat nigger *come and crawl* in de bunk with me 'fore I knows it. (Rose 436)
2. She was afraid to *come and bid* me good by, but she left a kind message with Betty. (Brent 114)
3. Ned Crittenden! Don't you lak it, don't you take it, heah mah collar *come and* you *shake* it! (Hurston, *Jonah's* 5–6)

There are several examples from later works. Kiswana Browne, a middle-class young woman in Naylor's *The Women of Brewster Place* makes the following statement:

4. As soon as they *come and paint*, I'm going to hang my Ashanti print over the couch. (81)

Other examples include *come and ask, come and stop, come and pick up*.

Here Come

Like the form auxiliary *come* discussed in the section on AAVE forms, the expression *here come* is sometimes used to express exasperation or indignation. I did not find examples in early works, but there are several in later works:

1. Soon as I got one day done *here come* a night. (Morrison, *Sula* 69)
2. now every Sunday *here come* Mr.____. (Walker, *Purple* 14)

This form is also used to express surprise or feigned surprise:

3. Then, lo and behold, *here comes* Pemberton out the bedroom. (Clair 90)
4. Well, *here come* the Reverend Mr.____, she say. (Walker, *Purple* 24)

Verbs Derived from Other Parts of Speech

Wolfram (1991) notes that some verbs are derived from other parts of speech. The following two examples come from the same work, and in both cases the verb is derived from a noun. Example 1 is from a middle-aged woman—a former slave. Her daughter produces example 2:

1. I *'spicion* him jes' the same. (Hopkins, "Hagar's" 177)
2. I *suspicion* him more and more every minute I'm alive, I do. (224)

Shifts in Semantic Reference

In the same section of the Wolfram book mentioned earlier, he describes this category as "broadened or narrowed semantic domain of the verb form" (287). I found some examples of this form. All of them come from later works, and the speakers are all adult females; the last two females are older women:

1. It's clear she *fixin to* take off. (Bambara, "Witchbird" 177)
2. What're you all *fixing to* do? (Tate 156)
3. I don't know no man who would sport a woman *fixing to* have a baby if she don't belong to him. (Clair 78)
4. Her baby's *fixin' to* come, ain't it? (Monroe 518)

Does as Auxiliary [Emphatic]

The use of *does* as an emphatic auxiliary appears in two contexts. It is used in a very early work where the speaker might have been using a form of plantation creole (example 1), and it appears in a later work that features West Indian speakers (example 2). The speakers are adult females:

1. We *does* owe on the mor'gage five hundred dollars. (Hopkins, "Hagar's" 175)
2. You *does* just be going there to meet boys. (Marshall, *Brown Girl* 42)

Absence of Auxiliary *Have*

Wolfram (1991) mentions absence of *be* forms as one of the characteristics of Vernacular speech. I discuss absence of *be* forms in the AAVE section, but there are also a large number of absences of *have* forms in the speech of the fictional Vernacular speakers that I examined. As a matter of fact, after the use of *done,* I have more instances of this form than nearly any other feature. There are patterns of absence that seem to be quite consistent.

In the following discussion, I adopt the use of the term NP to stand for nouns, pronouns, and proper nouns.

NP + *Been* + Verb-*ing*

Examples of this form appear in both early and later works. As early examples, the first two come from adult females; the last one, from an older woman:

1. Ain't got no money, an' *you been wurkin'* stiddy fer munfs! (Hopkins, "Hagar's" 176)
2. You jes took tuh buckin' 'im since *you been hangin'* round sich ez Beasley and Mimms. (Hurston, *Jonah's* 3)
3. But *you* allus *been triflin'.* Cain't do nuffin propah. (Larsen, "Sanctuary" 321)

In the later examples, the first speaker is an adult; the next two are older women:

4. *I been thinking* about it, Landlord. (Hunter 104)
5. *You been knowing* me a long time, ain't you, sugar? (Naylor, *Mama Day* 77)
6. *I been telling* you that for years. (Naylor, *The Women* 38)

NP + *Been* + Verb-*ed* (Participle)

An older speaker from an early work supplied the first example; example 2 comes from a later work, and the speaker is an adult female:

1. Unc' Ned conjure man; neber *been whopped* in all he life. (Hopkins, "Hagar's" 64)

2. *You been gone* too long, Sula. (Morrison, *Sula* 96)

In the following examples, the auxiliary *have* is absent in several different contexts. In most cases these constructions appear either in early works or where spoken by older females in later works.

NP + *Been* + Adjective

Both of these examples come from early works; the first speaker is an older, ex-slave; the second is an adult female:

1. Not lessen *you been keerless* an' let 'em smell you out gittin' hyah. (Larsen, "Sanctuary" 321)

2. an' Mis' Jenkins *been* mighty *kind.* (Hopkins, "Hagar's" 177)

NP + *Been* + Adverb

The first examples comes from an early work, and the speaker is an adult female. The next two come from later works; the speaker in example 2 is an adult female, and the last speaker is an older woman:

1. *Us been heah* too long. (Hurston, *Jonah's* 6)

2. Have you seen her since *you been back*? (Morrison, *Sula* 97)

3. How long *she been* like that? (Naylor, *Mama Day* 71)

NP + *Been* + Noun

The following example is from an adult female from an early work: "we *been kissin'-friends* for twenty years" (Hurston, *Eyes* 19).

Absence of Auxiliary *Do*

This form appears regularly in both early and later works. It often appears in question constructions using *what*. In the first two examples, taken from early works, the first speaker is an older woman; the second is an adult:

1. I says, "*What you* means, yo fool nigger?" (Rose 436)

2. Anyhow, *what you* ever *know* her to do so bad as y'all make out? (Hurston, *Eyes* 13)

All of the following speakers are adult females who appear in later works. The second example is set during an earlier time:

3. Dearie B! Chile! *What you* say! (Cooper, *Homemade* 51)

4. History? *What you* mean? (Morrison, *Beloved* 44)

5. *What I* got to tell you? (Meriwether 185)

Absence of Modal *Will*

This form is found in an early work and in a later work set in earlier times:

1. *You have* to 'scuse me, 'cause Ah'm bound to go take her some supper. (Hurston, *Eyes* 13)

2. *I be* sure to ask, but I know they take women at the slaughterhouse. (Morrison, *Beloved* 144)

Special Modals

Wolfram (1991) says that "[t]he forms *liketa* and *(su)poseta* may be used as a special verb modifier to mark special speaker perceptions relating to significant events that were on the verge of happening" (288–289).

In the works that I examined, the following examples are present; all come from later works.

Suppose[d] to

The first female is a Standard speaker who is style-shifting; the second female is an adult Vernacular speaker:

1. Here the three of us *suppose to* be traveling together and she just ups and leaves, ruining the rest of the trip for the two of us. (Marshall, *Praisesong* 27)

2. you *supposed to* be my friend lavender. (DeVeaux, "Tapestry" 172)

Like to [Liketa]

Both females in the following are Standard speakers who are style-shifting:

1. Ma *like to* had a fit. (Briscoe 68)

2. Mama *liketa* jumped down the man's throat. (Shange, *Betsey* 111)

Negation

There are two types of negation in the works that I examined; one type involves multiple negation, and the other involves *ain't* as auxiliary. Wolfram (1991) notes that there are four different patterns of negation in the Vernacular varieties of English (292–293). Following are examples of three of the patterns.

Marking of the Negative in the Verb Phrase and the Indefinite(s) Following the Verb

Example 1 comes from an early work; example 2 comes from a later work. Both of the speakers are adult females:

1. So Ah told her, "Ah *don't know nothin'* but what Ah'm told tuh do. (Hurston, *Eyes* 34)

2. I *ain't supposed to have nothing.* (Morrison, *Sula* 22)

Negative Marking of an Indefinite Before the Verb Phrase and Within the Verb Phrase

Adult females in early works produce examples 1 and 2; an adult West Indian female in a later work produces 3:

1. *Nothin' couldn't* ketch me dese few steps Ah'm goin'. (Hurston, *Eyes* 13)

2. Well, *nobody don't* know if it's anything to tell or not. (Hurston, *Eyes* 12)

3. *Nobody din* say he *can't* have the hot-*ass* woman. (Marshall, *Brown Girl* 31)

The speaker in example 2 also uses one positive indefinite pronoun (*anything*).

Inverting the Negative Element at the Beginning of the Sentence

There are several examples of this form, but all of them come from later works; the speakers are adult females:

1. *Can't nobody* spend every day in a shed for three years without being up to some devilment. (Morrison, *Tar* 13)

2. *Cain't nobody* hardly understand him lessen you came from wherever he be from. (Bambara, "Playin" 74)

3. Her mouth open showing all her teef and *don't nothing* seem to be troubling her mind. (Walker, *Purple* 33)

Two excellent examples of style-shifting come from older, Standard-speaking females. In example 4, Margaret-Elizabeth, in *Paper Dolls*, a play by Jackson, scoffs at her friend Lizzie's warning to behave with decorum:

4. *Ain't nobody* looking up here! (Jackson 394)

Bessie Delany, speaking about using certain words from her "hey day," says in a burst of defiance:

5. *Ain't nobody* going to censor me, no, sir! I'm a hundred-and-one years old and at my age, honey, I can say what I want! (Delany et al. 16)

Auxiliary *Ain't*

Wolfram (1991) notes that the auxiliary *ain't* may be used as a correspondence for various forms of Standard English, including forms of *be + not, have + not,* and *do + not*. He points out that the use of *ain't* as a correspondence for *do* is considered a uniquely AAVE feature, and that usage was discussed in the Chapter 3.

Ain't as a correspondence for the forms *be + not, have + not* appears extensively in both early and later works.

Be + Not

In all of the following examples, the *ain't* replaces the *be* auxiliary and the negative form *not* in progressive verb phrases. The first two examples come from early works; both of the speakers are adult females:

1. I hope you *ain't goin' ter have* sof'n o' the brain from drinkin' all Sam Smith's bad rum over to Buzzard's Nes'. (Hopkins, "Hagar's" 178)
2. You *ain't givin'* 'im nothin'. (Hurston, *Jonah's* 3)
3. I *ain't studying* myself with the niggers of this world. Besides, I have God and my Bible! (Rahman 215)
4. Leave him be. He *ain't botherin' nothing*. (Naylor, *The Women* 33)
5. I just know you *ain't singing* about me. (Dove, *Fifth Sunday* 26)

Have + Not

In the following examples, *aint* replaces the *have* auxiliary and the negative form *not* in past participle verb phrases. Although the first two examples come from early works, most of the examples come from later works. Both speakers are adult:

1. Obadiah, he *ain't done nuffin'*, Mistah Lowndes. (Larsen, "Sanctuary" 322)
2. she *ain't seen notin', nor hearn notin'*. (Brent 114)

In later works like the ones by Dove and Ansa, the form is used by adult females:

3. I *ain't got no* need for asking my husband nothing. (Dove, *Fifth Sunday* 27)
4. you go to grabbing and snatching it like you *ain't never had nothing* in your lives. (Ansa, *Baby* 58)

Many of the the later examples come from older females:

5. Guess you think I *ain't never loved*, huh, girl? (Sanchez, "Just Don't" 284)
6. Oh, I does all right for an old woman, but I *ain't had* me much school learning. (Taylor, *Circle* 96)

The last example comes from a younger female:

7. You *ain't done nothin'*. (Taylor, *Circle* 201)

I also found some examples of Standard speakers style-shifting into use of this form. The first example is from an older woman, and the second comes from a young girl:

8. That's why you *ain't made no* more movies to this day. (Jackson 399)
9. Mama's patients, niggahs what *aint got no* sense. (Shange, *Betsey* 26)

Other Forms of *Ain't*

Ain't is also used as a main verb in a number of utterances. In many cases it is coupled with another form of negation like *no* or *nothing*. The first two examples are from early works. The first speaker is an older woman, the second, an adult:

1. And the young ones *ain't no* better. (Larison 52)
2. Cap'n Mimms *ain't nothin'* but po' white trash. (Hurston, *Jonah's* 7)

The following examples come from later works; the speakers are older females:

3. Is a rudeness you have, talking to me so. Dog my age *ain't no* pup, you know. (Rahman 215)
4. Betsey, there *ain't nothin'* in the world to make you a nigger. (Shange, *Betsey* 83)

Ain't also appears as a main verb without other forms of negation:

5. It damn sure *ain't* me. (McMillan, *Disappearing Act* 84)

Finally, *ain't* replaces *be* forms in tag questions:

6. Mothers are something *ain't* they? (Cooper, *Homemade* 1)

All of the preceding examples are from later works, and the speakers are adults.

PRONOUN SYSTEMS

The pronoun system contains another set of features that seem to be used by the writers to signal non-Standard usage, informal uses, or style-shifting. The pronouns described next are different from those that are generally described as AAVE. However, I still believe that a few of these may be seen as part of a creole system, either from African languages or from American Indian languages. Wolfram (1991) lists five categories of differences in Vernacular pronoun use. Following are examples of each of them.

Using Non-Standard Forms of Possessives

This form (e.g., *hisself* for *himself*) appears in both early and later works. The first three examples come from early works. The last two come from later works. The speakers are adult females:

1. He jes rub *hisse'f* all ober wid goopher. (Hopkins, "Hagar's" 64)
2. Most of dese zigaboos is so het up over yo' business till they liable to hurry *theyself* to Judgment to find out about you if they don't soon know. (Hurston, *Eyes* 17)
3. He's round thirty his *ownself.* (Hurston, *Eyes* 12)
4. If you had any respect for the dead you'd be crying your *own self.* (S. E. Wright 262)
5. barely keep *hisself* in changing clothes (Sanchez, "Just Don't" 285)

Using *And Them* and *'nem* to Refer to Groups

This form is found only in later works; all of the speakers are adult females:

1. All them women is dirt poor with not people at all. Mrs. Wilkens and *them*. (Morrison, *Sula* 100)

2. Florence and *them*. (Bolton 9)

3. no matter what *mamma-nem* [mama and them] said; his eyes did sparkle. (Williams, "Meditations" 206)

Using a Variant of *You* for Second-Person Plural

It is somewhat surprising to me that only the first three of the following examples come from the early works. The speakers in the first and third examples are adults; the speaker in the second example is an older female. In the first example, the speaker is describing what her mistress said to her:

1. *Yous* am de portly gal and Rufus de portly man. (Rose 436)

2. Obadiah, he's too good to *youall* no 'count trash. (Larsen, "Sanctuary" 321)

3. De rest uh *y'all* get yo' plates and come git some uh dese cow-peas and pone bread. (Hurston, *Jonah's* 7–8)

In the later examples, the majority of the examples come from adults and older females:

4. *you all* done come in here, now go on to sleep. (Marshall, *Brown Girl* 41)

5. I know *y'all* wanta think the best of me, but I've been thru plenty of mess in my days. (Shange, *Betsey* 179)

The following example contains multiple use of the form in a single utterance. The speaker is an older female:

6. Come to bring *y'all* this here cow. Heard *y'all* lost *y'all's*, and you know we got more cows'n we can use the milk from. I figures *y'all* needin' a cow, *y'all* can jus' take this one off our hands awhile and put her to good use. jus' lending her to *y'all* till *y'all* get on your feet and can get ya one. (Taylor, *Circle* 200)

Note that in this passage, the speaker also says: *your feet* and *get ya* [you] one.

The adult speaker in 7 uses both Standard and Vernacular forms of the plural you:

7. *Y'all* calling on the wrath of God, feelin on each other like that. *You* better quit or somethin terrible gon' happen. I know. I swear fo' God, I know. (Shange, *Betsey* 41)

Other Vernacular forms of plural *you* include:

8. De massa wants *you-uns* fer to bring forth portly chillen.' (Rose 436)

Using *Them* for *Those*

Examples 1 and 2 are from early works; 3 through 5 are from later works. All of the speakers are adult females:

1. Why, in some of *them* shanties there are a dozen or more, whites, and blacks, and all colors, and nothing to eat and nothing to wear. (Larison 52)
2. She had some of *them* wite women she's always trailing around after. (Fauset, *Comedy* 305)
3. *Them* money orders sure helped. (Morrison, *Tar* 247)
4. one of *them* good to screw types. (DeVeaux, "Tapestry" 172)
5. I drops a hamhock in *them* string beans. (Guy, *Measure* 110)

A Special Personal Dative Use of the Object Pronoun Form

The examples come from later works; the speakers are adult females:

1. But I got *me* this go-ood job. (Guy, *Measure* 109)
2. Cause I loves *me* a fine man. (DeVeaux, "Tapestry" 169)

Wolfram (1991) notes that the preceding first four types of pronominal differences are well represented in most Vernaculars. He points out that the use of such terms as *you all* is southern, while Rose's use of *you-uns* is more likely associated with regions like those in western Pennsylvania (Rose, an ex-slave, lived in New Jersey). He also notes that the use of the personal dative is not particularly stigmatized in some contexts (295). Finally, he mentions examples of other pronoun forms that appear rarely. One form discusses the use of an object form with a simple subject. I found an example in an early work; the speaker is an adult female: "*[H]im* say nothin'" (Rose 435).

Other NS Pronouns

Adoption of Other Forms to Take the Place of Subjective Pronouns

I found other non-Standard forms that are not mentioned by Wolfram. Some of the most stigmatized forms appear only in the early works. They are produced by older females who live during or right after slavery:

1. *W'atall* [what all] bad news, Mistah Lowndes? (Larsen, "Sanctuary" 322)
2. When *we'uns* gits te de tradin' block. (Rose 435)

Relative Pronouns

Wolfram (1991) notes that form differences may range from the socially insignificant use of *that* for human subjects to the quite stigmatized use of *what.* Rose, the ex-slave mentioned earlier, uses this form regularly:

1. folks dere *what* come to look us over. (Rose 435)

2. Dere is 'bout 50 niggers *what* is growed and lots of chillen. (435)

Possessives

Wolfram identifies three categories involving possessive nouns and pronouns. I discuss one form under AAVE (*mines*). He notes that the one that is identified with Appalachian speech is the possessive *his'n* or *your'n*. The first two examples come from early works:

1. Them remarks o' *yourn* is suttingly curious. (Hopkins, "Hagar's" 178)

2. Pheoby, dat Sam of *your'n* just won't quit! (Hurston, *Eyes* 17)

3. It be more then a notion taking care of children ain't even *yourn*. (Walker, *Purple* 14)

OTHER GRAMMATICAL STRUCTURES

Several other grammatical structures have been commonly identified with Vernacular speakers. I briefly describe some of the ones that appear most often.

Pronominal Apposition

In a section on other grammatical structures, Wolfram (1991) notes that there are a number of these structures that might have been discussed, but were not. He explains that the structures often appear in the spoken language of many groups but because their use is so widespread, they often go unnoticed. One such structure is pronominal opposition.

This form is found in both early and later works. It appears most often in narratives. All of the following speakers are adult; examples from early works include:

1. *Obadiah, he* ain't done nuffin,' Mistah Lowndes. (Larsen, "Sanctuary" 322)

2. *Marse Sargeant he* lose heap money. (Hopkins, "Hagar's" 47)

3. *Massa Alf Pearson,* he got uh big plantation and he's quality white folks. (Hurston, *Jonah's* 11)

The next two examples come from later works:

4. My *mama she* fuss. (Walker, *Purple* 11)

5. *Marie—she's* my comedienne friend. (McMillan, *Disappearing Act* 20)

Prepositions

Wolfram (1991) notes that the discussion of different prepositions should take into account that each one is different from the other, and the differences are really more lexical than grammatical (296). I found that the use of certain prepositions is very often one of the clearest indications that a speaker is using Vernacular speech. Some of the forms indicate regional variation, others may well be examples of individual style. Most instances of use appear in early works. The first example comes from an older female:

1. Fore dat he shoot a mon *to* de college. (Hopkins, "Hagar's" 63)

2. Maybe us don't know *into* things lak you do. (Hurston, *Eyes* 12)

3. Humph! Talkin' *after* po' white trash! (Hurston, *Jonah's* 10)

Other examples include *iffen* [if], *outen* [out of].

In some of the utterances, the speaker leaves the preposition out: "Ah b'longs on de *other side de* Big Creek anyhow" (Hurston, *Jonah's* 6).

Plurals

Wolfram (1991) points out that there are several categories of plurals. I found an example of the most common form, "regularization of various irregular plural noun forms" (294). The next example comes an from early work; the speaker is an older female: "But dem last *lick* burnt me lak fire" (Hurston, *Eyes* 34).

Finally, I located several other structures that have been identified as non-Standard forms. These forms include the following.

Irregular Clausal Structures

The examples come from early works, and the speaker is an adult female:

1. If they wants to see and know, *why they don't come kiss and be kissed*? (Hurston, *Eyes* 18)

2. They don't know *if life is a mess of corn-meal dumplings, and if love is a bed-quilt!* (Hurston, *Eyes* 17)

Irregular Question Forms

The first example comes from an early work; the first three speakers are adult females. The last speaker is a young child:

1. *Who yo' folks is over* de Big Creek? (Hurston, *Jonah's* 19)

2. *What you two was talking today?* (Marshall, *Brown Girl* 44)

3. *Why ain't nobody known* Bernice is pregnant? (Naylor, *Mama Day* 71)

4. *what you brought?* (Marshall, *Brown Girl* 40)

Existential *It/They*

Wolfram (1991) writes that this form appears to be spreading. In the following examples *it* appears where Standard speakers would use *there*. I found the first two examples in early works; the last example comes from a later work. All of the speakers are adult female:

1. If it wuzn't for so many black folks *it* wouldn't be no race problem. (Hurston, *Eyes* 210)

2. Well, nobody don't know if *it's* anything to tell or not. (Hurston, *Eyes* 12)

3. *It's* some Black people that have whiter skin than some white people. (Cooper, *Homemade* 41)

The Use of *de* as an Indefinite Article

This form is used by the ex-slave Rose in an early work. In example 3, Rose quotes a man at a slave auction:

1. One man shows *de* intres' in pappy. (Rose 435)

2. and I sho' has *de* worryment. (435)

3. She's never been 'bused and will make *de* good breeder. (435)

This last form is interesting because its use suggests that there may be another language that is influencing her speech, possibly French.

SUMMARY

This section on non-Standard English features used by African American female characters reinforces the notion that non-Standard usage reflects a variety of different contexts.

As part of the examination of Vernacular speakers I've also described some features such as lack of subject-verb agreement (Oh, *I does* all right for an old woman); regularization of irregular verbs (I *would have sweared* it was a joke); and shifts in semantic reference (It's clear she *fixin to* take off).

I've also shown that some Vernacular speakers use features identified with regional differences, such as *a*-prefixing (*a climbin'*) or pronoun use (*you all, yun-uns*). Some use forms identified with certain time periods (*am* used with other than first-person singular; *gwine*). In addition, I've shown that the speakers' age might influence what features are used. For example, older females often use older or more archaic forms (*An' w'at am you lookin' foh me to do 'bout et?*). I also noted that in a few of the examples ethnicity influenced the speech of the female characters, as with the use of auxiliary *do* (You *does* just *be going* there to meet boys). Finally, I have pointed out that a person's individual speech style can also account for differences in the way that a female character speaks (One man shows *de* intres' in pappy). In Chapters 5, 6, and 7, I discuss grammatical structures. In Chapter 5, I focus on the females' use of Standard grammar. In Chapters 6 and 7, I focus on adjectives and adverbs—two forms that have received considerable attention from researchers on gender-based language differences.

5

Standard Structures

In this chapter, I discuss some of the differences in Standard structures that I found in works that I examined. The African American female characters use a wide range of structures that reflect their social class or level of education. Most of these features have been discussed in research literature that focuses on the subject of language and gender.

STANDARD GRAMMATICAL STRUCTURES

I look at some grammatical structures that have been identified as being part of the verbal repertoires of either educated speakers or middle-class female speakers. We begin with the verb phrase since Wolfram and Christian point out that "many of the socially significant grammatical structures concern the construction of the verb phrase" (136).

Auxiliaries *Shall*, *Do*, and *Must*

These forms appear in both early and later works. The early works contain examples of the exaggerated style often used to stereotype upper-class socialites. Examples 1 through 3 are from early works. The examples in the later works represent several different speaking styles. Example 4 is taken from a young girl daydreaming; example 5 comes from a schoolteacher who is addressing her class; and in example 6 a mother is speaking to her young daughter:

1. I hope I *shan't* be sick. (Kelley-Hawkins 16)
2. Oh, *do* try. *Do* put somebody else off. (Larsen, "Passing" 162)
3. *Must* you go? (Brent 87)

4. When I marry the President I *shall* call Eugene to be my escort. (Shange, *Betsey* 119)

5. we *shall* have to sacrifice for the next few days. We *shall* work, work, work. (Taylor, *Thunder* 13–14)

6. You *must* learn not to tell obvious lies. (Lee 31)

Modal Constructions

Modals (*will/would, can/could, may/might, ought*) have been identified as structures that are often used by females to signal politeness or deference. Though many might question this characterization, these forms appear in the speech of many Standard-speaking females in early works:

1. *Will* you join us? (Kelley-Hawkins 18)

2. O Master, *may* I go to meeting? (Veney, *Collected* 17)

3. But now I'm here, *may* I stay awhile? (Fauset, *Comedy* 199)

4. *Ought'nt* we really to stop and phone? (Larsen, "Quicksand" 40)

5. *Would* you like to watch me get things together? (Fauset, *Comedy* 202)

In the next two passages, Vernacular-speaking females welcome visitors and offer them refreshments. Example 6 comes from an early work, and the speaker is an older woman; example 7 comes from a work that was written in the 1980s but was set in an earlier time. The speaker is an adult female:

6. *Wont* yer hab a glass ob milk? (Harper 154)

7. *Won't* you have a seat? How bout a cool drink of water? (Walker, *Purple* 58)

Modals also appear in some of the later works that feature Standard speakers; examples 8 and 9 also show females offering refreshments:

8. *Will* you have another roll? (Lee 60)

9. *Will* you have a piece of chicken? (Guy, *Measure* 111)

10. Betsey! *Would* you see what's the matter. (Shange, *Betsey* 51)

11. Never a kindly how-do or *may* I help you. (Naylor, *Mama Day* 93)

Though most of the females who use this form are Standard speakers, a later work that features young speakers shows one young female identified as a Vernacular speaker producing the following sentence:

12. If she didn't want it, she *oughtn't* to have ask for it. (Guy, *Friends* 44)

Female Language Verbs

The three verbs, *dare [to]*, *needn't*, *can/could not bear*, are representative of the types of verbs that I have identified as classic female language verb stereotypes. Though they are often used by Standard-speaking females, they also appear in the speech of Vernacular speakers.

Dare + [*to*]

The form *dare* + [*to*] was used both in early and later works. Example 1 comes from an early work. Examples 2 and 3 come from later works:

1. Do you *dare to* take the responsibility? (Kelley-Hawkins 15)
2. If he so much as *dares to* put his infested, fat, red fingers in my personal, private belongings. (Jackson 353)
3. and you *dare to* speak of Ghana. (Angelou, *All God's* 50)

Vernacular speakers in two later works also use this form. The speaker in example 4 is a young woman from the South. The speaker in example 5 is West Indian:

4. I won't *dare to* come back to this old hick town. (Bolton 194)
5. with some woman called a Driver to wash yuh tail in licks if yuh *dare* look up. (Marshall, *Brown Girl* 45)

Needn't

This form is found in both early and later works. Examples 1 and 2 both come from early works, and both females are speakers of Standard English. Example 3 comes from a later work, and the speaker is a Vernacular speaker from the South:

1. Come back to bed—we *needn't* get up yet. (Kelley-Hawkins 9)
2. Well, you *needn't* trouble to answer. (Larsen, "Quicksand" 11)
3. You *needn't* go get an attitude and blame other folks 'cause you forgot. (Tate 72)

Can/Could Not Bear

Example 1 comes from early works; example 2, from a later one. Both females are Standard speakers:

1. she just *can't bear* any dark people. (Fauset, *Comedy* 54)
2. On the fifth night I *couldn't bear* watching them. (Meriwether 178)

The next sentence is produced by an apparition from the past in the book *Baby of the Family*, which is set in modern times:

3. But to be a slave on the ocean, I *could not bear* it. (Ansa, *Baby* 163)

Middle-Class Phrasal Verb Constructions

The following examples of phrasal verbs are perhaps more representative of stereotypic middle- or upper-middle-class language. None of these are produced by Vernacular speakers.

Examples 1 through 3 are from early works; examples 4 through 7 are taken from later works:

1. We have no Hotel. We *are intending* to stop at a private cottage. (Kelley-Hawkins 23)

2. I *had begun to cast about* for ways and means of bringing you over here. (Fauset, *Comedy* 224)

3. *Can't* something *be done* to stop it? (Brent 87)

4. I *should have called* when I knew I *might arrive* early. (Dove, *Ivory* 18)

5. *Could* you *have thought* of anything more banal! (Marshall, *Praisesong* 14)

6. *I'll see* you in court, Luther. (Naylor, *Linden* 245)

7. Why *am* I *left* alone night after night like some dried-up tree? (Rahman 214)

Tag Questions

This construction, like modals, has often been associated with female language use in sociolinguistic literature. It is used in a number of different ways in the works that I examined.

Asking for Compliance

The speakers in the first set are Standard speakers or those who style-shift regularly between Standard and Vernacular speech. The first example is from an early work; the other two come from later works:

1. Come to dinner with us tonight, *won't you?* (Larsen, "Passing" 156)

2. They're English, *aren't they?* (Naylor, *The Women* 87)

3. You *won't tense up* on me, *will you?* (Naylor, *Mama Day* 75)

Asking for Agreement/Confirmation

Both Standard and Vernacular speakers use this form. The first example is from an early work. The character is a Standard speaker:

1. He'll have to step over your dead body to get it; *won't he*, Vera? (Kelley-Hawkins 19)

Vernacular Speakers produce the following examples; all are from later works:

2. He finally come into his manhood today, *didn't he?* (Hansberry 110)

3. He really can strut some with a tomahawk though, *can't he?* (Hunter 99)

4. You're working, *ain't you*? (Meriwether 104)

5. What was so awful about it? She ask for it, *ain't she*? (Guy, *Friends* 44)

6. Mothers are something *ain't they*? (Cooper, *Homemade* 1)

In *Betsey Brown*, Shange has one of her characters use one tag question to accomplish two different things. In the following exchange, the mother corrects her children's language use and indicates that she wants them to let her know that they understand the correction:

7. "We don't fight in bed no more."
   "You mean anymore, *don't you*?" (Shange, *Betsey* 191)

Expressing Annoyance, Exasperation, Frustration

The next set of examples comes from adult female speakers who style-shift regularly:

1. You'll never understand, *will you?* (Naylor, *The Women* 83)

2. I thought if it was really important to you, you'd mention it. But you didn't, *did you?* (Cleage 71)

3. Here we go! You're gonna be depressing. You're gonna ring the ole bell again, *aren't you?* (Jackson 397)

Making an Indirect Request

The next speaker is a Vernacular speaker who is talking to her adult daughter: "You didn't happen to bring an extra old bra with you, *did you?*" (McMillan, *Mama* 259).

In the preceding section, the characters use the tag question in ways similar to those described in the early research literature (asking for agreement/confirmation or allowing someone else to have the last word), but other examples point to many different ways that this form may be used, many of which indicate differential power arrangements. For example, some examples show older females or more powerful females using the form when addressing those who were younger or less powerful. Some show peers using it to interact with each other aggressively, and several show females using it to express strong, sometimes negative emotion.

Irregular Past Tense

Since many Standard forms of irregular past tense have to be taught, evidence of their regular use may be a strong indication that the person who uses them is a speaker of Standard English. Characters in early works produce these forms:

1. Sally, I *have run* away. Let me in, quick. (Brent 98)

2. Oh, you darling—you *have come*. I *knew* you would; what made you so late? We *had* almost *given* you *up.*[emphasis in original] (Kelley-Hawkins 12)

3. I'*d* never in this world *have known* you if you *hadn't laughed*. (Larsen, "Passing" 152)

4. I, for one, wish that there was some way that they could forever stay out from the poisonous stuff *thrown* at them, literally *thrown* at them. (Larsen, "Quicksand" 13)

Later examples include:

5. I *brought* my bathing suit. (Marshall, "Brooklyn" 91)

6. We've *written* regularly. (Golden, *Migrations* 156)

7. He *drank* a lot. (Morrison, *Tar* 99)

8. Often I *fought* off the temptation to shake her. (Walker, "Everyday Use" 2368)

Subject-Verb Agreement

Regularly making the subjects and verbs agree is another indicator that the person is a Standard speaker. The following examples represent some of the types of agreement that I found.

Agreement with *There*

The first example comes from an early work, and the second comes from a later work:

1. And *there were* the *Scriptures*, and talks on morals and thrift and industry and the loving-kindness of the good Lord. (Larsen, "Passing" 159)

2. *there were* more *nymphs* in every corner. (Golden, *Woman's* 1)

Agreement with Forms of the Verb *Be*

Silvia Dubois, an ex-slave who lived in New Jersey during the time of the Revolutionary War, produces the following sentence:

1. At our tavern they used to stay, and *they were* a jolly set of fellows. I liked to see them come; *there was* fun then. (Larison 58)

Other early examples all show the presence of a copula:

2. O that *is* nothing; I should think you would be concerned about yourself. (N. Prince 78)

3. Oh yes; she *is* livin' with us in Cincinnati, and the smartest one we got too. She *is* about thirteen or fourteen. (Mattison 27)

4. I must confess that this wind *is* a little too much for me. (Kelley-Hawkins 23)

5. I replied, "If he *is* a puppy I *am* a puppy, for we *are* both of the negro race. It *is* right and honorable for us to love each other." (Brent 38)

6. her behavior *is* outrageous. (Larsen, "Quicksand" 60)

7. Ah! Surely! They *were* Negro eyes! mysterious and concealing. (Larsen, "Passing" 161)

In later works subject-verb agreement is much more commonplace. Examples 8 through 11 are Standard speakers. Example 11 is a very old woman. Example 12 comes from an older female who regularly style-shifts:

8. She *is* so normal. *She's* a lawyer, married, has a daughter, and *she's* happy. (McMillan, *Disappearing Act* 17)

9. I wouldn't worry if I *were* you. (Marshall, *Daughters* 42)

10. That old man *is* as flirtatious as a boy of twenty! (Lee 23)

11. If Sadie is *molasses*, then I am *vinegar*! Sadie is *sugar*, and I'm the *spice*. (Delany et al. 14)

12. Lord, that Lena Eggleston *is* a high-minded thing. (Hansberry 101)

Agreement with Compound Subjects

All of the following examples come from Standard speakers; the first one comes from an early work, and the rest are from later works:

1. *Those ladies and I were talking* on matters of the utmost importance. (Fauset, *Comedy* 201)

2. One lunch time *Vicki, Alice and I were occupying* our usual table when a voice louder than any tone we had ever used split the quiet air. (Angelou, *All God's* 24)

3. *Daddy and I were strolling* through the airport hand in hand. (King 229)

4. Sometimes I dream a dream in which *Dee and I are* suddenly brought together on a TV program of this sort. (Walker, "Everyday Use" 2367)

5. Allard, *you and I are going to have a talk* this evening. (Shange, *Betsey* 26)

A few points became clear to me as I collected the preceding sample of sentences. First, it cannot be claimed that the use of subject and verb agreement is solely a function of the writer's style since, in almost every case, other characters do *not* use these forms. Also, I noted that this form begins to appear very early in the literature, and even when the speaker is shown to use other non-Standard forms, the presence of this feature generally marks the speaker as one who is educated, of higher status, or both. It appeared to me that the presence of this form is a strong signal that that person's speech is closer to the Standard end of the dialect spectrum.

Use of Plural *You*

In the works that I examined, plural *you* is a form that is used to signal social status or regional or ethnic background. Speakers who regularly use the Standardized form are more likely to be perceived as members of the middle and upper classes. Examples of this form appear in both early and later works. In each of the examples, the speaker is addressing more than one person: Examples 1 through 3 are from early works. In example 1, a young adult female is addressing one of her brothers; in 2, a teacher is addressing her students. In example 3, an adult female is addressing her children:

1. But anyway Oliver and you are boys; *you* can get out of it all. (Fauset, *Comedy* 54)

2. Even if every last one of *you* did come from homes where *you* weren't taught any manners, *you* might at least try to pretend that *you*'re capable of learning some here, now that *you* have the opportunity. (Larsen, "Quicksand" 11)

3. It is too bad *you* have not a better day for your journey, my dears. (Kelley-Hawkins 11)

Examples 4 and 5 are from later works. The adult females are addressing children:

4. And I know your *evil* ways—all of *you*. (Naylor, *Linden* 12)

5. All right. I want *all of you* to go into that bathroom over there. Get that soot off of *you*. Then I want *you* to march back up those steps, sit down on that sun porch, turn on that

TV or get a book, and don't say two words to me or else I'ma be two minutes away from your asses. *You* understand me? (McMillan, *Mama* 33)

Negation with Indefinite Pronouns

Using acceptable forms of negation is yet another way that people identify themselves as Standard speakers. Following are some examples from early and later works of speakers who use negation with indefinite pronouns. Examples 1 through 3 come from early works:

1. He was*n't* doing *anything*. (Fauset, *Comedy* 131)
2. I *hadn't* asked *anything* about her own life. (Larsen, "Passing" 155)
3. Oh no, I *don't* want *anything* (Harper 94)
4. I *didn't* know *anything* about his living situation (McMillan, *Disappearing Act* 57)
5. I *don't* know *anything* about babies. (Giovanni 263)

Who/Whom Distinction

One of the most-recognized tests for Standard speakers is the way that they use the relative pronouns who and whom. There are examples of this form in both early works and later works. Examples 1 and 2 come from early works; examples 3 and 4 are from later works:

1. [It] [d]epends upon *whom* that one will be. (Kelley-Hawkins 14)
2. Helga felt that the Association secretaries had taken an awful chance in sending a person about *whom* they knew as little as they did about her. (Larsen, "Quicksand" 36)
3. Of all those educated colored teachers *whom* I knew and loved, it was my mother, the skinny bowlegged girl from Sparta with a ninth-grade education, *who* was the first feminist I ever knew. (Weems 128)
4. There was Caroline Piggee, *whom* I hated because of her long, soft, black curls. (Lee 24)

SUMMARY

The foregoing description of the use of Standard grammatical structures serves to point out what I consider one of the most important points of this book: African American speech is as complex as speech in any other healthy speech community. That means that it contains females who use the English language in a number of ways. These examples, taken from works written by African American female writers, show that from earliest times the community has had females who speak a range of dialects, from those that are almost exclusively Standard to those that contain varying numbers of Vernacular structures.

When describing a Standard speaker, often the absence of non-Standard features in the speech is the clearest indication that the person is speaking a Standard dialect. Of course, it is possible to talk about the presence of Standard features also, and in later chapters I discuss Standard female speakers' use of such forms as adjectives (Chapter 6), adverbs (Chapter 7), and address forms (Chapter 8), as well as others that have been identified as further markers of female and/or Standard structures.

6

Adjectives

In this section I discuss the differences in adjective use between African American Standard speakers and African American Vernacular speakers. I'm interested in this topic because I believe that African American females use adjectives not only to express their beliefs and attitudes but also to reflect their social roles. I have found that African American females use adjectives in a variety of ways that reveal their membership in various speech communities. Those ways include the use of gender-based language to reflect the fact that they are females; the use of Vernacular to reflect the fact that they are lower class, are from particular regions and/or ethnic groups, or are signaling metaphoric solidarity with these groups; and the use of Standard English to reflect that they are or aspire to be middle- or upper-class. The information in this chapter is gathered from works by African American female writers who wrote in the distant past, the immediate past, and those who are writing in the present.

DEFINITIONS OF ADJECTIVES

Adjectives have been defined in a number of ways. Veit (1986) defined an adjective as a word that describes (or modifies) a noun (82). He also notes that a noun phrase can have any number of adjectives in a series (29). Different types of adjectives include:

Common (*high, round, long*)
Proper name (*French* cuisine)
Possessive pronouns (*his* title, *his* plate)
Interrogative pronoun (*which* house)
Demonstrative (*this* minute, *that* pencil)
Numbers (*fifty* settlers, *nine* inches)

Colors (*white* sauce, *brown* shoes)

According to Huddleston (1988), "Adjectives function as head in AdjP [adjective phrase] structure. The two main functions of AdjP's are predicative in VP [verb phrase] structures and pre-head modifier in NP [noun phrase] structure, the latter involving what is called the attributive use of adjectives" (30). The examples that he supplies are: [the coat seemed] *too large*—predicative use; [an] *unusually large* [deficit]—attributive use (30).

Huddleston writes that most of the adjectives can be used both ways. He also notes that adjectives are gradable ("too large, quite good, very young"*)* and nongradable ("anthropological, female, phonetic, etc.") (30). Hacker (1995) writes, "Use a hyphen to connect two or more words functioning together as adjectives before a noun" (236). Finally, the description from *Longman Dictionary of Applied Linguistics* (Richards, Platt & Weber 5) includes the following list of adjective properties:

> can be used before a noun (*heavy* bag)
> can be used after *be, become, seem* (the bag is *heavy)*
> can be used after a noun (these books make the bag *heavy*)
> can be modified by an adverb (a very *heavy* bag)
> can be used in a comparative or superlative form (the bag seems *heavier* now)

EMPIRICAL EVIDENCE OF USE

Cheris Kramarae (1981) in *Women and Men Speaking* writes, "Women's everyday speech seems very similar to men's everyday speech. Empirical studies that compare, say, the number of adjectives or adverbs in men's and women's speech, or the particular words used, do not usually find significant differences" (70–71). Although Kramarae makes this general claim about the number of adjectives used by males and females, she does not focus, as I do, on the *types* of adjectives used by different groups of women. In other words, my comparisons are not between males and females but among African American females from different social backgrounds. In the works that I examined, I have found that there are recognizable differences in the way that these female characters are shown to use adjectives.

PATTERNS OF ADJECTIVE USE

Lakoff (1975) identifies two types of adjectives:

There is, for instance, a group of adjectives which have, besides their specific and literal meanings, another use, that of indicating the speaker's approbation or admiration for something. Some of these adjectives are neutral as to sex of speaker: either men or women may use them. But another set seems, in its figurative use, to be largely confined to women's speech. (11–12)

Lakoff (12) supplies examples of the two types of adjectives:

Neutral	*Women Only*
great	adorable
terrific	charming
cool	sweet
neat	lovely
	divine

In examining samples of languages used by Standard and Vernacular speakers, I find that both sets of speakers do, indeed, use adjectives in the way that Lakoff describes in terms of the categories, but I went further and decided to look at both single adjectives and adjectives in series. In addition, I noticed some differences in the neutral adjectives used by the two groups. I also decided to see if the manner in which these two groups use the neutral adjectives shows any obvious differences.

NEUTRAL ADJECTIVES—STANDARD AND VERNACULAR SPEAKERS

Both Standard and Vernacular speakers used single adjectives such as *white, po'* [poor], *decent, nice, plenty, colored, true, secure, pooty* [pretty], *pur'* [pure], *turrible* [terrible], *good*, and *bad*.

Both groups also used adjective phrases; some are compound adjectives (*nice, long*). A number of Standard speakers make use of idiomatic expressions: *like a toad under a cabbage leaf; wildgoose chase; single one; good and sorry*. This use of idiomatic expressions may be a further indication that Standard speakers are often shown using forms that reflect conformity. In the section on Vernacular speakers' adjective use, there are many examples of adjective phrases, but some are more idiosyncratic. This behavior represents what I believe to be Vernacular speaker's more creative or free-style use of language.

I do not mean to imply that Vernacular speakers do not make use of common neutral adjectives. For example, a pattern that I noticed in both sets of speakers is the use of the words *ol'* [old] or *po'* [poor] or *li'l* [little] with another adjective: *same ol', plain ol', ugly ol', nice ol', crazy ol', silly old, po' li'le* [little], *po' white, po' black, poor things, nice little, little old, little bit, little black*.

Others use unusual form or position. The first example comes from a Vernacular speaker; the second comes from a West Indian; the last two are Standard speakers from later works:

1. but Ah don't mean to chop *de first* chip. (Hurston, *Eyes* 45)

2. Not penny *one*. (Marshall, *Brown Girl* 42)

3. People learned not to mess with me from Day *One*. (Delany et al. 13)

4. we started to *bug each* from *day one*. (Briscoe 58)

Finally, both groups make use of common superlatives, for example: *best, old-est, youngest, darkest, the poorest, funniest, happiest, ugliest, scariest, most beau-tiful, mos' miserablest.* Several superlative phrases began with *"one of . . . "* All of the following sentences come from later works. The examples are from Standard speakers. The first speaker appears in an earlier work:

5. Were she not present I would say she is *one of the grandest* women in America. (Harper 244)

6. *one the prettiest* parts of Willow Springs. (Naylor, *Mama Day* 72)

This next example is a variation on the preceding pattern:

7. My father thinks Detroit is *the greatest place on earth.* (Golden, *Woman's* 17)

Another common phrase pattern is *"the -est . . . [ ] ever."* This phrase appears in both the early and later works. The following examples come from Standard speakers. The first two examples are from early works:

8. the *best* dancers up there that I *ever* saw. (Larison 59)

9. the *biggest* breakfast you *ever* saw. (Kelley-Hawkins 16)

10. I think that is the *stupidest thing I have ever* heard. (Lee 11)

The rest of the examples come from speakers who style-shift regularly:

11. *prettiest* Jewish girl I *ever* saw. (Meriwether 46)

12. a bunch of the *saddest* niggers *you'll ever* wanna meet. (Naylor, *Linden* 39)

13. She was the *whitest*—not beige, not pink, not rouge or lipstick—white woman we had *ever* seen. (Clair 24)

14. the *biggest* dinner we *ever* ate tonight. (Hansberry 109)

DIFFERENCES IN USE OF ADJECTIVES

In the following section I discuss differences in the way that some female speak-ers use adjectives. As with the other sections, these groups are not monolithic. There are internal differences that reflect time, region, age, education, and family background. In other words, only those speakers at the very ends of the spectrum can be comfortably placed in one category or the other. Therefore, the language of an uneducated slave may display the most instances of AAVE, while the language of a fourth- or fifth-generation professional female may contain the most instances of Standard English, but in between, the language of the two groups is much less predictable, making it necessary to refer to trends in the way that various speakers make use of language.

GENDER-BASED ADJECTIVES

Lakoff (1975) admits to a middle-class bias in describing women's language, and, indeed, many of the gender-based adjectives used in the works that I examined are produced by Standard speakers. Next I discuss some of those adjectives that fit into this category. They are divided into two subcategories—attributive and predicative—which are then subdivided into two groups: positive and negative.

Positive Attributive Adjectives

Within the subcategory of positive adjectives, I found a set of typical, gender-based adjectives, such as *delightful, marvelous, fantastic, magnificent*. In addition, I found that the speakers use a number of superlatives and words that indicate magnitude, quantity, or degree: *loveliest* sights; *kindest* thing; *nicest* man; *enormous* influence; *super-deluxe* lover. Also included were adjectives employing the word *little* or some other diminutive: cute *little* brown baby; *little-bitty* heel; *itsy-bitsy* resort; *tweenty* tots. Another group of adjectives included a form of endearment: *dear, sweet* man; *darling* infant; *beloved* Phineas. As in other sections, speakers style-shift from one style to another. In one of the works the same speaker produces these two examples:

1. one of them *good to screw* types. (DeVeaux, "Tapestry" 172)
2. On a *lovely* Friday evening. (173)

Negative Attributive Adjectives

Negative attributive adjectives in this subcategory also fall into sets. There are typical forms such as *ridiculous, disgusting, dreadful, loathsome, horrified, infuriating*. Others reflect the use of superlatives and other words indicating quantity or degree: the *most* impossible people; the *lonesomest place in the world*; the *least* idea; for the *hundredth* time; the *crudest* of people.

The use of negative attributive adjectives is consistent with Lakoff's description of women's talk: the female characters display the use of emotion or talk in italics. The characters also show conformity in that the examples all come from a small set of adjectives that are used over and over and that change very little over time.

Positive Predicative Adjectives

There is a smaller subcategory of positive predicative adjectives. Most examples are in the form NP + *be* + Adj, where the adjective was a word like *heavenly, delighted, grand, gorgeous, crazy, lovely, priceless, dainty*. The first three examples come from early works:

1. The vacation was *heavenly*. (Fauset, *Comedy* 88)
2. I am *delighted*. (Kelley-Hawkins 21)
3. It's *grand* to be alive! (Fauset, *Comedy* 234)
4. Your place is *gorgeous*. (McMillan, *Waiting* 162)

Slight variations on this pattern include the following examples; example 5 is from an early work:

5. I'm simply *crazy* to go. (Larsen, "Passing" 157)

6. *Lovely,* aren't they? (Morrison, *Tar* 117)

7. But they're *priceless!* (Walker, "Everyday Use" 2373)

8. You look so *dainty!* (Tate 152)

Negative Attributive Adjectives

As with the positive adjectives, most of the examples follow the pattern NP + *be* + Adj, with words like *horrid, unbelievable, frightening, repulsive, beastly, awful, ridiculous,* and *contrite* filling in the adjective slot. The first example comes from an early work:

1. *It's* just plain *horrid.* (Larsen, "Quicksand" 39)

2. *It's unbelievable.* (McMillan, *Waiting* 215)

3. Oh, *it was frightening.* (Lee 84)

Slight variations on this form include the following examples. Numbers 4 and 5 come from early works:

4. [That were . . .] entirely too *repulsive.* (Larsen, "Quicksand" 12)

5. Isn't it *beastly?* (Larsen, "Passing" 156)

6. That was *awful, awful.* (Morrison, *Tar* 209)

7. this is getting a little *ridiculous.* (McMillan, *Disappearing Act* 306)

8. I am *contrite.* (Dove, *Ivory* 18)

One adjective that is used regularly by both Standard and Vernacular speakers is *pitiful.* The first example comes from a Vernacular speaker in an early work. The other two examples come from Standard speakers in later works.

9. ain't he too *pitiful?* (Fauset, *Comedy* 203)

10. It's *pitiful* really. (McMillan, *Disappearing Act* 57)

11. you're too *pitiful* to be evil. (Hunter 22)

As with the other examples of adjectives discussed earlier, these examples also show a small set of forms used again and again, most of them showing the use of hyperbole.

Some female characters in the works that I examined do, indeed, make use of some of the features of Lakoff's "women's talk." What is interesting about this use is that it is not confined to a particular time period. Characters in Fauset's and Larsen's works used these forms, but so do the contemporary characters in works by McMillan, Morrison, and Tate.

Also consistent with Lakoff's description is the fact that many of these adjectives reflect emphatic or heightened emotion. It has been claimed that such talk is often characterized as speaking in italics. One other striking aspect of this list is the number of negative adjectives. It could be argued that this usage would be consistent with some descriptions of the middle class as being more conservative, more restrictive, and, perhaps by extension, more censorious. Finally, it is quite clear that this small group of adjectives may make a set of features that can be said to help define the speech of the middle-class African American female. It should be noted that few of the lower-class speakers are found to use these terms.

OTHER STANDARD ADJECTIVES

Though similar to the gender-based adjectives, other Standard English adjectives used by those women in the middle and upper middle classes seem to signal their class membership. These adjectives indicate (1) education or level of literacy or (2) middle-class status and values.

Literate Adjectives

The first set of adjectives includes those that I call literate adjectives. I use the term "literate" to describe forms that show either that the speaker is literate and educated or that the person is in regular contact with those who are. Like gender-based adjectives, these forms appear more often in the speech of middle-class female characters or those who control more than one dialect.

Some adjectives are used in both early and later works. The adjective *cruel* is used by an ex-slave in the first example, taken from an early work. In the second example, taken from a later work, the speaker is an educated, middle-class female:

1. Massa Black *am* awful *cruel.* (Rose 435)

2. How could he be so *cruel?* (Golden, *Migrations* 86)

Other adjectives are used by Standard speakers in early and later works. *Forlorn* is used in both an early work (example 3) and a later work (4):

3. the poor *forlorn* child that was me. (Larsen, "Passing" 155)

4. Looked as *forlorn* and neglected. (Golden, *Woman's* 19)

Some of the adjectives, like the word *distressed*, appear only in early works:

5. came to me with a very *distressed* countenance. (Brent 134)

6. He often left her, in the most *distressed* circumstances. (M. Prince 1)

Others appear only in later works:

7. Something *magical* happened between us, girl. (McMillan, *Disappearing Act* 57)

8. There's no reason to give up everything *gracious* on account of a few moments of hardship. (Shange, *Betsey* 21)

9. in conversation about the *underprivileged, misunderstood* and *oppressed* miscreants. (Angelou, *All God's* 7)

10. this *bizarre* baking soda story. (Jackson 358)

11. I had grown up in the *hermetic* world of old-fashioned black bourgeoisie. (Lee 4)

A few of the adjectives used are even more explicitly literary:

12. Margaret, . . . had in fact a positively *Brontëesque* conception of the ideal man. (Lee 97)

13. the *Machiavellian* notion that the end justifies the means. (Wade-Gayles 219)

Social Status Adjectives

Another set of adjectives belongs in this section. This set contains a mixed group of adjectives that have in common the fact that they provide information about the character's social status or aspirations: *respectable*; *self-respecting*; a *great race* woman; a *Big Ten* University; *vulgar*; *indiscreet*; a *five figure* income.

Summary

Besides using the gender-based adjective forms described in the literature, Standard-speaking characters use forms that reflect their level of education or at least the fact that they are in regular contact with people with some degree of literacy. But I also noted that sometimes Vernacular speakers use these forms also. In addition, I once again point out that some Standard speaker's style-shifted—sometimes using Standard forms and sometimes using Vernacular forms. I also found that some of these Standard speakers use adjective forms that reflect their social status. It is also possible that the use of adjectives by Standard females follows traditional patterns. Most of the creativity comes about by the speaker's use of various Standard adjectives available from her somewhat limited repertoire. There is little indication that the speakers make drastic changes in phrasal or clausal structures and little indication that they invent new forms of expression. This use of adjectives is yet another bit of evidence that one of the most salient features of language use for these female characters is the adherence to traditional and often conservative forms. It was also noted that those Standard speakers who do make use of style-shifting often do so to break away from the constraints of the more formal structures for some reason. Bessie Delany is a very good example of a female who is clearly an educated Standard speaker who makes use of informal language for emphasis ("People learned not to mess with me from Day *One*").

VERNACULAR ADJECTIVES

Most Vernacular adjectives appear in either AAVE or other NSE—usually regional or ethnic—dialects. They are less predictable than the traditional, stereotypical, gender-based, or Standard English forms. Some forms are readily used by a large number of speakers, but the combination, order, and number in any given expression are mainly a function of the user's skill and creativity. Other forms seem to be made up on the spot by the speaker.

African American Vernacular (AAVE) Adjectives

Creativity and style seem to be the most outstanding features of the adjectives in this section. If a rule of language use could be abstracted from their use, it would probably be: Make the expression of the idea as impressive or more impressive than the idea itself. For example, some characters make use of understatement: "she ain't got the reputation of being the quickest mind on the island" (Naylor, *Mama Day* 93). Others use exaggeration:

1. you switches a *mean* fanny round in a kitchen. (Hurston, *Eyes* 15)

2. jes' ez *barefooted ez uh yard dawg.* (Hurston, *Jonah's* 7)

3. The whites are just as good as the niggers, and both are as *bad as the devil can make 'em.* (Larison 52)

Stink

Some speakers make use of adjective forms that are often found in the African American community. One of these adjectives is *stink*. I found examples in both early and later times. Example 1 comes from an early work:

1. You kin get yo' ole *stink* hair comb any time. (Hurston, *Jonah's* 24)

The next two examples come from adult females; the first speaker is West Indian:

2. I tell yuh, that girl got the house *stink down with codfish.* (Marshall, *Brown Girl* 23)

3. there was a hogpen he had that was always *stink.* (Bolton 11)

The final example comes from a young Standard-speaking girl who style-shifts:

4. What do you think I'm gonna do? Go to school *stink* on accounta you take so long. (Shange, *Betsey* 17)

Raggedy

Another adjective used is *raggedy*, loosely defined as meaning "poor, broken down or worthless." It is found only in the later works, and most of the speakers are adult females who regularly style-shift. Some of the examples refer to people:

1. He was a *raggedy* black boy. (Meriwether 95)

Some examples refer to buildings and other structures:

2. She hated this *raggedy* house. (McMillan, *Mama Day* 1)

3. Not in that *raggedy* little broken-down storefront. (Dee 279)

Some refer to vehicles:

4. I'll de damned if I was coming into this city on a *raggedy* old Greyhound. (Naylor, *The Women* 58)

5. Then she drove up in a *raggedy* trap, old-time car with no top. (Clair 23)

One speaker uses the term to refer to both a structure and a vehicle:

6. *Raggedy* house . . . *raggedy* truck. (Tate 29)

One little girl produces this ambiguous expression:

7. Mary Louise Williams of Raggedy Town, Baltimore. (Bambara, "Raymond's" 27)

Many adjectives used by the characters in the works examined have their origins in Standard English, but their meanings have been altered in subtle ways. Some examples include the words *evil, simple, trifling, nasty, proper*, and various terms for *stuck up* and *fine*.

Evil

A rough definition of this *evil* is something like "very bad behavior/disposition." No examples of its being used this way are found in early works. In these examples, all of the females are adult Vernacular speakers who style-shift:

1. He sure was one *evil* black West Indian. (Meriwether 50)

2. *Evil*, triflin and simple minded is what I was. (Shange, *Betsey* 180)

3. I started acted mean and *evil*. (Bolton 185)

The following speakers are Standard speakers who sometimes style-shift.

4. No, Betsey wasn't being *evil*. (Shange, *Betsey* 60)

5. And I thought it would be a terrible thing for an *evil* militant like me. (Giovanni 264)

6. And I know your *evil* ways. (Naylor, *Linden* 12)

Simple

Some of the characters use the adjective *simple* to mean either "retarded, foolish, or stupid." This term in this form is not found in early works. A female in Cooper's *Homemade Love*, supplies the following description:

1. Now, in the city we would have called her "retarded," but in the country she was called "plain and simple" only. Just "*simple*" mostly. (48)

Dorinne, the narrator in Guy's *A Measure of Time*, uses the adjective in the following example when she sarcastically describes a woman she sits next to on a train:

2. Plain woman, plain ideas—even to the *simple* smile. (109)

Finally, young girls use this adjective. The next speaker is a young Vernacular speaker who style-shifts regularly:

3. So we shut up and watch the *simple* ass picture. (Bambara, "Gorilla" 15)

Triflin[g]

The adjective *triflin* '[g] is often used to roughly mean, "unreliable, petty, not serious behavior." The first comes from an early work, and the female is a Vernacular speaker:

1. But you allus been *triflin'*. Cain't do nuffin propah. (Larsen, "Sanctuary" 321)

The next two examples come from later works; the speakers are adult females who style-shift regularly:

2. Well, he run off with that *trifling* Peggy—from Elyria. (Morrison, *Bluest* 15)

3. Evil, *triflin* and simple minded is what I was. (Shange, *Betsey* 180)

In a dialogue between Eva and her adult daughter Hannah in Morrison's *Sula*, Eva asks her daughter if she plans to can some of the peas that she is shelling, and the following exchange takes place (Hannah speaks first):

4. "Uncle Paul ain't brought me none yet. A peck ain't enough to can. He say he got two bushels for me."
   "*Triflin.*"
   "Oh, he.all right." (Morrison, *Sula* 68)

Nasty

In the first example from a Standard speaker in an early work, the term *nasty* is used to mean "unpleasant or disagreeable." In all of the rest of the examples, the term roughly means that the person is doing or saying something improper that is related to sex.

1. Now, don't be *nasty*, Helga. (Larsen, "Quicksand" 61)

2. Mr. Floyd, you so *nasty*. (Jones, "Jevata" 133)

3. You look *nasty!* (Jackson 393)

4. *Nasty, nasty.* (Naylor, *Mama Day* 49)

5. some kind of *nasty* woman disease. (Walker, *Purple* 48)

The last two examples come from young children:

6. Frieda and Claudia are out here playing *nasty!* (Morrison, *Bluest* 27)

7. You *nasty* lil niggah. (Shange, *Betsey* 35)

Note that the *nasty* used in this section is not the one used in slang or informal language to mean "very good."

Proper

Another adjective that appears in some of the works is *proper*, meaning "extra good behavior," as in examples 1 and 2 or "paying close attention to speaking correctly," as in 3. There are examples of this usage in both early and later works. Example 1 comes from an early work:

1. Cain't do nuffin *propah*. (Larsen, "Sanctuary" 321)

2. I think you ought to be a bit more *proper*, now my child's back. (Shange, *Betsey* 190)

3. but said she was raised in Ohio. Talked real *proper*. Pemberton liked *proper* talkers. (Clair 72)

Closely associated with the word *proper* are the set of adjectives that follow. They have one thing in common: they can be defined as making a social commentary (negative) about another person or persons. The three words are *hincty, dicty,* and *saddity* [spelled different ways]. Roughly translated all of them mean "snobbish," "stuck up," or "thinking one is better than someone else." All of these examples come from later works. The speakers are adult females:

4. *Hincty,* that's why. Comes from handling money all day. (Morrison, *Jazz* 19)

5. an eye on these *hincty* misbehaving brats. (Shange, *Betsey* 55)

6. like *dicty* whores. (Guy, *Measure* 109)

7. like them *saddity* kids at school. (Williams 49)

8. Surely you could put that *ciddity* [saddity] old woman down. (Shange, *Betsey* 187)

Fine

Many females characters use the adjective *fine* to mean "especially good looking and desirable." All of the following examples come from later works. The speakers are adult females:

1. Cause I loves me a *fine* man. (DeVeaux, "Tapestry" 169)

2. this tall, *fine,* darker brother. (Guy, *Measure* 111)

3. this slight woman, not exactly plain, but not *fine* either. (Morrison, *Sula* 103)

Though I make no claim that the adjectives just discussed are exclusively used by African Americans in the works that I examined, I do say that these adjectives show up with great regularity among these characters, and there seems to be a very strong consensus among all of the writers about just exactly how these words are to be used.

Other NSE Adjectives

As with other features that I've discussed, the category of NSE adjectives encompasses all Vernacular forms except those explicitly identified as AAVE. They include those that I have labeled "general," those that are labeled "idiomatic," those that are related to "ethnic" (West Indian) usage, and those that I've labeled "individual."

General NSE Adjectives

The adjectives that I'm calling general NSE are mostly taken from older speakers or from earlier times. Some of the terms themselves are archaic (*blessed, likely, portly*); some show regional influence (*chanyberry* [chinaberry], *old time-y, Yankee, nable* [navel] *string*); many refer to quantities (*heap, plenty, mess, many a*), or degree (*turrible bad, powerful glad*); some seem to be almost superfluous (*bed* quilt; *stove* wood; *hair* comb). A few of these adjectives, like *nary,* are used in both early and later works. Both speakers are adult females:

1. befo' de fambly done seed *nary* leg of 'em. (Hopkins, "Hagar's" 48)

2. *nary* a fit house in sight. (Bambara, "Witchbird" 185)

Idiomatic Adjectives

The following expressions all contain adjectives that are used idiomatically. In some cases the terms merely reflect informal use; in others, they reflect slang from one time period or another. The first example comes from a slave narrative. I was surprised to see that this expression is quite old:

1. Well, de biscuits was *yum, yum, yum* to me. (Rose 436)

The next set of examples shows the word *smart,* roughly meaning, "attempting to put something over on someone." I found examples only in later works. The first example comes from an adult West Indian; the second, from an older female; and the last, from a young adult female:

2. Oh, you's playing *smart.* (Marshall, *Brown Girl* 44)

3. Oh, wasn't you *smart*, come fixing my hair and Oh Miss Lydia ain't we prettying me, sewing them short dresses so you can get that man away from his wife. (Clair 84)

4. I got so *smart* at it, I took the tobacco out of my cigarette and put some marijuana in. (Bolton 86)

Many of the expressions containing adjectives are slang expressions that are used in a particular time period. The next example comes from a later work set in an earlier time:

5. That just *fine and dandy.* (Walker, *Purple* 60)

The next set of examples comes from adult females; many of them style-shift regularly:

6. Cause you can stand *stark raving still* and life will still happen to you. (Cooper *Homemade* 1)

7. to make your summer a *fly* and *funky* affair. (DeVeaux, "Tapestry" 170)

8. Since when did you get *froggy* about folks' stealing? (Morrison, *Sula* 100)

9. It's a *hellafyin* thing. (Bambara, "Witchbird" 185)

The next two examples come from older females:

10. the *pure-dee* insult. (Jackson 354)

11. I ain't making her nothing, 'cause she's too *fresh.* (Naylor, *Mama Day* 37)

The last two examples come from young girls:

12. Old lady Lass sure did get *hot.* (Guy, *Friends* 45)

13. It's *boss.* (Guy, *Friends* 46)

Ethnic (West Indian) Use of Adjectives

Because several of the works feature speakers from the West Indies, I found examples of adjectives used by these speakers. Some of the terms and phrases hint of early British influence, as in examples 1 and 2:

1. and the *blasted* children ain nothing but a keepback. (Marshall, *Brown Girl* 30)

2. You's a *wicked* something. (20)

The next example contains an interesting turn of phrase:

3. This is all some *forge* up something. (25)

The final example uses duplication:

4. But look Adry got *big-big* childen! (Marshall, "To da-duh" 388)

Individual Use of Adjectives

Throughout the course of my examination of works by African American fe-male writers, I have been struck again and again by the skillful and creative use of language displayed by many of the characters. Both early and later works contain excellent examples.

Older Females

The speech of older African American females has been described, mimicked, and parodied for centuries. The main features that most note are the no-nonsense approach to language use, the choice of topic matter, and the style of delivery. Fol-lowing are examples from several older female characters who appear in both early and later works. All but the last two examples come from early works.

Nanny in Hurston's *Their Eyes Were Watching God:*

1. Ah don't want no *trashy* nigger, *no breath-and-britches*, lak Johnny Taylor usin' *yo'* body to wipe his foots on. (27)

Aunt Henny in Hopkins's "Hagar's Daughter":

2. Mis' Johnson's a *born lady cook or no cook*. (172)

3. 'pinted [appointed] mammy prominen'ly to a *firmamen'* [permanent] persition. (173)

4. *disrespons'ble* gal. (63)

An old ex-slave in Rose's *Documentary History of Slavery in North America:*

5. I's 'bout sixteen year old and has no larnin', and I's jus *igno'mus* chile. (436)

Mama in Hansberry's "A Raisin in the Sun":

6. you look just like *somebody's* hoodlum. (109)

Eva Peace in Morrison's *Sula:*

7. Awww, Mamma? Awww, Mamma? You settin' here with your *healthy-ass* self and ax me did I love you? Them *big old* eyes in your head would a been two holes *full of maggots* if I hadn't. (68)

Adult Females

Adult African American females are also shown using adjectives in creative ways. The following examples are taken from both early and later works. The first two examples come from early works.

Amy in Hurston's *Jonah's Gourd Vine*:

1. Dat's uh big ole *resurrection* lie. (3)
2. Uh *slew-foot, drag-leg* lie at dat. (3)

Dorine in Guy's *A Measure of Time*:

3. she raised her *high-class* eyebrows. (105)

Celie in Walker's *The Color Purple*:

4. If she so smart how come she *big* [pregnant]? (37)

Bessie Smith in Guy's *A Measure of Time*:

5. Bring down the goddamn ceilings on *sons-of-bitch* imitators. (104)

Mama in McMillan's *Mama* fusses at her daughter for going out without a brassiere:

6. It looks downright *nasty*. Gon' get your little *fast* ass raped again out here if you don't stop thinking you so *cute*. (129)

Fanny in Hunter's *The Landlord* describes herself this way:

7. I'm an artist. I need inspiration for my work. I can't work in some *grim old* place where the paint's *all peelin' off the walls* and the *rickety old three-legged* chairs are *all fallin' down* and the windows ain't been washed in twenty years. I said to the woman who owned one of them places, "You call this a beauty shop? It looks more like an *Ugly* Shop to me." (102)

Young Females

Young girls in both early and later works also make creative use of adjectives. Example 8 comes from an early work; example 9, from a later work.

Lucy in Hurston's *Jonah's Gourd Vine*:

1. Well, folks! Where you reckon *dis big yaller bee-stung* nigger come from? (13)

The young narrator in Bambara's "The Lesson":

2. So me and Sugar leaning on the mailbox being *surly*, which is a Miss Moore word. (88)

SUMMARY

In this chapter, after an overview of adjectives including definitions and descriptions of various types of adjectives, I discussed my findings on the way that African American female characters were shown to use adjectives in different social contexts. For example, I pointed out that some adjectives are used by both

Standard and Vernacular speakers, while others seem to be used predominantly by one group or the other.

Drawing from research on women's language use, I found that middle-class females, in certain circumstances, do indeed, use many of the adjectives that Lakoff and others have described. The heaviest, most consistent use occurred in the works of such writers as Fauset and Larsen, who wrote in the early part of the century. Standard-speaking characters in later works also use these forms, but they don't use them as frequently and they don't use them exclusively. I included another category—literate adjectives—to promote the idea that many of these educated and literate females regularly use adjectives that reflect their social situation. Overall, I found that the use of gender-based adjectives reflects the females' membership in the *female*, middle-class speech community, while the use of the literate adjectives reflects their membership in the larger, more general, middle-class speech community.

Although both Standard and Vernacular speakers use similar sets of neutral adjectives, the Vernacular speakers use some adjectives in ways different from the ways used by Standard speakers. With few exceptions, the Vernacular speakers do not use the same gender-based adjectives that mark the Standard speakers. This finding leads me to conclude that there might actually be some forms of language behavior that can be said to be almost exclusively the province of one group or the other. At this point, I am willing to claim that the frequent use of traditional, stereotypical, gender-based adjectives may very well be a sign of membership in the middle- or upper-middle class Standard speech community. Further, the absence of such forms may be one indication that the speaker does *not* belong to this group.

When examining adjective use among Vernacular speakers, I discovered that they make extensive use of both AAVE and other NSE forms. The most striking finding is the consistent presence of creativity and individualism in the use of these forms. Specifically, I noted that many of the features associated with both AAVE and NSE use—colorful language, individualistic treatment of linguistic forms, use of stress, rhythm, and other paralinguistic features, and expression of strong feelings—are used regularly by the characters who are identified as Vernacular speakers. This use is in contrast to the more traditional adjective use of Standard speakers.

Circumstances that seem to have a definite relationship to the type of adjective used are age (older speakers use more of the archaic forms; younger speakers used more slang), region (urban speakers seem to rely more on new slang forms; rural speakers often rely on more idiomatic expressions); individual style (some speakers display more skill in using the language than do others); and ethnicity (speakers from other areas like the West Indies have their own style of expressing themselves). This category, like others I have looked at, overlaps with other areas. For example, some adjectives appear in the chapters on "Expressive Behavior" and "Language Use."

7

Adverbs

Longman Dictionary of Applied Linguistics (1985) defines an adverb as "a word that describes or adds to the meaning of a verb, an adjective, another adverb, or a sentence, and which answers such questions as how?, where?, or when?" (Richards, Platt, & Weber 6). Huddleston (1988) notes also that the most important characteristic of adverbs is that a high proportion are derived from adjectives by suffixation of *-ly* (122). The most common forms for adverbs are adverbs of time, adverbs of manner, and adverbs of degree. Some of these adverbs are used by both Standard and Vernacular speakers; others are used predominantly by one group or the other. Most of the following examples come from adult females.

ADVERBS OF TIME

Though both groups use adverbs of time regularly, so far I have not found many striking examples of the use of these adverbs. One possible explanation is that these forms are used so much that their use has become regularized in both groups and that they are simply part of the neutral language that is available to members of both groups. I did notice the word *never*, however, because the use of this word does show some variation.

Never

Both groups of speakers use *never* to express simple negation. Standard speakers produce the following two examples. Example 1 is from an early work, and example 2 comes from a later work. The second speaker is an older female:

1. she'd *never* been merely the janitor's daughter. (Larsen, "Passing" 154)

2. But she *never* had me fooled. (Marshall, *Praisesong* 27)

Vernacular speakers also use *never* to show simple negation. One pattern that I found is the use of repetition for emphasis. Vernacular speakers from both early and later works show this pattern:

3. an Unc' Ned *neber* was whopped tell de day he died, *neber*. (Hopkins, "Hagar's" 58)

4. And I ain't *never* had no sty before. *Never*! (Morrison, *Sula* 117)

Both groups use *never* in set expressions, that is, expressions in which *never* regularly co-occurs with another word or words. The Standard speakers who produced examples 5 and 6 both appear in Kelley-Hawkins's *Four Girls of Cottage City*, an early work. Example 7 comes from Brent's *Incidents in the Life of a Slave Girl*; both books are early works:

5. it would *never do* to let these gentlemen know their situation. (23)

6. Well, *never mind*, Jess; we can't help the weather. (9)

7. I *never again* saw her who had so generously befriended the poor, trembling fugitive! (Brent 114)

Vernacular speakers used some of the same set expressions. Example 8 comes from a work written in the 1980s but set in the 1930s to 1940s:

8. *Never again* the brown bags of fried chicken. (Guy, *Measure* 112)

The expression *never mind* appears in a number of later works:

9. *never mind* the airs she gives herself. (Marshall, *Praisesong* 27)

10. *Never mind* who. (Jones, *Eva's* 89)

11. *Never mind* the rest. (Morrison, *Tar* 121)

Never appears in several set expressions using the auxiliary *did* or the modals *will*, *would*, and *could*. In each of these expressions the combination of *never* + the auxiliary or modal serves the purpose of emphasizing how impossible it is to accomplish whatever is being attempted.

Never + *Did*

Example 1 comes from an early work; the rest are from later works. The last example comes from a young girl:

1. *Never did* lak it over heah. (Hurston, *Jonah's* 6)

2. She *never did* even make any real close women friends after Miss Billie left. (Jones, *Eva's* 83)

3. I *never did* trust them things. (Naylor, *Mama Day* 36)

4. Miss Moore, who always looked like she was going to church, though she *never did*. (Bambara, "Lesson" 87)

One Standard speaker, Sadie Delany, an older female, writes in her autobiography:

5. Mama looked white but she *never did* try to "pass." (Delany et al. 9–10)

Never + *Will/Would/Could*

All of these examples come from later works:

1. *Never will* forget. (Dee 281)
2. Up to the day we separated, I *never would* let Joe Hunn fry me no chicken. (Jones, *Corregidora* 35)
3. I *never would* have made it if I had had to start back down the beach right away. (Marshall, *Praisesong* 169)
4. *Never could* carry a tune. (Walker, "Everyday Use" 2368)
5. We *never could* get Daddy to go to church with us. (Meriwether, *Daddy* 54)

This next example is an excellent demonstration of how this type of set expression can be used to show the utter futility of some enterprises:

6. I used to try, try so hard I'd break out in a sweat just wishing, but I *never could, never could* fly. (Ansa, *Baby* 163)

Never is also used with *a*. The following two examples come from later works:

7. *Never a* kindly how-do. (Naylor, *Mama Day* 93)
8. *Never a* curse word cross that woman mouth. (Marshall, *Brown Girl* 32)

The Standard speakers use *never* in ways consistent with traditional usage, but they also display use of what has been called by the literature "women's talk." In the case of *never,* the speakers use this term in expressive forms denoting exaggeration or hyperbole. Both of the following examples come from an early work:

9. I'll *never* forgive you. (Larsen, "Passing" 162)
10. I'd *never in this world* have known you. (152)

The Vernacular speakers also use *never* in a variety of ways. For example, many speakers use *never* with other forms of negation in a single utterance. Examples 11 and 12 come from early works; 13 comes from a work that is set in earlier times, though it was written in the 1980s; the rest come from later works:

11. *no* one *neber* goes nigh de old summer house. (Hopkins, "Hagar's" 63)
12. talkin' 'bout work when de race *ain't never* done *nothin'* else. (Hurston, *Eyes* 212)
13. You better *not never* tell *nobody* but God. (Walker, *Purple* 11)
14. We *never* allowed *no* one in here who wasn't decent. (Clair 74)

Forever

The word *forever* appears in a number of examples from both Vernacular and Standard speakers. Standard speakers produce the following. The first example comes from a young female in an early work, and the other two examples come from later works. The second example comes from an older female, and the third speaker is young girl:

1. She'll munch and read away *forever* and the day afterward. (Kelley-Hawkins 16)

2. it took her *forever* to do it. (Delany et al. 224)

3. It could take *forever* to finish one of Mr. Robinson's sodas. (Shange, *Betsey* 39)

Style-shifting Standard speakers or Vernacular speakers produce the following examples. The last two speakers are young girls:

4. He took *forever* writing it up. (Guy, *Measure* 113)

5. Puddin and Wanda Coles had lived across the street from us *forever*. (Clair 25)

6. She was *forever* in the kitchen laughing and talking with Big Ma. (Taylor, *Circle* 185)

Phrases of Time

Some of the adverbs of time used by Standard speakers appear in the form of phrases. One that is used by both groups is some variation of the phrase, *all these years*. Standard speakers produce the first two of the following examples; the first is from an early work:

1. to see Clare again after *all those years*. (Larsen, "Passing" 153)

2. I've been thinking about telling it after *all these years* (Dove, *Fifth* 67)

The next examples come from Vernacular speakers; both are from later works:

3. them blue periwinkles look painted fresh after *all these years*. (Naylor, *Mama Day* 95)

4. but we was on the good-house list for the school board *all them years*. (Clair 76)

Other time expressions using *years* include *in later years* and *for the first time in years*. In the next passage, one older Standard speaker is annoyed by the behavior of her friend. In speaking of her exasperation, she still manages to avoid referring to the exact number of years that they've known each other since the friend is sensitive about her age:

5. And I'm looking at you! I'm looking right at you ... for the first time in *all the ... "ho hum" years* I've known you, I just don't recognize you! (Jackson 354)

In the next passage, the same speaker as in 5 uses other adverbs of time:

6. *Occasionally*, but *very rarely*—you LAUGH!—a nerve-wracking, hysterical, nervous laugh. (Jackson 353)

Other time phrases are also used. The next one comes from an early work.

7. "I've thought of you *often and often*. (Larsen, "Passing" 154).

The one thing that I noticed about these passages is that many of the phrases express some element of hyperbole or exaggeration, which would be in keeping with early research literature's characterization of "female language."

Vernacular speakers also use adverbial phrases of time. One of the phrases that is used often in early works is *by and by*:

8. P'raps I'll come 'long *by and by*. (Brent 114)

9. But *by and by* the brandy began to wear off. (Larison 63)

As is true with many other features, the Vernacular speakers use these adverbs to reflect their regional (*for uh spell*) or social class background (*dis one time*; *dat quick*; *manys de time*) or their individual style (*too long to talk about*). Like their Standard-speaking counterparts, they make use of a number of set expressions (*every now and then*; *every so often*; *soon afterward*).

ADVERBS OF MANNER

Standard speakers use standard forms of adverbs such as *clearly, perversely, politely, bitterly, honestly, unobtrusively, voluptuously, tearfully, shamelessly,* and *ridiculously*. One speaker uses the word *quietly*. *Quietly* is a pattern of duplication that appears regularly in some West Indian Vernaculars. The adverbs themselves seem to reflect values, beliefs, and norms of behavior. Some of the adverbs, though neutral in terms of manner, still reflect the values of the speech community in that they reflect attitudes toward the use of Standard English. For example, as will be shown, Standard speakers actually use many -ly adverbs, while Vernacular speakers use this form less often, especially if the form is derived from an adjective.

The examples of adverbs of manner phrases are similar in style to those of adverbs of time. They usually employ hyperbole or exaggeration:

1. She's enough *to scare you silly*. (Marshall, *Brown Girl* 20)

2. Puddin would sit down and hit a note repeatedly, hard, with one finger until *he took us to the brink of nutty*. (Clair 30)

Vernacular speakers also produce several adverbs of manner, though, as I mentioned earlier, I didn't find many *-ly* forms. I found that it was often necessary to see how the adverbs are used in *context*, since they often appear in unusual or non-Standard forms. Vernacular speakers often use adjectives in place of adverbs. Example 3 is set in an earlier time but is written in the 1980s. The rest of the examples come from later works:

3. I'd look *favorable* on some water though. (Morrison, *Beloved* 143)

4. listen to me *good*. (Naylor, *Mama Day* 73)

5. I oughta find me a good man and settle down to live *quiet* in my old age. (Naylor, *The Women* 61)

6. If she's sick, she ain't *bad* sick. (Taylor, *Song* 12)

In the following examples, a West Indian speaker makes use of duplication of adjectives, and these duplications function as adverbs:

7. But the boy, God rest him in his grave, did lay *easy-easy* inside me. (Marshall, *Brown Girl* 30)

8. Sitting and thinking *hard-hard*. (30)

Vernacular speakers' use of adverb-of-manner phrases is similar to that of Standard speakers in that the phrases often demonstrate exaggeration or hyperbole: "Tell him he's not dressing *to meet President Roosevelt* this morning" [grandmother about young grandson] (Taylor, *Song* 6).

ADVERBS OF DEGREE

Veit (1986) lists some of the most common adverbs of degree: *very* quickly; *most* politely; *quite* happily; *too* soon; *almost* always (82). Standard and Vernacular speakers both make use of adverbs of degree. Several are used by both groups, and some are used mainly by either Standard speakers or Vernacular speakers.

Adverbs of Degree Used By Both Groups

Very

Standard speakers use this form in both early and later works. Examples from early works include:

1. I remember *very* well when my master come home from that battle. (Larison 55)

2. came to me with a *very* distressed countenance. (Brent 134)

3. But I'm not surprised to see you, 'Rene. That is, not so *very*. (Larsen, "Passing" 153)

The use of the term *very* in the truncated expression *not so very* is similar to the expression found in an utterance in a play by Collins that is set at a later time:

4. he's brown, Momma, not *very*, but a little browner than any of us. (Collins 324)

Other later examples include:

5. She repeats anything important twice, once *very* loud. (Golden, *Woman's* 18–19)

6. a fact you know *very* well. (Hunter 42)

7. She was quick to anger, and *very* outspoken. (Delany et al. 11)

I found fewer instances of Vernacular speakers using *very* as an adverb in early works. The following example comes from Hopkins's "Hagar's Daughter":

8. We was the *very* las' couple jined befo' the s'render. (221)

The following example is set in an earlier time but was written in the 1980s:

  9. they were *very* kindly but I'm not a sporty type person. (Childress, "Wedding Band"
  91)

Other, later examples include the following:

  10. I wouldn't put it past my *very* own boys to have sinned with you. (S. E. Wright, *This
  Child's* 80)

  11. I wasn't *very* fond of fish, but I ate it anyway. (Meriwether 37)

Almost/'Most

In the following pair of adverbs of degree, early Standard speakers generally use
the Standard *almost* form, while early Vernacular speakers generally use the
non-Standard *most* form. The examples come from early works featuring Standard
speakers:

  1. She's really *almost* too good-looking. (Larsen, "Passing" 156)

  2. We had *almost* given you up. (Kelley-Hawkins 12)

These examples come from early Vernacular speakers:

  3. an' beat de prefesser *'mos'* to def. (Hopkins, "Hagar's" 63)

  4. An' she jis' looked as ef her heart war *mos'* broke. (Harper 11)

In later works, the division of use is not as clear-cut. There are examples of both
Standard and Vernacular speakers using *almost* and *most*. Examples from Standard speakers are:

  5. I feel *almost* brave. (Marshall, "Brooklyn" 96)

  6. Whatta night they had at the Savoy. Why, she danced until she *most* fainted [thoughts
  of an adult female]. (Shange, *Betsey* 19)

Vernacular speakers produce the following examples:

  7. I *almost* broke my own hand hanging up that pay phone. (Bolton 161)

  8. But I'm an old woman, my life's *most* over. (Naylor, *The Women* 37)

Most

The superlative *most* is used extensively by both groups in both early and later
works. Examples 1 through 3 are from early works featuring Standard speakers;
examples 4 and 5 come from Standard speakers in later works:

  1. They used to say that General Washington was the *most* beautiful dancer in America.
  (Larison 61)

  2. You two can be the *most* provoking! (Fauset, *Comedy* 130)

  3. the *most* congenial member of the whole Naxos faculty. (Larsen, "Quicksand" 13)

  4. the hairline at the nape of the neck that harbored the *most* stubborn patches of hair.
  (Golden, *Woman's* 24)

5. the *most* beautiful, intelligent, everything baby in the world. (Giovanni 269)

Vernacular speakers use this form in both early and later works. The first example is from an early work:

6. you is de *mos'* 'quis'tive gal on dis plantation. (Hopkins, "Hagar's" 64)

7. The *most* contentious, cantankerous old witch that ever lived. (Walker, *Temple* 101)

Pretty

The adverb of degree *pretty,* meaning "fair" or "moderately" (Stein 695), is used by both groups, though Standard speakers were to use it most often. Examples 1 and 2 come from early works; examples 3 and 4 come from later works:

1. I thought it was a *pretty* big rain. (Kelley-Hawkins 11)

2. *Pretty* good salaries, decent rooms, plenty of men, and all that. (Larsen, "Quicksand" 14)

3. They're *pretty* complicated to operate. (Dove, *Ivory* 112)

4. Raleigh seemed *pretty* small. (Delany et al. 140)

The final example comes from a Vernacular speaker from a later work.

5. You gave up *pretty* easy. (Naylor, *Mama Day* 48)

Damn/Damned

The adverb of degree *damn/damned*, meaning "utter" or "very" (Stein 220), is used by both Standard and Vernacular speakers. I found all of my examples in later works. Standard speakers produce the following examples:

1. I'm really too *damn* gullible. (McMillan, *Disappearing Act* 16)

2. I'd have to be a *damned* good pickpocket to get away with all this. (Naylor, *The Women* 58)

3. You're *damned* right it's mine. (Naylor, *Linden* 244)

The next set of examples comes from later works. The first speaker is an older woman:

4. What's so *damn* personal about it? (Hunter 95)

This example comes from a Vernacular speaker:

5. id be so damn free from all my bar-stool affairs. (DeVeaux, "Tapestry" 169)

Certainly

The adverb of degree *certainly* is used extensively by Standard speakers in early and later works. The first three examples come from early works:

1. I *certainly* do. (Fauset, *Comedy* 142)

2. People didn't take their servants to the Shelby for dinner. *Certainly* not all dressed up like that. (Larsen, "Passing" 153)

3. She *certainly* ought to be ostracized. (Larsen, "Quicksand" 60)

The next set of examples comes from later works:

4. That would make a great sermon or poem and would *certainly* help me get some sleep at night. (Weems 129)

5. I'd *certainly* forgot about the pushing. (Walker, *Temple* 107)

6. Yes, my Frank would *certainly* have loved to hear your very own rendition in that dialect of our times. (Shange, *Betsey* 27–28)

There are not many examples of this form being used by Vernacular speakers. Examples 7 and 8 are from the same early work. Example 9 comes from a later work; the speaker style-shifts regularly:

7. he *cert'nly* must. (Hopkins, "Hagar's" 64)

8. remarks o' yourn is *suttingly* cur'ous. (178)

9. you *certainly* got it. (DeVeaux, "Tapestry" 168)

Hardly

Although both groups use the adverb of degree *hardly*, there are some differences in their use of this form. Standard speakers use it to mean roughly "barely," and it carries a sense of negation, but no other negative is used in the sentence with it. Vernacular speakers, on the other hand, generally include another negative in the sentences. Early examples of Standard speakers using this form include:

1. Naxos? It's *hardly* a place at all. (Larsen, "Quicksand" 19)

2. [From a letter] I have dreadful news for you and I *hardly* know how to tell it. (Harper 122)

3. he would not dare tell anyone that he gave me the money, and would *hardly* dare to whip me for it. (Mattison 13)

4. Our feet were so sore we could *hardly* walk. (S. Taylor 20)

Examples 5 through 7 come from later works:

5. You're so weak now you can *hardly* pull the comb through my hair. (Angelou, *All God's* 190)

6. I *hardly* spoke to him. (Lee 84)

7. she *hardly* looked to have the strength needed to swing the axe in such a hefty fashion, but her looks were deceiving. (Taylor, *Circle* 27)

I found one example of a young militant Standard speaker who uses the non-Standard version of this form when she addresses her mother, who insists on calling her "Melanie," although she changed her name to "Kiswana":

8. Oh, hi, Mama. You know, I thought I heard a knock, but I figured it was for the people next door, since *no one hardly* ever calls me Melanie. (Naylor, *The Women* 78)

One Standard speaker from a working-class background uses the form both ways:

9. I *hardly* ever go off campus. (Golden, *Woman's* 6)

10. I was mad at mama for a long time. Didn't *hardly* talk to her. (5)

As I noted earlier, Vernacular speakers generally use some form of negation with the adverb *hardly*. These examples below come from later works:

11. Ambush *ain't hardly* what you call the excitable type. (Naylor, *Mama Day* 70)

12. Cain't nobody *hardly* understand him. (Bambara, "Playin" 84)

13. *Wouldn't* let me *hardly* do *no* work at all. (Sanchez, "Just Don't" 285)

Steady

The adverb *steady* is found in some of the works. It is generally used in the way that *The Random House Dictionary* describes it: "1. firmly placed or fixed. 2. continuous or free from change. 3. regular or habitual. 4. free from excitement. 5. reliable and careful. 6. steadfast or unwavering" (Stein & Urdang 853).

Examples 1 through 3 come from later works. The speaker in example 1 is a Standard speaker; the speaker in 2 is a young female; and the speaker in 3, an old woman, regularly style-shifts:

1. So I tell her about this imaginary boyfriend I've got, this one *steady* guy. (Golden, *Woman's* 19)

2. he lost his house-painting job, which hadn't been none too *steady* to begin with. (Meriwether 21)

3. She had a *steady* paycheck through the entire Depression. (Delany et al. 226)

Vernacular speakers also use this form; examples 4 and 5 come from early works:

4. He looks at me *steady* for a minute. (Rose 436)

5. Ike's so *stiddy*. (Hopkins, "Hagar's" 175)

Example 6 is interesting because it comes from a young Vernacular speaker who uses *steady* in an idiomatic expression that captures some of the dictionary's definition, but, because of its placement in the utterance, shows a stylistic difference in use from that of Standard speakers:

6. We had never really been full too *steady*, but we had always had something! (Cooper, *Homemade* 3)

Wolfram (1991) observes that one form of *steady* is a structure of Black Vernacular English. He writes that "its use in a construction such as *They be steady messing with you* refers to an intense, continuous activity" (292; see Baugh 85 for a fuller explanation). The next two examples contain this construction. The first speaker is a young female; the second is an older woman. Both examples come from later works:

7. Later that night, under the covers, I was *steady* practicing. (Campbell 143)

8. If you had any respect for the dead you'd be crying your own self instead of *steady* looking up and down this line to catch you a boyfriend. (S. E. Wright, *This Child's* 262)

Female Intensifier *So* and *Such*

A special set of adverbs of degree has been identified in the literature as being part of women's talk. In the section "Items Which are Described as 'Women's Language,'" Robin Lakoff (1975) writes that women use the intensive *so* (54) and that they speak in italics (56). Also, in discussing "Syntactic Constructions," Key (1975) notes that females "make more use of *intensifiers,* the often-emphasized words such as 'so,' 'such,' 'quite,' 'vastly.' 'It was *so* interesting. I had *such* fun' " (75).

For the purpose of this study, I place the words *so* and *such* in the category of intensives. I discuss the use of words like *quite* in the section that discusses adverbs of degree used by Standard speakers. Adverbs of gross exaggeration like *vastly* I have placed in the section on female use of adverbs. My decision to make this separation is based on readings in other research literature on this area, which usually lists *so* and *such* as intensifiers. The pattern that I searched for was the one where these forms are *not* followed by the expected "that" clause that explains the extent or degree of the intensity. For example, the standard forms would be: "He is *so* tall *that he towers over his father*," or "It was *such* a bargain *that I had to buy it.*" The forms that I searched for would have the pattern: "It was *so* nice," or "We had *such* a good time." When the intensifiers *so* and *such* are used in this way, the females can be said to be using them in the way described by Lakoff, Key, and others.

Intensifier *So* + Adjective [no "that" clause]

This pattern is found in the speech of both Standard and Vernacular speakers. Examples 1 and 2 below are from Standard speakers in early works:

1. And then they were *so* damned clumsy. (Larison 60)
2. And Vera is so terribly honest. (Kelley-Hawkins 23)

The next set comes from later works:

3. She is *so* normal. (McMillan, *Disappearing Act* 17)
4. this building—it's *so* shabby and rundown. (Naylor, *The Women* 83)

Vernacular speakers are also shown using these forms. Examples 5 through 7 come from early works; the rest of the examples come from later works:

5. How'dy, honey! Ise *so* glad you's come. (Harper 275)
6. and it was Aunt Jane's praying and singing them old Virgina hymns that helped me *so* much. (Albert 11)
7. He did not care about waitin' *so* long for them in the mornin'. (Mattison 14)
8. You love me *so* much. (Wade-Gayles 230)

9. But this white stuff gets *so* dirty. (Hunter 105)

Intensifier *Such* + Adjective [no "that" clause]

Standard speakers use this adverb in both early and later works. The examples come from early works. The second speaker is a young girl:

1. It's *such* a frightfully easy thing to do. (Larsen, "Passing" 158)

2. But I like Marise best. She's *such* fun. (Fauset, *Comedy* 34)

Standard speakers in later works produce the following examples. The last speaker is a young girl:

3. You've been *such* a good girl all afternoon. (Ansa, *Baby* 76)

4. It's *such* a big journey. (Rooks 122)

5. Such a simple thing. (Morrison, *Sula* 98)

6. Grandma, that's *such* a long way off. (Shange, *Betsey* 77)

I found no early examples of Vernacular speakers using this form, but I did find a few examples in later works:

7. It was *such* a funny little name. (Taylor, *Circle* 92)

8. She had *such* pretty suitcases. (Dee 280)

Key (1975) says that early research notes that "males do not use the expressive patterns of emotion in intonation, or in the use of intensifiers and superlatives, nearly as much as females do" (98). In her explanation as well as that of Lakoff's, the women and men who were discussed were generally white and Standard-speaking. It is interesting to note that African American female characters, both Standard-speaking and Vernacular-speaking, were shown to use these intensifiers also.

Although *so* and *such* are usually cited as the most common female language intensifiers, another is used in a similar fashion. The adverb *too* when expressing the same type of intensity would normally be followed by an explanatory clause or phrase like: "He's *too* good *to be true*" or "He's *too* pretty *for a boy*" or "It's *too* funny *that we met here*." But when the following phrase or clause is left off, the sentence is very similar to those just discussed. For example, Janie in Hurston's *Their Eyes Were Watching God*, an early work, compliments her friend Pheoby on her cooking by saying about the meal, "Gal, it's *too* good!" (15). Aunt Linda, an ex-slave in Harper's *Iola Leroy*, on hearing that an old friend would be coming to live near her soon, exclaims, "Oh, dat is *too* good" (275). This use of *too* as an intensifier shows up in an early work featuring Standard speakers also: "It's simply *too, too* lucky!" (Larsen, "Passing" 151).

Adverbs of Degree Used by Standard Speakers

Some adverbs of degree are used almost exclusively by Standard speakers.

Quite

Female characters from both early and later works use this form. Examples 1 through 4 are from early works:

1. We are not *quite* ready to go up just now. (Kelley-Hawkins 23)
2. In order to leave the coast *quite* clear for me. (Brent 114)
3. I was made *quite* a pet by Miss Betsey. (M. Prince 1)
4. I made a large quilt of red, white, and blue ribbon that made *quite* a sensation. (S. Taylor 60)

The next set of examples comes from later works. The last speaker is an older female:

5. and there you were, butt naked and really *quite* messy. (Giovanni 268)
6. I was tall and lanky and light-skinned, *quite* pretty in a nervous sort of way. (Lee 4)
7. *Quite* a few escaped. (Golden, *Migrations* 216)
8. As a dentist, I had *quite* a few white patients. (Delany et al. 108)
9. We've done *quite* enough for the Negro race today. (Shange, *Betsey* 192)

Entirely

Examples 1 and 2 come from early works; example 3 comes from a later work:

1. *entirely* too repulsive. (Larsen, "Quicksand" 12)
2. the boat ran upon St. John bar and went *entirely* to pieces. (S. Taylor 53)
3. Portia . . . has an *entirely* different set of standards. (McMillan, *Disappearing Act* 17)

Truly

Example 1 comes from an early work; example 2 is set in an earlier time, though written in the 1970s:

1. I was *truly* attached to her. (M. Prince 1)
2. when a man and a women are not *truly* married. (Childress, "Wedding Band" 84)

In the works from later times, most of the following examples come from adult speakers, with the exception of example 3, which comes from an older female, and examples 5 and 7, which come from young girls:

3. But I have been a wealthy woman. *Truly* blessed. (Wade-Gayles 231)
4. That spot was *truly* special. (Ansa, *Baby* 52)
5. Mr. Jamison was one of the few adult white people that I *truly* liked. (Taylor, *Circle* 32)
6. whatever I saw surpassed good and bordered on the *truly* wonderful. (Coleman 23)
7. But my social worker mother was *truly* alarmed. (Campbell 164)

Other early examples of adverbs of degree include: *deeply* rooted aversion; *decidedly* rough; cared *greatly*; cut me *dead*; I could have done it quite *creditably* and *credibly*; not the *slightest* idea; a *blamed* hard time; a place *much* visited; the thin *intensely* feminine.

Examples of later forms include: *halfway decent* view; *definitely* a lot of work; *precisely* why I went; *remotely* close; *completely* lost; *progressively* more difficult; *truly* angry; it couldn't *possibly* be worse.

Adverbs of Degree Used by Vernacular Speakers

Vernacular speakers use several kinds of adverbs of degree that are not often used by Standard speakers. Some of these adverbs reflect regional, especially rural, usage.

Mighty

Mighty as an adverb of degree is used in both early and later works, often by older females. Most of these females lived or had been born in the South. Examples 1 through 4 come from early works, and all of the speakers are Vernacular speakers; most are slaves or ex-slaves:

1. I'se *mighty* 'fraid dat 'ere nigger vill pop on you some time. (Brent 114)

2. I hope the ol' lady's safe, but I mistrus' *mighty much,* I do. (Hopkins, "Hagar's" 173)

3. But ef she comes out yere looking *mighty* pleased, an' larffin' all ober her face, an' steppin' so frisky, den I knows de Secesh is gittin' de bes' ob de Yankees. (Harper 10)

4. Richard used to be *mighty* faithful to his prayer-meeting. (Albert 24)

In later works, most of the speakers, with the possible exception of the narrator in example 5, are older females:

5. Her mama, growing *mighty* old, had talked Deari B into marrying a old, old man! (Cooper, *Homemade* 49)

6. When I was handling this caul of hers downstairs I could feel some *mighty* power in it. (Ansa, *Baby* 30)

7. But down south they's *mighty* informal. (Shange, *Betsey* 56)

8. I've been working *mighty* hard for a lotta years. (Dee 280)

This form is also used by some Standard speakers. In the next example, the female in this early work is speaking informally:

9. Well, that's *mighty* mysterious, (Larsen, "Quicksand" 38-39)

In a later work is an older Standard speaker who style-shifts regularly:

10. Knowing people like Miss Moseley and our white grandfather, Mr. Miliam, made this Jim Crow mess seem *mighty* puzzling. (Delany et al. 101)

Right

Right as an adverb of degree is also used in both early and later works. This form is used by both older females and young adults who either lived in, or were from, the South. In the following examples from early works, 1 and 2 are spoken by older females, and 3 is spoken by a younger female:

1. Obadiah's *right* fon' o' you. (Larsen, "Sanctuary" 321)

2. I felt *right* set up an' mighty big wen we counted all dat money. (Harper 154)

3. it's gittin' on toward seven *right* smart. (Hopkins, "Hagar's" 169)

In later works, both older and younger females use the form; example 5 is from an older speaker:

4. No, you didn't have to, but it speaks *right* well of you that you did. (Naylor, *Mama Day* 50)

5. Boys, one of you run in the fish house *right* quick and get me some pretty mullet. (Ansa, *Baby* 30)

Heap

Heap as an adverb of degree shows up in both early and later works; as with most of the adverbs in this section, the speakers were usually older females who lived or had lived in the South. The first three examples came from early works; the three speakers are older women who are ex-slaves. Example 4 while set in a later work, is spoken by a ghost who had been a slave, and examples 5 and 6 come from later works:

1. but I got a *heap* 'o hope [help] outen dem whilst dey ben limber. [Old lady speaking about her legs.] (Hopkins, "Hagar's" 175)

2. Emspesial' seein how he allus set such a *heap* o' store by you. (Larsen, "Sanctuary" 321)

3. But Jake's listenin' all de time wid his eyes and his mouf wide open, an' ketchin' eberything he kin, an' a *heap* ob news he gits dat way. (Harper 11)

4. You gonna see a *heap* more like me before you dead, too. (Ansa, *Baby* 158)

5. Well, that grin tells me he musta gotten a *heap* better. (Naylor, *Mama Day* 75)

6. The Lord done put a *heap* of glory in the bodies of many a young man. (Shange, *Betsey* 123)

Near

Near is used in both early and later works, but I found most of my examples in later works. As with the other forms in this section, the speakers are generally older females or young adults who either lived or had lived in the South. Example 1 is from an early work; the speaker is an older woman, an ex-slave:

1. He was over forty; I guess pretty *near* fifty. (Mattison 19)

In later works, most of the speakers are young adult females:

2. Nurse Bloom, who acted like she wasn't anywhere *near* ready to leave. (Ansa, *Baby* 29)

3. Pretty soon, as they got older, the cheek wasn't anywhere *near* her lips. (Shange, *Betsey* 116)

4. and Adam was standing up in the pulpit with his arms outstretched, looking handsome and *near* white. (Meriwether 184)

Other Adverbs of Degree

Other adverbs of degrees used by Vernacular speakers are listed here. Examples 1 through 3 are from early works. Example 4 comes from later works; the speaker is a West Indian:

1. wid a pissle [pistol] pinted *plum'* at me. (Hopkins, "Hagar's" 48)

2. Mammy and pappy *powerful* glad to git sold. (Rose 435)

3. Dat's a *gracious* plenty. (Hurston, *Eyes* 14)

4. nothing *a-tall, a-tall.* (Marshall, *Brown Girl* 29)

Summary

Although both Standard speakers and Vernacular speakers use many of the same adverbs of degree, they do not always use them in the same ways. In some cases I found no early examples for either group (*damn/damned*). In other instances I found no early use in Vernacular speakers (*pretty*). But in many cases the use is harder to explain because of the presence of style-shifting (*hardly, steady*).

Several adverbs of degree are used almost entirely by Standard speakers or by Vernacular speakers. I found that Standard speakers generally use traditional forms in traditional ways. In some cases, those forms identified with female language could be seen in such behavior as using clichés (the *very* same; she cut me *dead*), exaggeration (entirely *too* repulsive), and reduplication (*very, very* special; simply *too, too* lucky); and the use of the two intensifiers identified with female use, *so* (I was *so* afraid) and *such* (*so* terribly honest; *such* fun).

Vernacular speakers use the traditional forms in traditional ways also, but they also use regional varieties (*mighty, right, plum', heap*), and they use these adverbs in idiosyncratic, if creative, ways (a *gracious* plenty; been full too *steady*). It can also be seen that both groups make some use of "rough talk" (too *damn* gullible, *damn* near). However, it should be noted that rough talk shows up more often in the later works when young Standard speakers style-shift more often.

OTHER ADVERBS

Besides using adverbs of time, manner, and degree, the speakers in the works examined use other adverbs. Some are used by both groups; some are used almost exclusively by one group or the other.

Adverbs That Appear in Both Groups

Enough

The Random House Dictionary gives one definition of *enough* as an adverb meaning "sufficiently. fully or quite. tolerably or passably" (Stein & Urdang 289). The pattern of adjective + *enough* + infinitive is found in both groups and in early and later works. The examples are from Standard speakers. The first three are from early works:

1. Two or three others were fortunate *enough* to find some other defects in the wood-work. (Larison 56)

2. What white girls had she known well *enough* to have been familiarly addressed as 'Rene by them? (Larsen, "Passing" 151)

3. La, me, child! I never thought any body would care *enough* for me to tell of my trials and sorrows in this world! (Albert 27)

The next example comes from a later work that is set in an earlier time:

4. my mother didn't stay around long *enough* to see. (Morrison, *Jazz* 208)

The rest of these examples also come from later works:

5. You ain't old *enough* to marry nobody. (Hansberry 109)

6. It took me long *enough* to get your behind out here. (McMillan, *Disappearing Act* 315)

7. Can you tom long *enough* to work on a way to get out of here? (Golden, *Migrations* 217)

8. She'd probably be backward *enough* to put them to everyday use. (Walker, "Everyday Use" 2372)

Vernacular speakers use this form in early and later works also. The first three examples come from early works; example 9 is uttered by a young girl; examples 12 through 14 are from later works:

9. Ah wuz nice *enough* tuh len' it tuh yuh. (Hurston, *Johah's* 24)

10. Ah . . . —wuzn't lucky *enough* tuh raise but dat one. (Hurston, *Eyes* 211)

11. Well, you oughter, ef you's mean *enough* to wote [vote] dat ticket. (Harper 177)

12. Make em know ya get mighty upset, if somebody is fool *enough* to come round bein hurtful. (Shange, *Betsey* 186)

13. So when your father got to be grown *enough* to fix his own breakfast, there was the problem of Carrie. (Dove, *Fifth* 63)

14. someone who is ignorant *enough* to be kind to him? (Walker, "Everyday Use" 2368)

Although *The Random House Dictionary* defines *sure* + *enough* as an informal adjective meaning, "as might have been supposed" (Stein & Urdang 876), most of the examples use *sure enough* as an adverb. This form appears in the speech of both Standard and Vernacular speakers, and, like many other adverbs, it can and does appear in various positions and serves many functions. The form is used mainly by Vernacular speakers. Examples 15 and 16 come from early works. Examples 17 and 18 come from later works:

15. Ah'm liable to have something *sho nuff* good tomorrow. (Hurston, *Eyes* 15)

16. That's so, *sho' 'nuff*, baby. (Hopkins, "Hagar's" 221)

17. I was *surenuff* hungry now! (Cooper, *Homemade* 22)

18. Late frost gonna kill 'em *sure enough*. (Naylor, *Mama Day* 67)

Standard speakers produce this form occasionally. In example 19, the young narrator of Shange's *Betsey Brown* makes the folllowing statement:

19. Grandma *sure enough* had the coffee done. (18)

In some ways, I find myself reluctant to include this statement as a "real" example of the form used by the Vernacular speakers earlier. When I considered what about it seemed odd, I discovered that the placement of "sure enough" in this sentence doesn't follow the patterns evident earlier. In some of the examples, *sure enough* modifies adjectives, and it appears *before* them (*sure enough good*, *sure enough hungry*), or it modifies verbs and appears *after* them (that's [that is] so *sure enough*; kill 'em *sure enough*). But in example 19, *sure enough* comes *before* the verb, which might be an individual stylistic difference.

The other example of a Standard speaker using *sure enough* shows the speaker using the form as an adjective:

20. French-kissy, hickeys on the neck, *sho'- 'nuff* love. (Campbell 227)

Downright

The Random House Dictionary defines this term as an informal adjective meaning "thorough or absolute" or as an adverb meaning "thoroughly" (Stein & Urdang 264). The first example comes from an early work:

1. Mother, who is at the bottom of this *downright* robbery? (Harper 106)

The next set of examples comes from later works. The last two come from young girls:

2. It looks *downright* nasty. (McMillan, *Mama* 129)

3. Best serve him with a summons for being so *downright* ugly. (Bambara, "Witchbird" 182)

4. It makes you *downright* embarrassed being part of the Negro race. (Naylor, *Mama Day* 92)

5. so it's pleasant and *downright* comforting. (Shange, *Betsey* 111)

Particularly

Particularly, meaning "especially," was used by both Standard and Vernacular speakers. The first two examples come from Standard speakers in early works:

1. The Rev. Mr. Young, who lives in the next house, has shown me much kindness, and taken much pains to instruct me, *particularly* while my master and mistress were absent in Scotland. (M. Prince 22)

2. And it seemed, too, that Audrey Denney was to her *particularly* obnoxious. (Larsen, "Quicksand" 61)

The next set comes from Vernacular speakers. The first example is from an early work:

3. everything worked *preticularly* fine. (Hopkins, "Hagar's" 241)

4. he did admit that Adam had done a lot of good in Harlem, *particularly* last year when he opened a free food kitchen and fed a thousand people a week. (Meriwether 54)

Adverbs and Adjective Pairs Used as Adverbs

In the following groups of words Standard and Vernacular speakers sometimes show different patterns of use.

Really

According to *The Random House Dictionary*, *really* is an adverb that means "actually," "truly," or "indeed" (Stein & Urdang 731). This form is use extensively by both groups, and it appears in both early and later works. Following are some of the patterns that I discovered.

Really + Verb

In this pattern, Standard speakers use this form in both early (1 through 3) and later (4 through 8) works.

1. and had no one to help her in her old age, when she *really* needed help. (Albert 15)

2. Are you *really* going to leave, . . . come into the country with me. (M. Prince 20)

3. You've *really* got to help me. (Fauset, *Comedy* 130)

4. Well, you should wait until someone who *really* cares asks you a question. (Angelou, *All God's* 50)

5. I *really* felt as if I might faint from the stifling heat of the room and the smell of liniment. (Lee 85)

6. I catch myself studying her out of the corner of my eye, wondering what *really* drove her to drink. (Weems 129)

7. Never *really* wanted to be rich with money and things. (Wade-Gayles 231)

8. But we also knew that she *really* just enjoyed kissing Daddy on everybody else's sugar spot. (King 227)

Vernacular speakers use this form also, but I found no examples in early works. In the later works example 9 comes from a young girl, example 10 comes from an old woman, and example 11 comes from an adult West Indian female:

9. my pinafore scratching the shit outta me and I'm *really* hating this nappy-head bitch and her goddamn college degree. (Bambara, "Lesson" 88)

10. Yes, baby, like Papa Luke and Mama Rachel, except they were born right here in Mississippi. But their grandparents were born in Africa, and when they came there were some white people who thought . . . that black people weren't *really* people like white people were. (Taylor, *Thunder* 96)

11. You mean to say that after all you are *really* going to be the kind of woman who the baker won't let near the bread? (Kincaid, *At the Bottom* 5)

Really + Auxiliary Do

An interesting twist on the way that this form is used concerns the placement of auxiliary *do* in relation to the adverb *really*. In the first three examples, which come from Standard speakers in later works, *really* precedes *do*. Example 3 comes from a young girl who regularly shifts between Standard and Vernacular, and her pattern matches that of Standard speakers:

1. i *really* dont know how you do it jet. (DeVeaux, "Tapestry" 168)

2. It . . . *really* doesn't matter what we call it. (Jackson 359)

3. But Mr. Scott *really* didn't want us "boarders" living in his home (Delany et al. 142)

In the next two examples, which come from Vernacular speakers in later works, auxiliary *do* precedes the adverb *really*:

4. She didn't *really* act twenty-seven. (Jones, *Eva's* 87)

5. I wanted to ask him was he a barber, but I didn't *really* think he was, so I didn't ask. (Walker, "Everyday Use" 2371)

Really + Predicate Adjective

Both groups use this pattern. Examples from Standard speakers come from early works (1) and later works (2 through 4):

1. I'm *really* awfully grateful. (Larsen, "Quicksand" 13)

2. I thought if it was *really* important to you, you'd mention it. (Cleage 71)

3. he just smiled as though what I said was new or *really* funny. (Morrison, *Jazz* 207)

4. The patterns are *really* basic. (Dove, *Through the Ivory* 109)

I found no early examples in works featuring Vernacular speakers. In the next two examples, which come from later works, both of the speakers are young girls:

5. And we heard a noise outside, and we all were *really* frightened. We were *really, really, really* frightened. (Bolton 17)

6. Girl, we were *really* worried—weren't we. (Clair 168)

Really + Predicate Nominative

I found a few examples of this pattern. Example 1 comes from a Standard speaker in an early work, example 2 comes from a Standard speaker in a later work, and 3 comes from a Vernacular speaker in a later work:

1. Jessie! Is it *really* you? (Kelley-Hawkins 21)
2. My cousin Michael told me that it was *really* candy and I should eat some. (Campbell 32)
3. Life is *really* something too. (Cooper, *Homemade* 1)

Real

When *real* is used as an adverb, according to *The Random House Dictionary*, it is informal usage, and it means "very" or "extremely" (Stein & Urdang 730). This pattern appears in both groups, but fewer examples are found among Standard speakers. The first three examples come from Standard speakers. Example 1 comes from an early work, example 2 comes from a young girl, and example 3 comes from a young college student who occasionally switches between the Standard and the Vernacular:

1. One time a colored woman came there, *real* genteel. (Mattison 29)
2. I washed my Afro down the drain, feeling *real* pissed off. (Campbell 253)
3. The ceiling was *real* high. (Golden, *Woman's* 1)

Vernacular speakers are responsible for examples 4 through 7. With the exception of example 4, which comes from an early work, all of the other examples are from later works. Example 5 comes from an older speaker:

4. He's *real* smart. (Hurston, *Eyes* 211)
5. Talked *real* proper. (Clair 72)
6. And if she was *real* ugly, it would cost her fifteen. (Hunter 102)
7. She never did even make any *real* close women friends after Miss Billie left. (Jones, *Eva's* 83)

Other examples include *real* sweet, *real* thick, *real* close, *real* hard, *real* sick, *real* good, *real* slow.

Awfully

Awfully, as defined by the *The Random House Dictionary*, means "very" or "extremely" (Stein & Urdang 58). The pattern of *awfully* + adjective is found among Standard speakers in both early (1 through 4) and later works:

1. She was *awfully* frightened. (Larison 62)
2. It's *awfully* surprising. (Larsen, "Passing" 152)
3. Thanks *awfully*. (Larsen, "Quicksand" 13)
4. Then he whipped him *awfully*. (Mattison 9)

5. Well, it's *awfully* strange. (Naylor, *The Women* 78)

6. It was *awfully* hot in there. (Lee 86)

Awful

The Random House Dictionary notes that *awful* may be used as an informal adverb meaning "very" or "extremely" (Stein & Urdang 58). The pattern of *awful* + adjective is found among Vernacular speakers in both early and later works. The first two examples come from narratives of ex-slaves, and the last two examples come from later works:

1. Massa Black am *awful* cruel. (Rose 435)

2. Then he got *awful* mad. (Mattison 19)

3. You're making it *awful* hard. (McMillan, *Disappearing Act* 308)

4. He was *awful* clumsy the first time. (Naylor, *Mama Day* 75)

Surely

The Random House Dictionary defines *surely* as an adverb meaning "without doubt" (Stein & Urdang 876). It is used by both Standard and Vernacular speakers. Example 1 comes from an early work, and the person talking is a Standard speaker. In later works the person using this form is often an older female who style-shifts between Standard and Vernacular forms; examples 2 and 3 contain this kind of usage. Example 4 comes from a Vernacular speaker who is using the form in a set expression:

1. *Surely,* she'd heard those husky tones somewhere before. (Larsen, "Passing" 151)

2. God was *surely* going to strike Etta. (Naylor, *The Women* 68)

3. You can't be serious about apples. *Surely.* (Morrison, *Tar* 34)

4. You're *surely* welcome. (Bambara, "Mississippi" 52–53)

Sure

The Random House Dictionary says that this form is informally used as an adverb (Stein & Urdang 1431). There are many examples of its use in both groups. In early works it is usually pronounced without the *r*. The first five examples come from early works; all of the females are Vernacular speakers. Examples 1 through 3 come from older women, and example 5 comes from a young girl:

1. I *sho'* has de worryment. (Rose 435)

2. Oh, *sho*! (Harper 185)

3. Ah *shuah* don' see nuffin' in you but a heap o' dirt. (Larsen, "Sanctuary" 321)

4. That's so, *sho'* 'nuff, baby. (Hopkins, "Hagar's" 221)

5. *Sho* don't. (Hurston, *Jonah's* 14)

In later works this form is used by Vernacular speakers in all age groups. The first two examples come from young girls; the rest come from adults:

6. But you *sure* know my name. (Bambara, "Happy" 65)

7. I *sure* am glad they told that old heifer off. (Guy, *Friends* 44)

8. I *sure* had you figured wrong. (Hunter 93)

9. but the house *sure* does run good. (Shange, *Betsey* 190)

10. I *sure* hope it's two oh two. (Meriwether 43)

In one example, the adult speaker is represented as pronouncing *sure* without the *r*:

11. They *sho* do. (Jones, *Eva's* 86)

In another example an older Standard speaker who sometimes style-shifts produces the following:

12. It *sure* was obvious to me. (Delany et al. 107)

But in another context, she also says, "they would *surely* come home" (145).

Indeed

Indeed is listed in *The Random House Dictionary* as both an adverb meaning "truly" and an interjection expressing "surprise, incredulity, irony, etc." (Stein and Urdang 446). I found that both Standard and Vernacular speakers use this form in both ways in early and later works.

Standard speakers produced the following five examples of *indeed* meaning "truly." All of them except 5 come from early works:

1. she must, *indeed*, be my mother. (Harper 201)

2. Was she, *indeed, a* descendant of naked black savages of the horrible African jungles? (Hopkins, "Hagar's" 57)

3. I was very sick—very sick *indeed*. (M. Prince 19)

4. Yes, *indeed*. (Harper 167)

5. And *indeed*, we have no plans to hire a gardener who comes by more than once every two weeks. (Shange, *Betsey* 177)

Examples 6 through 10 come from Vernacular speakers. With the exception of 6, all of the examples are from later works:

6. Yes, *indeed*. (Hurston, *Eyes* 16)

7. And that you can't be learning through no books. No, *indeed* not. (Ansa, *Baby* 184)

8. Yes, *indeed,* and I'm sure a shepherd like you has helped to turn many back to the fold [to a minister]. (Naylor, *The Women* 68)

9. and jesus knows a good man can make me feel real and happy yes *indeed* umph umph umph. (DeVeaux, "Tapestry" 171)

Example 10 is a slight variation of this form; it too, comes from a later work.

10. No, *indeedy*. (Clair 72)

Indeed is also used as an interjection. A Standard speaker in an early work produces example 11; in later works Vernacular speakers who style-shift regularly, are responsible for examples 12 and 13:

11. Working *indeed!* (Larsen, "Passing" 153)

12. Fried chicken—*indeed!* (Guy, *Measure* 111)

13. After that sermon, Reverend, I'm thinking of coming back—indeed! [one friend mimicking the other's speech]. (Naylor, *The Women* 69)

Summary

There are several patterns of usage found in this section. Some forms are used by both Standard and Vernacular speakers (*enough, particularly, really, sure, indeed*). The adverb *surely* is used by Standard speakers in early works and by older, Vernacular speakers in later works. This pattern of older, Standard forms being carried into the present by older speakers is one that I noticed in other areas. In most cases the older speakers are females who regularly style-shift between the Standard and the Vernacular. In the section that describes adverbs and adjective pairs, I don't find the expected correspondence between speaker and form in all cases. In other words, Standard speakers do not always use only Standard adverbs forms and Vernacular speakers do not always use informal adjective forms. In fact, the only pair that is used this way is *awfully* (used by Standard speakers) and *awful* (used by Vernacular speakers). I find a few adverbs that are used mostly by Vernacular speakers (*sure enough, real, downright*). As is true in other sections, the picture of other adverb use shows a wide variety of ways of using these forms.

ADVERBS USED MOSTLY BY STANDARD SPEAKERS

Female Adverbs

Key (1975) notes that females "make more use of *intensifiers,* the often-emphasized words such as so, such, quite, vastly" (75). She points out that Lord Chesterfield wrote that women have a "fondness for hyperbole" (14). Key also notes, "Female language demonstrates greater use of hyperbole, accompanied by strong emphasis patterns: 'I'll just *die!* He'll *never* forgive me! It was the most extraordinary hat!' The 'cackling hens' effect of women's higher voices and rhythms were superbly stylized in a voice choir performance in *The Music Man*" (37).

Coates (1986), in the section on vocabulary, writes: "An anonymous contributor to *The World* (6 May 1756) complains of women's excessive use of certain adverbial forms." Some of these forms were *vastly, horridly, abominably, immensely, excessively,* and *amazingly* (18). Coates notes further, "The use of adverbial forms of this kind was a fashion at this time, [early 18th century] and was evidently associated in the public mind with women's speech" (18). Though these forms don't appear with much regularity nowadays, I did find some examples; all come from Standard speakers.

Absolutely

Example 1 comes from an early work; examples 2 and 3 come from later works, and the speakers are young females:

1. And you'll see *absolutely* everybody. (Larsen, "Passing" 156)

2. crammed in a paper bag, were the remnants of a junk feast that would be *absolutely* forbidden in Philadelphia. (Campbell 54)

3. I had a wonderful day. An *absolutely* wonderful day. (Shange, *Betsey* 79)

Perfectly

I found this form in both early (examples 1–5) and later (6–9) works:

1. Yesterday was a *perfectly* delightful day. (Kelley-Hawkins 9)

2. nice live crinkly hair, *perfectly* suited to her smooth dark skin. (Larsen, "Quicksand" 14)

3. Now isn't that *perfectly* manlike. (Harper 242)

4. one was *perfectly* white. (Mattison 9)

5. This work was *perfectly* new to me. (M. Prince 10)

6. I'm *perfectly* capable of saying what I mean. (Naylor, *The Women* 81)

7. My eyes were small diamonds. *Perfectly* cut. (Golden, *Woman's* 25)

8. But . . . but what about our Mercury? It was *perfectly* good! (Taylor, *Cadillac* 57)

9. It seemed *perfectly* obvious to me what I was doing. (Taylor, *Circle* 185)

Terribly

In these passages, examples 1 and 2 come from early works; 3 and 4 come from later works:

1. she was *terribly* sorry. (Fauset, *Comedy* 237)

2. And Vera is so *terribly* honest. (Kelley-Hawkins 23)

3. That's *terribly* dishonest, Lizzie. (Jackson 398)

4. he himself seemed too terribly still. (Dove, *Fifth* 60)

Other Female Adverbs

There are other examples of female adverbs used in both early and later works. The first four examples come from early works:

1. She gave me some medicine which she thought helped me *amazingly*. (Larison 63)

2. "You've been really poor, Phebe?"
   "*Horribly*. . . . You've no idea" (Fauset, *Comedy* 274)

3. It's such a *frightfully* easy thing to do. (Larsen, "Passing" 158)

4. It's *positively* obscene. (Larsen, "Quicksand" 61)

The next examples come from later works:

5. what you and I have are two *totally* different things. (Naylor, *The Women* 83)

6. I love you *madly*. (Wade-Gayles 231)

The preceding passages come from works that feature Standard speakers, and so far it is fair to say that I've not found instances of this exact type of usage in many Vernacular speakers. The closest examples are from later speakers who style-shift, for example, "Mama, puleeze. Have you *completely* lost it?" (McMillan, *Mama* 162).

Other Adverbs Used By Standard Speakers

Standard speakers use two other adverbs in many of the works—*simply* and *actually*.

Simply

Simply is used by speakers in both early and later works. The first two examples come from adult females in early works:

1. You've *simply* got to stay and talk. (Larsen, "Passing" 151)

2. it's *simply* no go. (Fauset, *Comedy* 155)

In later works this adverb was used by all ages. Example 3 comes from an older female; example 4, from a younger one; 5 and 6, from adults.

3. Certainly Mr. Barnett had *simply* forgotten about T. J.'s order. (Taylor, *Thunder* 83)

4. That would be *simply* perfect (Dove, *Ivory* 109)

5. So I *simply* got up in the middle of the night and started packing, (Marshall, *Praisesong* 171)

6. He'll *simply* never let me have Tunde. (Golden, *Migrations* 217)

The last example comes from an adult female who regularly style-shifts.

7. I was *simply* stating a fact about you. (Hunter 42)

Actually

Actually is also used by speakers in both early and later works. The first two examples come from early works; both of the speakers are adults:

1. most of her charges had *actually* come from the backwoods. (Larsen, "Quicksand" 12)

2. even I was uncertain whether I was *actually* there in the flesh or not. (Larsen, "Passing" 154)

In later works older speakers (example 3), younger speakers (4 and 5), and adults (6 through 9) used this adverb.

3. And you *actually* think you can compete with that? (Golden *Woman's* 4)

4. I needed some souvenir, some proof that he had *actually* come from Pittsburgh. (Dove, *Fifth* 60)

5. I *actually* turned once and headed toward the store. (Taylor, *Thunder* 85)

6. when I woke up the next morning I was *actually* hurting, physically hurting. (Marshall, *Praisesong* 170)

7. We *actually* got started about 7 A.M. (Giovanni 263)

8. so I don't *actually* sing yet. (McMillan, *Disappearing Act* 165)

The last example in this section comes from a speaker who regularly style-shifts.

9. Well, *actually*, . . . I been thinking about it, Landlord. (Hunter 104)

ADVERBS USED MOSTLY BY VERNACULAR SPEAKERS

Some adverbs are used mostly by Vernacular speakers and those who style-shift.

All

All is used by some Vernacular speakers to mean "totally, entirely or completely." I found instances of this form in both early and later works. Examples 1 through 4 are from early works:

1. While she sot dar *all* white an' trimbly. (Hopkins, "Hagar's" 63)

2. Your grandmother is *all* bowed downed wid trouble now. (Brent 98)

3. They was *all* cheerin' and cryin' and shoutin' for de men dat was ridin' off. (Hurston, *Eyes* 32)

4. She's put it *all* wrong. (Harper 10)

5. Me, I done got *all* fat. (Jones, *Eva's* 84)

6. Suppose Shirley was *all* splayed out in front of you? (Morrison, *Sula* 97)

7. He got down, *all* trembly, on one knee and asked her to be his wife. (Dove, *Fifth* 27)

The next two examples come from Standard speakers who regularly style-shift:

8. She was walking around the house *all* bent over backward. (Giovanni 264)

9. Don't go getting yourself *all* hung up on another one. (McMillan, *Disappearing Act* 61)

Other examples from later works include: *all* nice and neat; *all* screwed up; *all* clogged up; *all* creaky; *all* trembly; *all* wrong; *all* well again; *all* sweaty; *all* shriveled.

All is also used by some speakers to emphasize such feelings as exasperation, indignation, or scorn. Items 10 through 15 are examples of this type of usage. All of the examples come from later works:

10. Don't you see her bags *all* packed over there near you? (Marshall, *Praisesong* 22)

11. The short stocky fellow with the hair to his navel is *all* grinning. (Walker, "Everyday Use" 2369–2370)

12. Real bangle bracelets, *all* on her arm. (Bolton 90)

13. So one night he was by my place *all* drunk up and snoring. (Naylor, *The Women* 58)

14. The girls was *all* nicey-nicey to each other. (Clair 78)

Barely

Barely is another adverb used by Vernacular speakers. I found examples only in later works:

1. Just *barely*, Mattie, just *barely*. (Naylor, *The Women* 62)

2. *Barely* enough to wash, let alone press and curl. (Golden, *Woman's* 25)

3. and started tracing her finger along my hand, but *barely* touching the lines. (Jones, *Eva's* 89)

4. I could *barely* see her. (Dove, *Fifth* 60)

5. *barely* keep hisself in changing clothes. (Sanchez, "Just Don't" 285)

Naturally

I found one example of this adverb in early works (1), but, like *barely*, this form is used mostly by speakers in later works:

1. I'd *be nachally* obleeged [obliged] to giv' up the ghos'. (Hopkins, "Hagar's" 173)

2. *Naturally* he wants some, he's always hungry. (Hunter 51)

3. *Naturally*, he was crazy as hell. (McMillan, *Disappearing Act* 21)

ADVERB PHRASES

There are adverb phrases that appear with some regularity in both early and later works.

Better Not

The first two examples are from early works; the speaker in example 1 is a Standard speaker; in example 2, a Vernacular speaker:

1. It was the advice of the best physicians that I had *better not* remain in Russia during another cold season. (N. Prince 40)

2. Nobody *better not* criticize yuh in mah hearin'. (Hurston, *Eyes* 284)

The first speaker comes from a later work that is set in an earlier time. The female is a Vernacular speaker. The other speaker style-shifts regularly:

3. You *better not* never tell nobody but God. (Walker, *Purple* 11)

4. But he *better not* be looking for you. (Clair 165)

Other Adverb Phrases

There are other adverb phrases used that appear in both early and later works. The next three examples all come from early works. The first example comes from the narrative of an ex-slave, an older woman. The second example comes from an adult female who speaks in a Vernacular dialect, and the third example comes from a young girl who also spoke in a Vernacular dialect:

1. the *devil knows* where all. (Larison 53)

2. He done whipped niggers *nigh to death*. (Hurston, *Jonah's* 7)

3. Git back *outa mah face*, Phrony. (Hurston, *Jonah's* 24)

In later works, examples 4 through 6 come from older speakers, and 7 comes from a West Indian adult. The rest of the examples come from books by Terry McMillan, whose characters use adverbs extensively and creatively:

4. No, you didn't have to, but it speaks *right well* of you that you did. (Naylor, *Mama Day* 50)

5. That girl sho' do favor you, George, ... *Right long* in here. (Campbell 62)

6. She wasn't *nowhere near* light skin. (Clair 72)

7. I tell yuh, that girl got the house *stink down with codfish*. (Marshall, *Brown Girl* 23)

8. or else I'ma be *two minutes away from your asses*. (McMillan, *Mama* 33)

9. He was crazy *as hell*. (McMillan, *Disappearing Act* 21)

10. I've got gigs coming *out of my ass*. (McMillan, *Disappearing Act* 316)

TRANSITIONAL ADVERBS

Several words are used by both groups to introduce a sentence or to resume a conversation or a narrative.

Why

This form is used most often by older female speakers, both Standard and Vernacular. They employ it as a transitional device in the course of some kind of narrative or as a way to begin a sentence, especially sentences that are responses to questions. Examples 1 through 4 come from Standard speakers. The first two examples come from early works:

1. Helga Crane, do you know what time it is? *Why,* it's long after half past seven. (Larsen, "Quicksand" 13)

2. *Why,* of course, I know you! (Larsen, "Passing" 150)

3. Who's guaranteed her a flight right away? *Why,* some of these little islands don't see a plane going anywhere but maybe two, three times a week. (Marshall, *Praisesong* 25)

4. *Why,* Denver, ... Look at you. (Morrison, *Beloved* 247)

Vernacular speakers use this form also; in most cases, the speaker is an older woman. Examples 5 through 7 are from early works; the rest, from later works.

5. Den someone say, $525.00 and de auction man say, "She am sold for $525.00 to Massa Hawkins." Am I glad and 'cited! *Why,* I's quiverin' all over. (Rose 435)

6. *Why,* in some of them shanties there are a dozen or more, whites, and blacks, and all colors, and nothing to eat and nothing to wear. (Larison 52)

7. *Why,* old marster used to make me go out before day, in high grass and heavy dews, and I caught cold. (Albert 3)

8. What could a tired old woman like me do to a powerful hoodoo doctor? *Why,* that little mess I got out at the other place wouldn't hold a candle to—. (Naylor, *Mama Day* 51)

9. And—we can put up them new curtains in the kitchen. . . . *Why* this place be looking fine. (Hansberry 102)

10. *Why,* by the time I was your age, I was on my second husband. (Naylor, *The Women* 37)

11. *Why,* one reason to live there was cause there were so many children. (Shange, *Betsey* 14)

12. *Why,* I'd love to. (Dove, *Ivory* 109)

Still

This form is generally used in narratives as either a conjunction or an adverb that signals the meaning, "in spite of that" or "even" or "yet" (Stein & Urdang 857). It is used mostly by Standard speakers in later works. I found only two examples from early works: example 1 comes from a Standard speaker, and example 2 comes from a Vernacular speaker:

1. It was a hard life for a girl of sixteen. *Still,* I had a roof over my head, and food, and clothes. (Larsen, "Passing" 159)

2. *Still,* 'siderin' all an' all, how Obadiah's right fon' o' you. (Larsen, "Sanctuary" 321)

The rest of the examples come from Standard speakers. Example 3 comes from an older female; examples 4 and 5, from adults:

3. *Still,* that first picture she saw of Greer was most like a monkey-man she'd ever seen. (Shange, *Betsey* 30)

4. *Still,* her mother insisted that she was "delicate," easy to wear out, easy to bruise, seeming to enjoy the myth of her delicacy. (Ansa, *Baby* 57)

5. *Still*, I didn't want him to think I was trying to set a "mood." (McMillan, *Disappearing Act* 63)

Well

Well is used extensively by both groups in early and later works. It is generally used "to introduce a sentence or resume a conversation" (Stein & Urdang 990). This adverb is also used to resume narratives.

A few Standard speakers in later works use *well* to introduce sentences. Example 1 comes from an older female:

1. *Well* what am I supposed to think? (Jackson 354)

2. *Well*, I had pulled the curtain so we could be alone. (Giovanni 270)

Vernacular speakers use *well* this way in both early and later works. Examples 3 and 4 are from early works; example 3 is from an older speaker:

3. *Well*, I hear she was in Texas, and I keep writin' to Texas. (Mattison 27)

4. *Well*, honey, I foun' a big pile o' greenbacks—mus' a bin 'bout a million dollars, I reckon,—one night when I was sweepin', an' I jes' froze to 'em all night. (Hopkins, "Hagar's" 253)

Example 5 is from a work that is set in an earlier time but written in the 1980s:

5. *Well* I have to cut out six dozen paper roses today. (Childress, "Wedding Band" 92)

The next two examples are from later works; both speakers are adult females:

6. *Well*, soon we got the name out of the way. (Walker, "Everyday Use" 2371)

7. *Well*, sometimes you have to do thangs in this world that you don't want to do. (McMillan, *Mama* 52)

Standard speakers use *well* to resume a conversation and to resume narratives in both early and later works. Examples 8 and 9 are from early works:

8. The dear sweet man! *Well*, they couldn't tell him because they didn't know it. (Larsen, "Passing" 160)

9. the students are coming out from breakfast. *Well*, let them [internal monologue]. (Larsen, "Quicksand" 13)

Examples 10 through 12 come from later works; all of the speakers regularly style-shift: the speaker in example 12 is an older woman:

10. The only thing I see is that you're telling me I'm not good enough for a man like that. . . . *Well*, I'll tell you something, Mattie Michael. I've always traveled first class. (Naylor, *The Women* 69)

11. I can't stand Claudette, you know? She thinks she's hot shit. *Well*, since ain't nothing happening out here today, I might as well get wet. (McMillan, *Disappearing Act* 86)

12. I had to borrow $25 from the school. *Well*, I paid that money back as fast as I could. (Delany et al. 150)

Vernacular speakers also use *well* in the way described earlier. I found examples in both early and later works. Examples 13 through 15 come from early works; all of the speakers are older females:

13. I used to be subject to the cramps, and sometimes I used to have it very bad—so that my mistress used to give me medicine for it; and once, a little while before, I was so bad with it that she thought I was going to die with it. *Well*, I thought now I had better have the cramp, and then maybe I wouldn't get licked. (Larison 62)

14. I's never tasted white flour and coffee and mammy fix some biscuits and coffee. *Well,* de biscuits was yum, yum, yum to me, but de coffee I doesn't like. (Rose 436)

15. Dem Jews hez been right helpful to cullud people wen dey hab lan' to sell. I reckon dey don't keer who buys it so long as dey gits de money. *Well,* John didn't gib in at fust. (Harper 155)

Examples 16 through 19 come from later works; an older speaker produces example 16; adult females produce the rest:

16. Child, when do think is the time to love somebody the most; when they done good and made things easy for everybody? *Well* then, you ain't through learning—because that ain't the time at all. (Hansberry 106)

17. but I said to her, "Look, if you'll be good and behave yourself, maybe we can get along." *Well,* she didn't say nothin'. (Hunter 101)

18. I wasn't going to no beauty parlor in the snow. *Well*, October Brown said she would do it. (Clair 80)

In the following example, the speaker uses *well* in both ways: once to introduce a sentence and once to resume a conversation:

19. Yeh, *well* I noticed something long time ago. Ain't said nothing 'bout it 'cause I wasn't sure what it meant. *Well* . . . I did mention it to Ivy but not nobody else. (Morrison, *Sula* 115)

Summary

In the preceding examples, it appears that a transitional word like *why* is used most often by older women in later times. *Still* is used by Standard speakers and mostly in later works. The word *well* is used extensively by both groups both in early works and in later works; Vernacular speakers use it both to introduce sentences and to resume conversations or narratives; Standard speakers use it most often to resume conversations or narratives. Overall, it appears that these forms are used most extensively in early works or by older speakers. This makes sense when we consider that the rhetorical style of the older females reflected traditional conventions of narration—introducing the topic, making comments on the topic, and signaling transitions. It would be interesting to see if these words are used with the same frequency among older female speakers in other racial and ethnic groups.

ADVERB USE IN AFRICAN AMERICAN FEMALE CHARACTERS

I feel confirmed in my ideas that even when we talk about social class differences between African American female speakers, we are really talking about the same old continuum of language use. In essence, what I've discovered is:

1. Early works show very distinct differences in the language used by speakers identified as higher status; this is true even during slavery, there were some slaves who interacted on a regular basis with Standard speakers and slaves who had little or no contact with anyone other than other plantation creole speakers.

2. The distinctions between Standard and Vernacular remain constant throughout the time periods that I investigated, but the *degree* of difference changes subtly over the years so that, although the earliest works show some Standard speakers using no non-Standard features whatsoever, the later works show that many of the Standard speakers often style-shift to include aspects of AAVE or NSE language in their speech. Works featuring Vernacular speakers follow a similar pattern: early literature shows the Vernacular speakers using non-Standard language all the time; later works showed that these speakers also use style-shifting to include elements of Standard language into their speech.

3. A consistent pattern that emerges is that Standard speakers conform to more traditional forms, while non-Standard speakers use more creative and individualistic styles.

4. As with other sections, we can see that the age of the speaker emerges as an important component. In all of the works examined, writers show marked differences in the way that very old and very young females use language.

5. Finally, some features of language use can be considered African American whether they occur in the speech of Standard speakers or in the speech of Vernacular speakers.

8

Forms of Address

According to Trudgill (1983) and others, language has to be appropriate to the speaker using it. He writes,

Language, in other words, varies not only according to the social characteristics of the speaker (such as his social class, ethnic group, age and sex) but also according to the social context in which they find themselves. The same speaker uses different linguistic varieties in different situations and for different purposes. The totality of linguistic varieties used in this way—and they may be very many—by a particular community of speakers can be called that linguistic community's *verbal repertoire*. (84)

Fasold (1990), in describing the ways the speakers use language, writes:

When people use language, they do more than just try to get another person to understand the speaker's thoughts and feelings. At the same time, both people are using language in subtle ways to define their relationship to each other, to identify themselves as part of a social group, and to establish the kind of speech event they are in. (1)

Use of address forms is certainly one way that speakers can indicate the relationship that they have with the person or persons to whom or about whom they are talking. Brown and Gilman (1960), when discussing certain kinds of pronoun use, claims that pronoun usage is governed by two semantics, which they call "power" and "solidarity." In other words, certain pronoun use can help us understand along a continuum of use whether the speaker is signaling an intimate and informal relationship or a distant and formal one. Further, speakers can also say something about the social context of the situation by their choice of forms. Much of what is said about pronoun use can be said about the way that we in America use forms of address. Brown and Ford (1961) developed a schema that describes the American address system that goes from "title," the most formal and distant, to "multiple name," the most informal. In this section, I make use of parts of this system for organizing the information that I found about the way that African American females are shown to use address forms in the works that I examined. I begin with an overview of names; then I examine titles and multiple names. In the last section I discuss the use of forms that I call "labels." As with other chapters, whenever possible, I divide the sections into areas that reflect different social groups.

FIRST NAMES

Chaika (1982) writes, "The actual rules of address in society are as complex as society itself" (47). Others have pointed out that different groups follow different patterns when choosing first names. Names can be examined from the point of view of social differences in the African American community. Some of the names are neutral in the sense that they represent traditional naming practices for females in the United States. Looking at such names, it might be possible to decide *when* a particular name was popular, but we might not be able to assign the use to a particular social group. So, for example, in a certain Zora Neale Hurston novel, which is set in rural Florida in the early part of the twentieth century, Janie's best friend is named Pheoby, and in a Jesse Fauset's novel that is set in Boston, New York, and France and that chronicles the lives of a group of upper-middle-class professional African Americans in about the same time period, one of the main characters is also named Phebe (spelled differently, but probably pronounced the same).

Still, names of females in these works can give us clues about their social environments as well as the time periods. Some of the women changed their names from one thing to another for various reasons; for example, in Morrison's *Beloved,* Jenny Whitlow changes her name to Baby Suggs because "Suggs" is the name of her slave husband, and "Baby" is his name for her. After he leaves, she holds onto the incongruous name as a way of remembering him. Another name change that appears with some regularity in the 1960s and the 1970s is that from a Westernized name to an African name. The author Toni Cade changed her name to Toni Cade Bambara, and in one of her books a character changes her name from Dee to Wangero Lewanika Kemanjo. Also, in Gloria Naylor's *The Women of Brewster Place*, one of the characters changes her name from Melanie Browne to Kiswana Browne.

One character's decision to change her name was described this way: "She told me her new name was Belle, said 'who wants to be named Is-so-bel?' Said, 'Now that I am free, I can change my name if I want to! Change my whole life if I want to!' Now!" (Cooper, *Some* 52).

Names may also tell us other things about the social environment of the person. For example, it is reasonable to assume that Rosie Giraffe and Sally Brown are likely to live in one neighborhood and that Laurel Dumont and Mrs. Olivia Blanchard Carey are likely to live in another. Because most parents are more likely to choose the first and middle names of their children, we are often able to obtain some insights into the parents' and the community's norms of naming by looking at some of the first names that appear in the works that I examined. Following are some examples of first names that are used by different groups in the African American female community.

Names Used by Both Standard and Vernacular Speakers

A few names are used by both Standard and Vernacular speakers. It can be seen that this list contains female first names that are traditionally used: Bernice, Bessie, Bunny, Claudette, Ida, Jane, Linda, Lena, Mary, Ruth.

The term "Standard speaker" has two different meanings in the early works. For example, some of the information on these speakers comes from slave narratives where the speakers are identified as being educated, and, indeed, many say that they were responsible for writing their own accounts of their lives. I have called these females Standard speakers. A problem arises when these writers refer to other people, especially relatives. It is sometimes difficult to determine if these other people are also Standard speakers, though in many cases it would seem logical to conclude that they are not, since the writers are usually females who came by their education in exceptional ways. My solution to this dilemma is to identify as Standard speakers only those females whose language use I can see and assess. Some of the first names of these speakers include Iola, Louisa, Marie, Nancy, Silvia, Susie.

The second set of speakers is easier to identify. They appear in books written a little later (although I still classify the books as "early"), and the characters are either overtly or covertly portrayed as educated, middle-class Standard speakers. The first names of these speakers include Alicia, Allie, Clare, Emma, Garnet, Gertrude, Helga, Irene, Jesse, Margaret, Maritze, Nettie, Olivia, Phebe, Polly, Teresa, Vera.

There are many more works produced in later years, and there were hundreds of female names used. Most of the names represent traditional female first names. The names below represent only a small sample. Those in italics are names that were used many times: Abigail, Alice, Ann, Anne, Barb, Bebe, Belle, Betsey, *Beverly*, Bonnie, Bunnie, Cassie, CeCe, Cecelia, Carrie, Charmaine, Charlotte Ann, Christie, Christine, Clarice, Crystal, Darlene, Debra, Dorcas, Dorcy, Doris, Emily, Ethel, Eugenia, Evelyn, Faith, Fanny, Folami, Gaile, Irene, Jane, Janey, Jean, Jerry, *Julia*, Kate, LaTisha, Laurel, Libby, Liliana, Luciela, Lydia, Margaret-Elizabeth, *Margaret*, Margot, Marguerite, Marion, Mary Esther, Maude, Mavis, Miranda, Naomi, Nellie, Nisi, October, Odetta, Onika, Pauline, Pearl, Portia, Rita, Roxanne, Sadie, Sharon, Sierra, Silvia, Sofia, Suzella, Tamu, Teresa, Thomasina, Ursula, Vida, Vicki, Violet, *Virginia*, Wanda, Zora.

Many of the early Vernacular speakers also have traditional female first names; if there is anything noteworthy about the following names, it is that several of them are diminutives: Amy, Annie, Bertha, Betty, Charlotte, Elizabeth, Hagar, Haley [Mehaley], Harriet, Hetty, Jane, Janie, Jinnie, Martha, Marthy, Merrilee, Pearl, Pheemy, Phrony, Rose, Sarah, Susanna, Sylvia, Venus, Zulena.

In later works featuring Vernacular speakers, I found that, with a few exceptions (e.g., China, China Doll, and Poland are the names of prostitutes), many of the names follow the traditional first-name pattern for females: Avey, Be-A-trice, Beryl, Bootsey, Burlee, Carole, Chaundra, Cora Lee, Corabelle, Dearie B., Deidra, Dicie, Doll, Edith, Elo, Ernestine, Eula Mae, Eva, Florence, Francie, Freda, Georgia, Gussie Ann, Hannah, *Hattie*, Ina, Jocelyn, Johnette, Johnnie Mae, Juanita, Kaye Francis, Kitty, Lanie, Laura, Lillie, Lissie, Lulu, Maggie, Maizelle, Malaika, Mamie, Marge, Marriage, Mary Elouise, Mildred, Naomi, Patsy, Phyllis, Priscilla, Rachel, Rebecca, Reema, Rhoda, Rowena, Ruby, Sally, Sarah, Selina, Sheila, Shug, Silla, Sophie, Suggie, Sukie, Timika, Valentine, Veejay, Virgie, Willa, Willie Bea, Yolanda, Zurletha.

In Meriwether's *Daddy Was a Numbers Runner*, two members of Father Divine's Church are called Beloved Theresa and Sweet Morning Glory.

FIRST AND LAST NAMES

In some communities a few females are referred to by both their first and last name at least part of the time. Examples from Standard speakers include October Brown, Judy Long-Carter, Ann Marie Cooper, Laurel Dumont, Princess Childs, Albertine Scott, Clara Davis, Emancipation Sheridan.

Vernacular speakers also use this form. For example there is a character in McMillan's *Mama* whose name is Sally Noble. The author notes that "folks always said both of her names as if they were one" (40). Other examples from Vernacular speakers include Rosie Giraffe, Janey Wagon, Suggie Skeete, Mattie Michael, Viola Prunebrough.

The preceding examples show that, although both groups of speakers make use of some traditional names, the Standard speakers use these types of names most often. Standard speakers, however, have a few names that might be seen as unusual; for example, one young female is named Suzella. Folami is the name of another young female who belongs to a separatist, African-based religious group; Maritze is a character in an early work who is described as being both dark and exotic; and October Brown was a young schoolteacher whose eccentric behavior meets with the disapproval of many of the more conservative members of the African American community in which she lives.

The naming patterns for the Vernacular speakers follow a pattern also. There is more evidence of the use of diminutives (Janie, Annie, Rosie) as well as unusual and perhaps coined names (Burlee, Chaundra, Dearie B., Jet, Lavender, Maizelle, Marriage, Mehaley, Pheemy, Phrony, Timika, Zulena, Zurletha). This difference in the ways that first names are used points up once again the fact that, generally, the Standard speakers display conformist behavior, while the Vernacular speakers use more creative, individualistic behavior. In the following descriptions, this pattern is evident again and again.

TITLES

Anthropologists and other social scientists have looked at the way that address forms are used in communities. Brown and Ford (1961) offer a scheme that says that, generally, Americans use address to signal a range from formality to informality and from intimacy to distance, for example, Doctor, Doctor Hudson, Doctor Barbara Hill Hudson, Barbara, Barb, Booch.

This set leaves out a number of other possibilities, but it illustrates the point that, generally in the United States, title alone represents a high level of formality and distance, while Barb and Booch, nicknames, represent one of the lowest levels of formality, and also indicate a degree of intimacy quite different from that of the first form.

Not only do different communities make different use of the typical range of titles and names, but they may also have a set that represents other types of relationships along the formality-informality and distance-intimacy continuums.

The characters that I examined use all of the forms mentioned by Brown at one point or the other, but certain communities make use of other forms and also put traditional forms to novel uses.

TFN (Title + First Name)

Miss + First Name

Sociolinguists say that this form is common in the South and areas settled by people from the South. It denotes both a sense of formality and intimacy. Neighborhood children call older women (at least ten years older) by this title if they are in regular and intimate contact. Regular and intimate contact may include being neighbors (loosely), being members of the same church, or knowing the women because they are friends of the family. An example of this usage occurs in the following passage in which a speaker describes how a young girl has grown up: "Yeah, Jeffrene's grown now. They calling her Miss Jeffrene, except her mama, her mama still call her Jeffy or sometimes Jeff" (Jones, *Corregidora* 200–201).

Adults might use this term with older women (approximately fifteen years older). *Miss* + first name may also be used by peers in the community and often signals friendship or a special bond, so that two adult women might playfully refer to each other as Miss Anne, Miss Grace, Miss Janet, Miss Wilma. This form is used in both early and later works and among both Standard and Vernacular speakers. Some of the examples that I found are Miss Abigail, Miss Aussie, Miss Betsey, Miss C, Miss Candy, Miss Cathy, Miss Celie, Miss Effie, Miss Elaine K, Miss Eva, Miss Frances, Miss Hagar, Miss Hazel, Miss Ina, Miss Iola, Miss Isabele, Miss Jessie, Miss Jewel, Miss Julia, Miss Lena, Miss Lizzie, Lula, Miss Lydia, Miss Marge, Miss Mary, Miss Nan, Miss Nellie, Miss Rose, Miss Rowana, Miss Ruby, Miss Sadie, Miss Suggie, Miss Sula Mae, Miss Vida, Miss Virginia, Miss Wilhelmina.

Mrs. + First Name

This pattern is found in two works. In both cases a young girl refers to, or addresses, an older female. In Ansa's *Baby of the Family*, the Standard-speaking female narrator refers to her beautician as Mrs. Maureen. In S. E. Wright's *This Child's Gonna Live*, the author calls a prayer leader in a church Mamma Bertha Ann, but a young girl addresses the woman as Mrs. Bertha.

TLN (Title + Last Name)

Miss + Last Name

This form is used by various segments of the African American community to signal formality and distance. In the middle-class community it is the proper way to address young ladies in a number of different circumstances. In earlier times, young men had to address an unrelated, unmarried female by this title until he was given permission to use her first name. The young lady was referred to by this title by all speakers at all formal gatherings unless she was intimately involved or related to those who spoke to her. Examples that I found include: Miss Baeta, Miss Boswell, Miss Bowen, Miss Brown, Miss Calhoun, Miss Carey, Miss Cates, Miss Crane, Miss Crocker, Miss Coralle, Miss Dare, Miss Delany, Miss Denney, Miss Dumas, Miss Earle, Miss Furber, Miss Hunt, *Miss Jackson*, Miss Jefferson, Miss Johnson, Miss King, Miss Leroy, Miss MacGooden, Miss Madison, Miss Michael, Miss Moore, Miss Packer, Miss Pennyfeather, Miss Perkins, Miss Peters, Miss Picnkney, Miss Poole, Miss Ross, Miss Skipper, Miss Thompson, Miss Wangero, Miss Willback, Miss Wilson.

In the lower-class African American speech community, the title is usually reserved for older women who are in authority (a teacher, a supervisor) or for strangers or for people *in* the community but not *of* the community.

For example, Bambara described one type of woman who was referred to by title + last name in this way:

Miss Moore was her name. The only woman on the block with no first name. And she was black as hell, cept for her feet, which were fish-white and spooky. And she was always planning these boring-ass things for us to do, us being my cousin, mostly, who lived on the block cause we all moved North the same time and to the same apartment then spread out gradual to breathe. And our parents would yank our heads into some kinda shape and crisp up our clothes so we'd be presentable for travel with Miss Moore, who always looked like she was going to church, though she never did. ("Lesson" 87)

DeVeaux (1980) describes two other types of *Miss* + last name: one, a white woman who owns a business in the community, and the other, an eccentric:

1. *old miss goldberg* in the door of her laundromat. ("Remember" 112)

2. *miss king.* always dressed in black. summer or winter. (112)

Naylor's Etta Mae Johnson, a woman of questionable morals, also fits this description:

Any who bothered to greet her never used her first name. No one called Etta Mae "Etta," except in their minds; and when they spoke to each other about her, it was Etta Johnson; but when they addressed her directly, it was always *Miss Johnson. (The Women* 57)

Mrs. + Last Name

This form is used throughout the African American community to address a married woman in a formal, but not necessarily distant, manner: Mrs. Avery, Mrs. Blackman, Mrs. Bracken, Mrs. Briscoe, Mrs. Browne, Mrs. Burnett, Mrs. Cary, Mrs. Coles, Mrs. Cumberson, Mrs. Crandall, Mrs. Crooms, Mrs. Dare, Mrs. Davies, Mrs. Dumont, Mrs. Harrison, Mrs. Hayes-Rore, *Mrs. Jackson*, Mrs. Johnson, Mrs. Lewis, Mrs. Mackey, Mrs. Mitchell, Mrs. Mozelle, Mrs. Parnell, Mrs. Peck, Mrs. Powell, Mrs. Oliver, Mrs. Sargeant, Mrs. Scott, Mrs. Sheridan, Miss Stevens, Mrs. Sumpkins, Mrs. Russell, Mrs. Tilson, Mrs. Trace, Mrs. Turner, Mrs. Vane, Mrs. Vet, Mrs. Watson, Mrs. Wicker, Mrs. Will, Mrs. Wilkens, Mrs. Wood.

TFN + LN (Title + First Name + Last Name)

Miss + First and Last Names

This address is generally used to describe a woman who is known to the speaker, but who may not be an intimate. The usage reflects more formality than first name only but less than title and last name, for example, Miss Sula Mae Peace, Miss Daisy Crocker, Miss Mamie Nightlaw. The title may also be used to comment on the personality or behavior of certain females. So, for example, in a book by Shange a very spirited young girl is referred to as Miss Betsey Brown, and a schoolteacher whose behavior is deemed scandalous by some members of the community is sometimes referred to as Miss October Brown.

Mrs. + First and Last Names

There seems to be a social difference in the way that this form is used. Both Standard speakers and Vernacular speakers use the pattern that includes the title along with the first and last name of the female: Mrs. Baby Suggs, Miz Alfronia De Costa Meriwether, Mrs. Rosalie Johnson, Mrs. Olivia Blanchard Cary. In other cases, the first and last names are those of the female's husband: Mrs. Hendrick Harrison, Mrs. John Sturtevant, Mrs. Morgan Rogers, Mrs. Silas Lanier. This latter pattern reflects a middle-class and upper-middle-class practice.

Others

Miss + Label

This form is often used as a spur-of-the moment nickname and often serves as a commentary on the female's attitude or behavior, for example:

1. Miss Quicksilver herself. (Bambara, "Raymond's" 27)
2. Miss Busy [said of a neighborhood gossip]. (Jones, "Jevata" 137)

It is also used in set patterns like Miss Know-It-All, Miss Smarty, and Miss Thing/Thang (referring to someone who thinks she is "cute"), Miss Hot Stuff, and Miss Lady.

Miss + Title

A few works contain names of titles that reflect the African American community's interests and concerns:

1. MISS INTERNATIONAL SEPIA—1980. (Jackson 360)
2. Miss Emancipation Proclamation. (Jackson 384)
3. Little Miss Ebony Calvary County. (Tate 195)

Madame/Madam + Last Name

In some communities this form is used in a way similar to *Miss* + last name to denote formality and, in some cases, authority and high position. In early works the title is generally used for white women of substance: Madame Randolph, Madame Cook. In later works the females with this title often come from the West Indies or New Orleans or from regions that have a large French speaking population, for example, Madame DuFer, Madame Mico. Sometimes this form is used to refer to spiritualists, fortune-tellers, or "root workers" (women who practice folk medicine). In a passage from Ansa's *Baby of the Family*, one of the characters refers to "Madame Hand out on Highway 17" (32). In a work by Guy that is set in an earlier time, the main character, Dorine, tells a story about how, with the help of a friendly porter, she passes herself off as a person of importance by adopting a particular way of acting and speaking and by calling herself Madam Davis.

Madame + First Name

Generally, when this form is used, it is used in the same way that Madame Hand is used earlier. A character in Meriwether's work refers to "Madame Zora's dream book"(11).

Madame + Other

Madame is sometimes used with other forms, for example, first initials and last name, like real life millionaire Madame C. J. Walker. Another form includes first and last name, like real-life educator and social activist Madame Mary McLeod Bethune. Sometimes the title is used with a label. Meriwether uses the expression

"Madame Queen" (98) to refer to a social worker who puts on airs and looks down upon the narrator and her family.

Mademoiselle + Last Name

This is used in those contexts when the female is a patron of a high-status establishment: Mademoiselle Childs, Mademoiselle Cary.

Sister + Last Name

Female members of some churches are addressed by this title. In a work by Morrison that is set in an earlier time, a white female is called Sister Bodwin. Examples from later works include Sister Taylor, Sister Johnson, Sister Michael, Sister Monroe, Sister Henderson.

Sister + First Name

In one work, a fortune-teller goes under the title of Sister Aurorelia. In another work, set in West Africa, the narrator addresses West African friends using this form, for example, Sister Efua, Sister Grace.

Nurse + Last Name

In some communities, certain nurses are addressed with this title, for example Nurse Jacobs, Nurse Bloom.

Aunt + First Name

An interesting title is *Aunt*. In many instances, this word is not used as a kinship term. In slavery and just after, the title Aunt was given as a title of respect to trusted and highly valued African American female slaves. It denoted a certain position in the household, and it also implied a certain amount of authority over some of the other slaves and often over the younger members of the slaveholder's family. Aunt Jemima is probably the best-known character holding this title. Other examples include Aunt Henny, Aunt Lefonia, Aunt Charlotte, Aunt Jane, Aunt Linda, Aunt Milly, Aunt Katie.

In later works female characters occasionally use the form to address or refer to fictive or "play" kin in a manner similar to that used for *Miss* + first name discussed earlier. One example of this use is Aunt Zurletha, the title given to a roomer in a family household.

Tante + First Name:

This form is another variation of the title *Aunt* that is used in some parts of the country, for example, Tante Rosie. The form sometimes used for a community root worker.

Titles from Slavery

Female slaves or ex-slaves often refer to their owners or to other white females who had high status by one of the following: Mistress, Old Miss, Young Mistress, Missee Enson, Missee Jewel, Old Miss Pickney.

In later works I found several instances of Vernacular-speaking females using the TFN + first name for the name of their white female employees: Miss Mary, Miss Eleanor Jane.

Kinship Terms and Titles

Schneider (1980) discusses some differences and similarities between "family" and "relative" in his book on American kinship:

"Family" can mean all of one's relatives, but "my family" or "the family" means a unit which contains a husband and wife and their child or children, all of whom are kind of relatives. "The immediate family" is another way of restricting the all-inclusive scope of "family" from all relatives to certain very close ones. Family and relatives are thus coordinate categories in American kinship in that they share one of their meanings, though certain of their other meanings diverge. Every member of the family is at the same time a relative, and every relative is, in this sense, a member of the family. The cultural definition of a relative thus applies to members of the family insofar as they are relatives. (30)

Wardhaugh (1986) writes about the role that kinship systems play in society:

One interesting way in which people use language in daily living is to refer to various kinds of kin. It is not surprising therefore that there is considerable literature on kinship terminology, describing how people in various parts of the world refer to brothers, sisters, uncles, aunts, cousins, and so on. Kinship systems are a universal feature of language because kinship is so important to social organization. Some systems are much "richer" than others, but all make use of factors as sex, age, generation, blood, and marriage in their organization. (219)

In the works that I examined, members of the female African American speech community use the common forms of kinship terms used in America. These terms include mother, father, daughter, son, aunt, uncle, niece, nephew, cousin, grandmother, grandfather, great-grandmother, great-grandfather, great-aunt great-uncle, and so on.

In addition, the members of the community use other terms to denote these and other fictive relationships.

Aunt

This title is used either to signal real or fictive kinship. An example of fictive kinship would be having one's children call one's best friend *Aunt*. For example, in one story by Ruby Dee, the narrator makes a distinction between the main character, called "Aunt Zurletha," and her "for-real aunt Marie."

Aunt + First Name

Most of the examples that I found used are in this form. Examples of Standard speakers' use include Aunt Barbara, Aunt Carrie, Aunt Ellen, Aunt Jane, Aunt Janet, Aunt Lily, Aunt Lucille, Aunt Pat, Aunt Rosa, Aunt Ruth, Aunt Sister.

Examples of Vernacular speakers include Aunt Beezy, Aunt Bell, Aunt Carrie, Aunt Dee, Aunt Di, Aunt Dicie, Aunt Ellen, Aunt Hazel, Aunt Henny, Aunt Katie, Aunt Lily, Aunt Linda, Aunt Mae, Aunt Sarah, Aunt Saro Jane, Aunt Treece.

Aunt + First and Last Names

I found one example of this form in the speech of a Standard speaker in an early work: Aunt Jane Lee.

Auntie

This form is used in a way similar to the way *Aunt* is used. In terms of a formality continuum, it may be a little closer to the intimacy pole. In some works it appears with a first name; in others, with a last name. Both Standard and Vernacular speakers use this form: Auntie Barb, Auntie Cheryl, Auntie Julia, Auntie Mattie, Auntie Maya, Auntie Griffin.

Cousin + First Name:

This form is used to denote kinship or intimacy with a family; most of the examples come from Standard speakers, and the person referred to is usually an older female: Cousin Daisy, Cousin Emily, Cousin Lucille, Cousin Mary, Cousin Mattie, Cousin Polly.

Terms for *Mother*

There are many variations on the terms for *mother* or for a mother figure; they include: Mother, Mama, Mammy, Ma, Mom, Mother-Dear, M'Dear, Mud Dear, and Blessed Mother.

Sometimes attempts at calling a mother by another term are rejected. In the following passage, a young woman calls her mother "Mother" for the first time. This is the resulting exchange (the mother speaks first):

What did you call me?
Oh, I've gotten into the habit of calling Ethan's mom that. Does it bother you?
You ain't been calling me no damn mother, and don't start now. (McMillan, *Mama* 233)

Mama/Mother + First, Last, or Nickname

These terms may refer either to a grandmother or to an older woman who has a position of respect in the community. All of these terms are used by Vernacular speakers or those who regularly style-shift: Mamma Bertha Ann, Mama Day, Mama Effie, Mamma Hattie, Mama Teddy, Mother Bloom, Mother Delany,

Mama Drewery, Mother Lee. Sometimes another title precedes this form, for example, Miz Mama Mae.

Terms for *Grandmother*

Like the term *mother*, *grandmother* has variations. These examples come from Vernacular speakers: Big Ma, Big Mama, Big Mamma, Little Mama, Other Mother, Nanny, Mammy, Gran, Granny, Granny Dorcy, grandmama, Grandma, Grandma Baby, Grandma Dee, Grandma Renfrew.

Standard speakers use the following terms: Grandmother, Grandmother Black, Nana.

Many discussions of kinship note that there is often an element of choice in whom people decide they are related to. A work by Schneider (1980) suggests that there are some circumstances in which an individual will decide to deny kinship with those whose might obviously be a relative and claim kinship with others who might be far more distant (but more desirable). An earlier work by Schneider and Smith (1973) suggests that some people in the middle class focus on the nuclear family unit and on self-sufficiency, while those in the lower classes often find it advantageous to include more distant relatives and even some nonrelatives as part of the family in order to benefit from mutual help and cooperation. One result of including a wider range of people is that in some Vernacular communities females speak of fictive or "play" relatives.

In this section, I found many of the patterns of use of kinship terms. The Standard speakers use more forms that relate to the traditional family, and the Vernacular speakers have a wider and looser range of terms that include both kith and kin.

NICKNAMES

Nicknames are used to reflect intimacy or familiarity. The ones that I found include traditional, shortened versions of given names as well as names given to people because of physical appearance, attitude, or other distinguishing characteristics.

Traditional Nicknames

These names are used by all social groups. These examples come from Standard speakers: Barb [from Barbara], Betsey [from Elizabeth], Bessie [from Elizabeth], Ciel [from Luciela], Deb [Debra], Tess/Tessa [from Teresa], Net/Nettie [from Garnet], Lizzie [from Margaret-Elizabeth], Janey/Janie [from Jane], Jess [from Jessie], Phyl [from Phyllisia], 'Rene [from Irene], Sadie [from Sarah], Yoki [from Yolanda].

The following examples come from Vernacular speakers: Cat [from Catherine], Dee [from Dicie], Jeffy/Jeff (Jeffrene), Ruthie [from Ruth], Zu [from Zurletha].

In both groups there are names that have a diminutive form, but it is not clear if the name is a nickname or a given name. Examples from Standard speakers include Jackie, Rosie, Mattie.

Examples from Vernacular speakers include Francie, Nikki, Rosey, Bessie, Maggie, Mattie, Nettie.

Descriptive Nicknames

These forms appear quite frequently in some of the works that I examined; many come from Vernacular speakers. Some are quite obvious, and others are so obscure that often the nickname will not be understood unless the story behind it is known.

Following are examples of descriptive nicknames from Vernacular speakers: Big Butt [this is used by a young, urban female describing a young male]; Gal; Squeak [name for young woman with high voice]; Squeaky [little girl].

These descriptive nicknames come from Standard speakers: Badbird [used by a mother for her tough-acting little daughter); Nazi Youth [woman's description of a white chemist]; Fur Coat [used to refer to a woman who wore a full-length fur coat]; Mr. Sealskin [a man who bought someone a sealskin coat].

Creative Nicknames

Most of the following names come from Vernacular speakers or from those speakers who regularly-style shift: Tea Cake (name given to an attractive young man by females); Nanadine [combination of Nana (grandmother) and Ondine, the grandmother's name]; Miss Johnny Cake; Queen Honeybee; Big Boy [young girl's name—a bully]; Nurse J[acobs]; Mr. Yes ma'am-no ma'am. Examples of obscure nicknames include: Pot Limit, Cocoa, Sin-Sin.

As with the other sections, there are some differences in the way groups use nicknames. Though both make use of traditional forms and descriptive forms, the Vernacular speakers also make use of creative and obscure forms.

TERMS OF ENDEARMENT

I use this term to represent ways of addressing females in an affectionate manner. I also use it to represent the terms that females use in an intimate or affectionate manner to others.

Although many common terms of endearment are used by all segments of the African American female speech community, once again, there seems to be some differences in the way that some of these forms are used.

Some common forms used by all segments include: Child [in Standard speakers, mostly to young child]; Darling; Dear; Dearest; My Dears; My dear; Honey; Kid; Precious [in Vernacular speakers, mostly to young children].

Some forms favored by Standard speakers include: Handsome; Lamb; My dear girl; my dear child; Pookah-pookah; Silly [used for both men and women]; Sugar Sweetie; Little Pumpkin Seed [grandmother to granddaughter].

Some forms favored by Vernacular speakers include: Baby; Baby Doll; Baby Girl; Beautiful-ugly [West Indian]; Brown Sugar; Chile; Chittlin' Honeychile; Gal; Girl; Girl friend; Little daughter; Little Honey; Miss [grandmother to granddaughter]; Miss Z[ora]; Old sweetness; Pigmeat; Puddin'; Soul [West Indian]; Sucker [said affectionately, wife to husband]; Sweet Daddy; Sweet Pea.

Some patterns of use seem quite clear-cut. I found fewer different forms of endearment among the Standard speakers, although many of the ones that are listed are used extensively. The terms of endearment used by the Vernacular speakers show more variety, but many fit into categories; for example several refer to "being sweet" (Sugar, Honey, Peaches), several refer either to age or to size (Baby, Little, chile) or to gender (girl, gal, daughter). As with nicknames, a few are so obscure that a reader would need the context to understand them (Chittlin', Pigmeat, Little Pumpkin Seed).

LABELS

The address forms that I've discussed represent traditional areas of investigation. The ones to which I now turn are similar in some ways and different in others. I have collected them under a category that does not normally come under the term "address forms," but they represent ways in which these females talk to or about other people. I call this group of forms "labels"; they are similar to what many would call references, but I am interested in looking at only a subset of that category.

Some of the labels that I found include those that place people into a familiar (to the speaker and listener) group, labels that use location of the person as a means of identification, stereotypes of all kinds, labels that use physical characteristics as a means of identification, and labels that use origin or ethnicity as a means of identification. Other labels describe social status, activity, relationship, a striking characteristic, attitude, or kinship.

Again, I separate the descriptions of label use into those that may be used commonly by all segments, labels used by Standard speakers, and labels used by Vernacular speakers.

Some forms used by all segments include general descriptions, such as: a bad character; a sweet girl; city girl; colored woman/girl [marked for time and age]; poor kid; that Logan boy.

Standard speakers use labels such as: My young men (archaic); beau (archaic); she's a judge's daughter; Mrs. Bivens of Xenia; The Simmons girls; The Chestnut Hill Nashes.

Some of the labels are quite long: these miserable white women who traffic with Negroes; One of these Portuguese down on the cape in Cranberry bogs (Fauset, *Comedy* 143).

Vernacular speakers use labels such as these: House niggas; my white folk [folks that own her or the ones for whom she works]; all of my people [family/relatives]; one of my folks [relative]; Mrs. Wilkens and them; mamma-nem; the woman who does heads at Mamies; the widowman up there on Edgecome [Avenue]; the man from the barber shop; Marshall the trumpet player; the Chinamen [restaurant]; that old West Indian lady; one of old Slack Bessie's girls; a nice good church woman like Della; the two in 312 were *that* way [lesbian]; her sometimey lover; kissin-friends [archaic]; the lover; her nigger.

Vernacular speakers also use labels that are long. The first example comes from an early work; the second comes from a West Indian speaker; all of the speakers are adults:

1. I'm a temprunce 'ooman. . . . I b'long to de High Co't of Gethsamne, and de Daughters of de Bridal Veil. (Hopkins, "Hagar's" 255)

2. A big-shot cricketeer back home—a big-time wicket keeper. (Guy, *Measure* 219)

3. Some old dude named James Noughton, had a crooked back and worked at the post office at night, and knew everything about everything, read all the time. (Bambara, "Medley" 258)

The preceding examples show how African American females use descriptive labels to characterize themselves and others. These labels serve to give insights into the norms of behavior as well as the beliefs and values of the communities in which these women live.

SUMMARY

The study of address forms can yield valuable insights into how language is used in various social contexts. This chapter has supplied examples of how the use of names, nicknames, titles, and terms of endearments used by African American female characters in literature can shed light on the norms, values, and beliefs of the African American female speech community. Further, this section once again points out that the pattern of language use that forms the continuum between Standard (traditional) and Vernacular (creative) is clearly demonstrated.

9

Word Choice and Wordplay

Chaika (1982) in her book *Language: The Social Mirror* writes,

The vocabulary of a language, then, indicates what is important to its speakers. It also indicates how certain aspects of culture or society are valued: whether favorably or unfavorably. It tells us what makes speakers uncomfortable and what they feel about the rightful role and behavior of different members of society. (220)

In this chapter I discuss some of the word choices and wordplay that help to characterize the speech of various segments of the African American speech community. Though the examples are by no means exhaustive, they help to give a feel for some of the choices that are available to members of this community. The first section focuses on word choice.

WORD CHOICE

Lexicon

This section describes words used by females that reflect their place in time or their membership in various speech communities. This small set represents words that appear regularly in many of the works. They reflect regional, social class, or ethnic use.

Studying

This is an older form, possibly regional, since it appears to be associated with the old South in phrases like *study war no more* from the spiritual "Down by the Riverside." In the following examples, it is used to mean roughly "to pay attention

to" or "to think about deeply." It is used by adult Vernacular speakers. The first
two examples come from early works; the first speaker is an an older woman:

1. He ain't *studyin'* 'bout the dear ol' so'l. (Hopkins, "Hagar's" 220)

2. Ah ain't *studyin'* bout none of 'em. (Hurston, *Eyes* 42)

The rest of the examples come from later works; the first two are produced by
older speakers:

3. I *ain't studyin'* that boy. (Taylor, "Friendship" 36)

4. I ain't *studying* myself with the niggers of this world. (Rahman 15)

5. But Walter Gee, he ain't *studyin'* about no war. (Hunter 97)

6. She'd always stand kind of at a distance when she even talked to Floyd Coleman, and I
   know nobody would think she was *studying* him. (Jones, *Eva's* 83)

7. I wasn't even *studying* her mon. (Jones, *Corregidora* 82)

Cute

This word is used in two ways in the works that I examined; in the older way, the
form means something like "clever and shrewd" (Stein & Urdang 217). In an example from an early work, an adult ex-slave makes the following statement:

1. Then Mr cook turned it off very *cute*. (Mattison 11)

Another ex-slave uses a noun variant of the form:

2. That Jake is a *cuter*. (Harper 11)

The third example comes from a later work and was produced by an older adult
who style-shifts regularly:

3. You must've thought you were *cute* taking him out of town so no one could see till you
   got his nose open good. (Clair 84)

The next example is also from a later work; the speaker is a young girl:

4. At first she tried to be *cute*. (Taylor, *Thunder* 137)

Cute also appeared in a phrase containing some variation of the verb *think*, and
cute generally means "pretty, handsome, desirable." The interpretation is something like, "Although X thinks she [or he] is cute, in reality, she [or he] is not." This
phrase is most often used by younger females who are either Standard speakers or
those who style-shift regularly. Examples 5 through 7 come from younger females:

5. You think you're so *cute*! (Tate 190)

6. he thinks he's *cute*, but he's an asshole. (Meriwether 178)

7. She must think she *cute*. She ain't poot. (Brown 33)

An older speaker makes the following statement to her adult daughter:

8. Gon' get your little fast ass raped again out here if you don't stop thinking you so *cute*. (McMillan, *Mama* 129)

The last example is a variation on the preceding one. In this case, *too cute* means approximately "too good." The speaker is a young, Standard-speaking adult:

9. Some women think they're *too cute* to suck dick. (Sister Souljah 129).

Mess

This word is used extensively in the works that I examined. It is most often used as a verb or a noun. I found examples in both early and later works.

As a verb it roughly means "to disturb," "to bother," "to annoy," or "to have romantic or sexual relationships." The following examples come from early works; the first speaker is an older ex-slave, and the second speaker is an adult Vernacular speaker.

1. Ah shuah wouldn't be letting you *mess* up my feather baid this ebenin'. (Larsen, "Sanctuary" 321)

2. He's easy to love if you *mess* roun 'im. (Hurston, *Eyes* 209)

Later examples of *mess* used as a verb come from both Standard and Vernacular speakers. The next four examples come from Vernacular speakers. The first example comes from an older woman, and the last two come from young girls:

3. Awready there was a house fulla chirren and she wouldn't stop *messin'* with that Greer. (Shange, *Betsey* 18)

4. I hear tell that some of you been *messing* a good friend of mine. Well, let me tell you one thing. If anybody in this room feel like *messing* with a monkey chaser, I got your monkey and I got your chaser. So come on and try me. (Guy, *Friends* 37)

5. Don't you come *messing* with me, T.J.! (Taylor, *Thunder* 181)

Standard speakers and those who style-shift regularly use *mess* as a verb also. The first example comes from an older woman, and the other one comes from an adult.

6. People learned not to *mess* with me from Day One. (Delany et al. 2)

7. They'll *mess* up ever' time! (Marshall, *Praisesong* 27)

Mess is also used as a noun, roughly meaning "untidiness," "disorder," or "something/someone that is undesirable or unpleasant." I didn't find examples of *mess* used in this way in early works, but in later works I found that it is used by both Vernacular and Standard speakers. The following example comes from an adult Vernacular speaker:

8. Well ain't it a *mess* in here though? (Hansberry 101)

The rest of these examples come from Standard speakers or females who style-shift regularly. All but the last two examples come from older females:

9. Don't mind the house, child. I know it's a *mess*. (Naylor, *The Women* 32)

10. You need to stop this *mess* right now. (Campbell 164)

11. Some *mess* this is. (Morrison, *Tar* 125)

12. [Mother referring to what she called, "all that nasty colored music"] Betsey turn that *mess* off and go to bed. (Shange, *Betsey* 114)

13. Think you gonna beat and bang on me like that white *mess* does to their women up on Nighaskin road? (S. E. Wright 37)

Fresh

The definition that comes closest to the meaning of *fresh* in *The Random House Dictionary* is "forward or presumptuous" (Stein & Urdang 352). It is used by females to imply that a young person is acting in a manner that is inappropriate. It often carries the implication that the behavior is potentially sexual in nature.

The first example comes from an early work, and the young, Standard-speaking female is commenting on the fact that a young man that she hardly knows kissed her goodnight:

1. He is *fresh*, I'll say that. (Fauset, *Plum* 125)

Most of the speakers are older adults, and many use the term as a form of real or mock scolding. All of the following examples are from later works. The next two examples come from females who are Standard speakers or from those who style-shift regularly:

2. Some among you have sinned. I wouldn't put it past my very own boys to have sinned with you, flirting in their faces the way some of you *fresh*-tailed girls do. (S. E. Wright 80)

3. Eugene Boyd, you take your *fresh* behind and that basketball right on away from here this very minute. (Shange, *Betsey* 196)

The final example comes from a young female who is quoting an older female relative:

4. messing with them boys and doing all them *fresh* stuff. (Bolton 28)

Shame

In the next two examples, the word *shame* means roughly "to be embarrassed." The speaker in the first example is a young adult: the second speaker is an older woman. Both are speakers who style-shift regularly:

1. a dude that can put in a good appearance so you won't be *shame* to take him round your friends. (Bambara, "Johnson" 168)

2. Anyone build a green house on the equator ought to be *shame*. (Morrison, *Tar* 13)

[Home] *Training*

This expression is used by female characters to mean, roughly, "proper upbringing." I found two examples of its use: both speakers are Standard speaking females who style-shift regularly:

1. she told me, "you have to act like you got some *home training* and don't go wandering through their house."(Clair 28)

2. No person with an ounce of *home training* ever actually chewed gum in the House of the Lord. (Campbell 192)

A variant of this expression, *training*, is used by a West African woman in a work by Maya Angelou:

3. A spell must have been on me, then, because I lost all of my *training*. I talked. I raised my voice. (Angelou, *All God's* 192)

Colored/Negro/Black/African American/West Indian

The women in the works use various terms such as *colored*, *Negro*, *Black*, *African American*, and *West Indian* to describe themselves and others. Most of the terms are popular within a specific time period or are used for a very specific purpose.

Colored

Of all of the terms listed, the one used most often and in the most time periods is *colored*. I found examples of its use from slavery times until the present. In later times the word is used most often by older females. When adult females use it, it is to talk about an earlier time. These examples come from early works; the speakers are adult female ex-slaves:

1. A *colored* man, unknown to us. (N. Prince 15)

2. He found out I was *colored*. (Mattison 8)

3. he would have been remanded to the *colored* car. (Harper 245)

4. Nobody knows the trouble we poor *colored* folks had to go through. (Albert 4)

5. At the gate I found Peter, and a young *colored* man. (Brent 114)

6. he shot the *colored* man dead. (S. Taylor 73)

In later works the term is used by all age groups. The first two examples come from older females. The women are Standard speakers or those who style-shift regularly:

7. She supposed the young *colored* men of Link's generation could have manners like Mr. Powther's. (Petry, *Narrows* 12)

8. Even the *colored* people down here don't eat mangoes. (Morrison, *Tar* 33)

The next set of examples comes from young females who are Standard speakers:

9. Well. . . . The nuns are white, and the Short-Neck Store-man is white, and Father Mulvoy is white and we're *colored*. (Lorde 58)

10. We were no longer two ordinary *colored* girls. (Campbell 63)

11. I am not *colored*, Cassie. (Taylor, *Circle* 184)

The rest of the examples come from adult females who are either Standard speakers or those who style-shift regularly:

12. No matter how white the rest of us are, we're just as *colored* as Laurie. (West 54)

13. a *colored* grade school. (Marshall, "Brooklyn" 3)

14. Nine *colored* boys are condemned to die. (Meriwether 104)

15. those lovely *colored* teachers. (Weems 127)

16. Banks wouldn't lend a *colored* family a cent. (S. E. Wright 13)

17. Like many *colored* women of her generation, she was vain of her skin. (Lee 63)

18. My grandmother would voraciously read the Pittsburgh Courier, the *colored* people's newspaper. (Brown 21)

Negro

The term *Negro* is in many of the works that are set in the period beginning about the turn of the century and going up to at least the mid-1960s. It is used to define and describe things associated with race and racial characteristics: a *Negro* girl; the *Negro* man; the freed *Negro*; a typical *Negro*; a Cuban *Negro*; *Negro* bishop; *Negro* blood; *Negro* eyes; the *Negro* vernacular; *Negro* society; the *Negro* race; *Negro* neighborhood; the *Negro* Women's League; Universal *Negro* Improvement Association; *Negro* insurance.

Black

I found fewer references to the word *black*, but those that I did find are also used to describe or define those things associated with race or racial characteristics. Most of the examples come from later works written after the 1960s. Several of the examples are produced as part of some kind of political statement. Only the first one comes from an early work; the speaker is an old woman, an ex-slave: dat *Black* face; *Black* women; a huge *Black* woman; *Black* working women; all those great *black* men; *Black* dancer; *Black* is baaaaad; *Black* is beautiful; a few *black* families; the *Black* American residents; *Black* community; *Black* folks; *Black* newspapers.

West Indian

Within the works that I examined, I found several references to West Indians. The examples all come from later works: a tall very black *West Indian;* the *West Indian* grocer; A *West Indian* family; the old *West Indian* lady; *West Indian* accent; *West Indian* speech; *West Indian* Negroes; *West Indian* money.

African American

I found many references to Africans, but I didn't find many occasions when the words *African* and *American* co-occur. One example of the term appears in the following passage, spoken by an older, Standard-speaking female: "I am a colored woman or a Negro woman. Either one is OK. People dislike those words now. Today they use this term *African American* [emphasis hers]. It wouldn't occur to me to use that. I prefer to think of myself as an American, that's all!" (Delany et al. 106–107).

Set Expressions

I found a number of expressions that could be placed together into recognizable categories. These categories make up one of the elements of speech that helps to identify a Vernacular speaker. Of course, on occasion, Standard speakers would also use these terms, especially when they are style-shifting. Some of the most striking and prevalent terms that I found are those that I call *self* terms and *ass* terms, since at least one of these words appears in each expression.

Self Terms

The word *self* is sometimes used to point to, or to call attention to, a particular characteristic. It is also used to make an emphatic statement. Older speakers, adults, and children use this term. The typical pattern is personal pronoun + adjective + *self*. All of the following examples come from later works, and the females are either Vernacular speakers or those who style-shift regularly. The first four examples come from older females:

1. So take your *frog-eyed self* and your frog-eyed son out of here. (Naylor, *Linden* 12)
2. Bring your *fresh self* here. (Naylor, *Mama Day* 73)
3. Just bring your *blasphemin' self* on downstairs. (Naylor, *The Women* 62)
4. She's just trying to make you feel guilty with her little fat, *phony self.* (Campbell 164)

The next four examples come from adults:

5. Tell 'm all about his *sanctified self.* (Bambara, "Happy" 65)
6. Go on, girl, with your *bad self.* (Weems 122)
7. He was much better than boring-ass Lakim with his *no-hitting-on-nothing self.* (S. E. Wright 85)
8. How he used to go swaggering through the bushes with his *brave-acting self.* (S. E. Wright 85)

The last two examples come from young girls:

9. Big Boy [a bully, after being called a monkey]: You got some nerve with your *pigeon-face self.* (Tate 1)
10. there she stood with her *moriney* [skin color] *self.* (Meriwether 177)

Ass Terms

Ass is used as an intensifier in some sentences. When used this way, it works in a way similar to *self* in that it calls attention to a particular characteristic. In the following examples *ass* is attached to a modifier in order to emphasize that attribute.

All of the examples come from later works, and the speakers are females who are Vernacular speakers or those who style-shift regularly. The first example comes from a young girl; the second example, from a West Indian adult. All of the rest of the examples come from adult speakers:

1. Who wants to know about your *smelly ass* stationery? (Bambara, "Lesson" 91)

2. Nobody din say he can't have the *hot-ass* woman. (Marshall, *Brown Girl* 31)

3. If you bring your *unfit ass* to my house to get my child, I'm going to call the police. (Bolton 161)

4. let her keep her *tired ass* at home with that *fine ass* husband of hers and that big-headed baby. (McMillan, *Disappearing Act* 61)

Other examples include: fast-*ass*; stupid *ass* son of mine; smart *ass*; pregnant *ass*; some sad-*ass* saga; nosy-*ass*.

Ass was also used to refer to body parts. In children, it usually refers to their buttocks:

5. Well, don't let your mouth start nothing that your *ass* can't stand. (Morrison, *Sula* 92)

6. sit down on that sun porch, turn on that TV or get a book, and don't say two words to me or else I'ma be two minutes away from your *asses*. (McMillian, *Mama* 33)

In adults, it might refer to sexual organs or by extension sexual activity:

7. Mildred's *ass* ain't gold. (Guy, *Measure* 186)

Most often, the word *ass* is used to refer to the whole person.

8. Now get your *ass* up. (Walker, *Third* 139)

9. Alderman Henry Peoples, is going to put some fire to his *ass*. (Bambara, "Christmas Eve" 193)

10. I'll be the first to drag your *ass* all the way to Washington, D.C. (Naylor, *Linden* 245)

11. Here was the pulse of a woman whose black *ass* shook the world once. (Goss 285)

The last example in this section shows both *self* and *ass* used in the same sentence. The speaker is an older female who is speaking to her adult daughter:

12. You settin here with your *healthy ass self* and axe me did I love you? (Morrison, *Sula* 68

Various other synonyms for *ass* (*behind, butt, booty, hind parts, tail*) are used the way the *ass* term is used.

Other Synonyms for *Ass*

Many of the same females who use *ass* terms also use *behind*. This expression is also used to refer to a child's buttocks. The following speakers are adults:

1. Take that book across the street and get those groceries or I'll blister your *behind*. (Meriwether 93)

2. before I tear up each and every one of your black *behinds*. (McMillan, *Mama* 32)

It is also attached to a modifier to emphasize an attribute. The speaker is an adult:

3. Eugene Boyd, you take your *fresh behind* and that basketball right on away from here this very minute. (Shange, *Betsey* 196)

It is also used to represent the whole person. The speaker is a young girl:

4. Deidra says she's gonna kick everybody's *behind* getting the most ads for the pageant. (Tate 140)

Butt is also used the way the *ass* terms are used. In the first two examples, *butt* is attached to a modifier to emphasize an attribute. The speakers are adults:

1. she can bring her *old fashioned butt* in here. (Morrison, *Tar* 34)

2. I listen to mama talk about my *uneducated butt* most all my life. (Cooper, *Some Soul* 42)

It is also used to represent the whole person. All of the speakers are adults:

3. shipped their *butts* to Saigon. (Golden, *Woman's* 21)

4. fix his *butt* in more ways than one. (Naylor, *Mama Day* 69)

5. Soon she'll be glad to get his *butt* out of the house. (Briscoe 59)

Tail is also used to refer to the buttocks or sexual organs. The first speaker is an older, Standard-speaking female who regularly style-shifts:

1. Margaret! People are looking up here! I bet they could see your *tail*! (Jackson 393)

The person who produces the following sentence is an older, Vernacular speaker:

2. Must be you like white *tail*. (Shange, *Betsey* 45)

In the next example, *tail* is used to refer to the whole person. The speaker is a Vernacular-speaking West Indian adult:

3. With some woman called a Driver to wash yuh *tail* in licks if yuh dare look up. (Marshall, *Brown Girl* 44)

The female characters that I investigated use other terms as substitutes for *ass*. The first example, featuring the word *buns*, comes from an adult female; *buns* is used to represent the whole person: "So I just took my *buns* right to her house, cause she my friend and what else a friend for?" (Bambara, "Witchbird" 185). Another adult female uses *hind parts*: "Get your *hind parts* out of that truck" (Clair 164).

Finally, the term *boody/booty* is used to refer to sexual organs or, by extension, sexual activity. Both of the examples come from song lyrics in the works that I examined. The first example comes from an early work; the second example comes from a later work:

1. If you want good *boody* [sex] Oh, go to Ella Wall. (Hurston, *Mule* 150)

2. I got it
   You know I got it

It's in my *booty*
Tutti Frutti. (Rahman 215)

Summary

As with any normal speech community, the African American speech community represented in the works that I examined uses words that reflect different social contexts. Some of the words are used in both earlier and later times (*studying, mess, colored, boody/booty*). Some words are used in a slightly different way in earlier times (*cute*). Some words appear only in later works (*self; ass*; and its variations, *behind, tail, butt, buns, hind parts*). Some words are used more by one group than another. For example, older female characters are most likely to use words like *studying* and *colored*. Young girls and young adults are more likely to use *cute*. Adult females are most likely to use *ass* and *self* terms—two terms that appear with regularity in many of the later works.

There are probably any number of reasons that *self* and *ass* terms are used with such regularity among some of the female characters. One possibilty is that the urban environment that became a part of more people's experience after the 1930s might have been an influence (these terms do not appear regularly before then). This urban environment might be instrumental in encouraging the rifflike, jazzy rhythms that often accompany the use of these two terms. Another possible reason to claim that these terms might have an urban influence is the presence of *ass* in dialects used by many urban West Indian characters (the term *self* is also used among West Indian characters but in a slightly different way). This argument, if it can be called that, is very tenuous, but it bears looking into since the usage of both of these terms still seems to be current among certain populations in the African American speech community. As one final note about the *ass* term, *ass* is discussed in both Smitherman (1994) and Major (1994). I have not found a reference to the use of *self* in the way that I've discussed it, but, of course, that doesn't mean that there aren't very good discussions of its use existing somewhere.

WORDPLAY

Researchers in the area of AAVE have often described the verbal skills and creative use of language displayed by members of the African American speech community (see Labov [1973], [1981]; Smitherman [1994]; Baugh [1983]; and Daniel [1974], among others). In addition, several researchers in the area of women's language also note that certain female members of some speech communities show great verbal skill and creativity (see Thorne, Kramarae, and Henley [1983]; Mitchell-Kernan [1972]; and Penfield [1987], among others). In the following section, I put together a small collection of passages to demonstrate some creative aspects of the language use in the African American female characters that I examined. The sample is small for two reasons. First, many of the early works do not supply the types of conversations that call for clever use of words or for quick-thinking comebacks. In the later works, I found many examples, but several come from the same source. Since I want to show the wordplay in a variety of contexts, I limit the number of examples from a single author. Another reason that this section does not contain a large number of examples is that creative language appears in various other chapters.

Playing with Words

The first set of examples displays a general ability to play with words. The first two come from the same early work, and the characters are Standard-speaking females. In both cases the female makes a humorous remark based on the wordplay. In the first case several young women are on a vacation trip together. They are engaging in lighthearted banter while preparing to go to bed. One of them has been dubbed "Mother," and the speaker is teasing her about her slight build:

1. There isn't too much to "Mother" when she is in *dishabilly* is there! (Kelley-Hawkins 42)

In another part of the book the speaker, a young woman, affects a non-Standard dialect to make the following pronouncement:

2. Men are nice *creeturs*, but you don't want to see too *meny* of them at once; *likeways* with *wimmen*. (Kelley-Hawkins 79)

Another example from an early work features an adult Vernacular speaker who produces the following expression:

3. if you *buys me* for a fool you *loses your money* shore. (Harper 10)

Sometimes the wordplay consists of putting two concepts together and then rhyming them. In the following passage, a young girl, a Vernacular speaker, tells her sister that their mother doesn't like the idea that she never wants to stay at home:

4. Momma says you got *street feet* too much. (Tate 119)

In the next passage an older Standard speaker uses two metaphors to describe the difference between her sister and herself:

5. If Sadie is molasses, then I am vinegar! . . . Sadie is *sugar*, and I'm the *spice*. (Delany et al. 14)

Some of the wordplay can be seen as a form of "smart talk"—the kind of talk that is meant to be provocative. The female who produces the next passage is an adult Vernacular speaker in an earlier work:

6. Mah mama didn't tell me ah wuz *born in no hurry*. So what business ah got *rushin' now*? (Hurston, *Eyes* 52)

In the following passage, a Vernacular-speaking mother uses sarcasm and wordplay to describe what she thinks one of her daughters is doing in college:

7. And that doll, she in college too, but as far as I'm concerned, *all she majoring in is being cute.* (McMillan, *Mama* 174)

In the following example, an older Vernacular speaker uses a play on words to remind a young girl to act like a female, not a male:

8. Take that ball out of your sock girl. How *many time got to tell you your name ain't Henry?* (DeVeaux, "Remember" 21)

Comeback

I define a comeback as an immediate retort that makes use of at least one word from the other person's comment. Sometimes the exchange is short, as in the following example, when a drunk addresses a Vernacular-speaking female, and she answers back sharply:

1. *Hey* baby.
   Hey baby yourself. (White 132)

In the next example two Vernacular speakers, a young girl and her grandmother, have the following exchange:

2. Can't I just go up and say *Hey*?
   I'm gonna *"Hey"* you . . . you keep pesterin' me. (Taylor, *Thunder* 80)

In Morrison's *Sula*, two Vernacular-speaking adults discussing childbirth produce the following exchange:

3. Patsy: She told me not to have 'em *too soon.*
   Valentine: Any time a tall is *too soon.* (57)

In Naylor's novel, *The Women of Brewster Place*, Mattie and Etta, two good friends, produce the following two exchanges:

4. Mattie: My God, woman. You *stole* the man's car?
   Etta: *Stole*-nothing. He owes me that and then some. (58)

5. Etta: My, my you the most *impatient Christian* I know.
   Mattie: Probably, the *only Christian* you know. (62)

Morrison supplies what I consider a classic example of this form in the following exchange, Sydney and Ondine, two Standard-speaking house servants, are discussing the elaborate plans that their employer is making for the holidays. They live in the tropics, and the arrangements call for Ondine to cook such things as a turkey and an apple pie. Ondine style-shifts as her husband explains and she makes her comeback:

6. Sydney: She wants an *old fashioned* Christmas.
   Ondine: Then she can bring her *old fashioned* butt in here and cook it up. (Morrison, *Tar* 34)

Sometimes the exchanges are a little more elaborate, as is the case in the following example with the two young Vernacular speakers. After Raisin tries to explain her younger sister's behavior using the word *crazy*, Big Boy, the other young girl, follows up with a comeback that plays on the word twice:

> 7. Raisin: Hattie's just actin *crazy*.
> Big Boy: She's gonna be *crazier* if she calls me monkey again, and I'll make you *crazy* right along with her, see? (Tate 1–2)

Sarah Wright supplies a similar example, but this time the speakers are two adult Vernacular speakers. The man makes the first remark, using the word *start* and the female makes the comeback using the word three times:

> 8. Shut up woman! Ain't never hit a woman in my life and ain't gonna *start* now.
> You ain't gonna *start* to do nothing now neither, Jacob. You might *start* but you ain't gonna get not further than *start*. (37)

In the next exchange Pecola, a young girl, repeats an expression uttered by Marie, a prostitute friend whom she is visiting. She aks Marie what the expression means, and as Marie answers Pecola's question, she uses the phrase *taught me*. China, another prostitute, enters the conversation and makes a comeback using a variation of the original phrase, *teach you*. As part of her comeback, China uses the word *drawers*. Then Marie makes a comeback to China's comeback, ending the exchange by using *drawers* in the answer. All of the females are Vernacular speakers. I have modified the form of this set of exchanges somewhat in order to keep all of the conversational turns together:

> 9. Marie: Whoa Jesus, ninety-nine.
> Pecola: How come you always say "Whoa Jesus" and a number?
> Marie: Because my mama *taught me* never to cuss.
> China: Did she *teach you* not to drop your *drawers*?
> Marie: Didn't have *none* . . . didn't have a pair of *drawers* till I was fifteen. (Morrison, *Bluest* 46)

Walker uses a comeback in an exchange between Celie and Harpo, the son of Celie's husband. Both are Vernacular speakers. Harpo uses the word *bright* to describe his girlfriend, and Celie thinks that he means *smart*. Harpo clears up the misunderstanding by explaining that he means light-skinned, but he adds that she is also *smart* in the way that Celie originally meant. Then Celie makes her comeback:

> 10. Harpo: She pretty, *Bright*.
> Celie: *Smart?*
> Harpo: Naw. *Bright* skin. She *smart* though. I think. Sometimes us can git her away from her daddy.
> Celie: If she so *smart* how come she big [pregnant]? (*Purple* 37)

Sometimes the comebacks appear as a string of short exchanges that build on each other. In the following set, which comes from Morrison's *Beloved*, almost ev-

ery line either introduces a word that will be used in the comeback of the next line
or introduces an image or concept that will be elaborated on the next line (*Whip-
ping her/like she was batter*). These are adult Vernacular speakers:

11. You *talking about flesh?*
    I'm *talking about flesh.*
    Whipping her?
    Like she was *batter.*
    Guess she had it coming.
    Nobody got that coming.
    But, Ella—
    But nothing. What's fair ain't necessarily right.
    But *you can't just up and kill your children.*
    No, *and the children can't just up and kill the mama.* (256)

Sometimes the comebacks are used playfully or to build on the preceding statement. In the following passage, a young female is allowed in on a conversation between older adults. The comebacks come in a string, building on the word *bitch*.
The young narrator describes the exchange and tells how she joined in. The fact
that she notes that her contribution is accepted points to the fact that this type of
wordplay is, indeed, considered a skill. All of the females are Standard speakers
who style-shift regularly. This exchange begins with Gail:

12. "One day I'm gonna have it all and right on the same plate. Cause a la carte is *a bitch.*"
    "*Being a together woman is a bitch,*" say Marcy.
    "*Being a bitch is a bitch,*" say Gail.
    "*Men a bitch,*" is my two cents, which seems to get over. (Bambara, "Johnson" 169)

Signifying

Mitchell-Kernan, in her article "Signifying and Marking Two African American Speech Acts" (1972), differentiates between two forms of signifying by classi-
fying them by function. When describing the second function, she writes: "When
the function of signifying is to arouse feelings of embarrassment, shame, frustra-
tion, or futility, to diminish someone's status, the tactic employed is direct and in
the form of a taunt" (316).

In the following passage, Roxanne, a middle-class, Standard- speaking female,
greets Willie, a lower-class friend of her brother whom she dislikes:

1. And Willie? Haven't see you in ages—*I thought you were in jail.* (Naylor, *Linden* 54)

Her observation that she thought he was in jail signifies that she thinks that he is
capable of, and likely to commit, criminal acts. This taunt, which she probably
doesn't believe herself, is meant to provoke both her brother and his friend.

In another example, a young female adult signifies about the weight loss of an
acquaintance. The speaker is a Standard speaker who style-shifts:

2. Girl, if I didn't know any better *I'd swear you was smoking that crack over the holiday.* (Sister Souljah 81)

Euphemisms

The Random House Dictionary defines a euphemism as "the substitution of a mild, indirect or vague expression for one thought to be offensive, harsh, or blunt" (Stein & Urdang 298). Both Vernacular and Standard speakers use this form of expression. I found examples in both early and later works and among both older and younger speakers. The following examples come from Vernacular speakers. The first one comes from an early work, and the speaker is an older Vernacular speaker who style-shifts regularly:

1. they have a *blamed* hard time of it, too. (Larison 52)

The next one also comes from an early work; the speaker is an adult:

2. Ah change jes' ez many words ez ah *durn* please! (Hurston, *Jonah's* 5)

The rest of the examples come from later works; the following examples are produced by adult speakers:

3. I ain saying that we don catch *H* in this country. (Shange, *Betsey* 70)

4. My *foot.* (Taylor, *Circle* 223)

Younger females produce these three examples:

5. What's so *daggone* funny? (Tate 27)

6. Ah, *shoot*, boy you're a *story* [a liar]. (Taylor, *Thunder* 174)

7. She makes me so *doggone* mad. (Taylor, *Circle* 218)

The first two of the following examples come from Vernacular-speaking West Indians, and the last one comes from an older female:

8. And the *blasted* children ain nothing but a keepback. (Marshall, *Brown Girl* 30)

9. *What-the-france* do you need with an election? (Lorde 61)

10. Oh, *sugar*, . . . I forgot all about it. (Ansa, *Baby* 100)

Standard speakers produced the following euphemisms; the first one comes from an early work, and the speaker is a young adult:

11. so *plaguely*-polite. (Kelley-Hawkins 88)

The rest of the following examples come from later works; the first set (examples 12–15) is produced by young girls:

12. that *confounded* Lillian Jean. (Taylor, *Thunder* 95)

13. He wasn't even there. *Daagone* (Campbell 35)

14. Oh mama, *darn* it. (Naylor, *The Women* 88)

15. *Dog*, my feet are getting mushy. (White 129)

The next two examples come from a young female who is a Standard West Indian speaker. In both instances, she is addressing her younger sister:

16. Well just you be careful. You know these New York boys. They don't care *who* they pick up as long as they think they can do *rudeness*. (Guy, *Friends* 94)

17. Phyllisia, you don't even know the boy. Suppose he does *nastiness* to you? (161)

Adult, female Standard speakers also use euphemisms. In the next set the last example comes from an older adult:

18. *Forget* you. (McMillan, *Waiting* 217)

19. What *the devil* does anybody need with three quarts of milk? (Morrison, *Bluest* 22)

20. Why was Shawn shouting *the devil* out in the hall? (Shange, *Betsey* 17)

21. *Darn* it, Lizzie! I'd almost forgotten that movie. (Jackson 394)

Hyperbole

Hyperbole is defined as "an intentional exaggeration not intended to be taken literally" (Stein & Urdang 431). The use of hyperbole is evident in the speech of both the Standard and the Vernacular speakers. I found examples among young girls, adults, and older females in early and later works.

The form of hyperbole used in early works featuring Standard speakers often takes the form of clichés or trite expressions. All of the following speakers are young adults. Larsen's "Passing" supplies many of these examples:

1. You're the *last person in the world* I'd have expected to run into. (Larsen, "Passing" 153)

2. Isn't it too *marvelous for words*? (167)

3. He's really *too funny for words*. (169)

4. You'd *die laughing* if you saw him. (169)

5. I'd rather *see her dead*. (Fauset, *Comedy* 143)

Sometimes the Standard speakers produce examples that display some creativity: the first speaker makes use of a powerful metaphor to describe her remorse, and the second speaker uses an analogy to describe her friend, who is dripping wet and standing under a large umbrella:

6. Forgive me! *I feel like seven beasts*. (Larsen, "Passing" 196)

7. Oh Allie Hunt! If you don't look too comical for anything—*just like a toad under a cabbage leaf*. (Kelley-Hawkins 11)

In later works, Standard speakers also use hyperbole. In the next example a young speaker uses a very creative hyperbole in the next example. Employing the expression "Queen Ashy Mae," the speaker uses a play on words to describe a skin condition that is *Queen* [extremely] *ashy* [dry]. The inclusion of *Mae* could signal that the speaker is following a common practice in the African American community of adding second names like "Lou" or "Mae" to indicate that they are referring to the country or to southern areas:

8. I held my face in my hands and gulped in the scent of the jergens lotion I'd soaked myself in earlier that morning. I didn't want to go to North Carolina *looking like Queen Ashy Mae.* (Campbell 33)

In the following three examples, which come from adult speakers, the first one is a trite expression, and the second two show more creativity:

9. *I wish I could die*! (Cooper, *Some* 134)

10. Howard's a fool. He's half educated. *And there's no bigger fool in the civilized world than a half educated colored man.* (Petry, *Narrows* 237)

11. I've got gigs *coming out my ass.* (McMillan, *Disappearing Act* 316)

Vernacular speakers often show creativity in their use of hyperbole. In the following two early examples, the first speaker is an adult female, and the second is an older woman. Both make use of gross exaggeration and colorful language to construct striking images:

12. Ah means *tuh beat her 'til she rope lak okra, den agin ah'll stomp her 'til she slack lak lime.* (Hurston, *Jonah's* 67)

13. and Ah betcha you want some dressed dude *dat got to look at de sole of his shoe everytime he crosses de street tuh see whether he got enough leather dere to make it across . . . you can buy and sell such as dem wid what you got. In fact you can buy 'em and give 'em away.* (Hurston, *Eyes* 42)

The next example comes from a work that is set in an earlier time but was written in the 1970s. The speaker is responding to a statement from a woman who has described to her how her young son died:

14. That must-a *left a fifty pound weight on your soul.* (Childress, "Wedding Band" 84)

In the next example, from a later work, a young girl produces an example of hyperbole that shows little creativity:

15. But, mama, that Lillian Jean *ain't got the brains of a flea*! How come I gotta go 'round calling her "Miz" like she grown or something? (Taylor, *Thunder* 95)

The adults, on the other hand, produce hyperboles that display wit as well as creativity. In the first example, the speaker is an American Standard speaker who style-shifts. She has listened in disbelief when she is told that, although they are living on an island in the West Indies, her employer wants her to prepare a traditional Thanksgiving meal, including an apple pie:

16. She wants it she can come in here and cook it. *After she swim on back up to New York and get the ingredients.* Where she think she is? (Morrison, *Tar* 34)

The rest of the examples in this section also show either creativity or wit or both. The last example comes from a young girl. All of the rest come from Vernacular-speaking adults or those who style-shift regularly:

17. I told Lisa that man's *no better for her than chitlins for high blood pressure.* (Woodson 173)

18. Puddin' I got *money's mammy.* (Morrison, *Tar* 45)

19. *He thinks you shit diamonds and pee Chanel Number Five.* (Bambara, "Johnson" 167)

20. But the second you see me with a bag in my hand, you go to grabbing and snatching it like you ain't never had nothing in your lives. *You'd think you were born in Switchblade Alley.* (Ansa, *Baby* 58)

21. She came marching into the yard *with her behind high up on her shoulders.* (Tate 83)

Older females also produce both trite and creative hyperboles. The first one is a cliché:

22. I know! *You've told me a thousand times!* (Jackson 394)

The next three examples show more creativity. In the first one, an indignant older woman compares her work habits with those of others:

23. I done worked round the clock, *did more work in twenty-four hours than there good-timing niggers out here on Fulton Street done for the year.* (Marshall, *Brown Girl*, 29)

In the next example, a grandmother describes how her granddaughter looks in one of the Afro hairstyles that are popular at the time:

24. *Queen of the electrified Zulus.* (Campbell 252)

In the last example, a grandmother tells her grandson what she'll do to him if he starts any more fires:

25. Allard, I told you WWII was over *but WWIII gonna start between you you and me, If I so much as hear you gotta flame, near you or anybody else. Yo' behind's gonna be on fire. You can believe that.* (Shange, *Betsey* 168)

Slang

Vivian de Klerk writes, "*The American Heritage Dictionary* defines slang as 'a style of language rather than a level of formality . . . the distinguishing feature . . . is the intention—however often unsuccessful—to produce rhetorical effect, such as incongruity, irreverence or exaggeration' (1969: xivi)" (278). De Klerk, quoting Crystal (1987, 53), further points out that slang "serves diverse functions often determined by context alone: to show disrespect for authority, to be witty or humorous, to show solidarity by the use of a shared style, or to exclude others who do not use the style: the chief use of slang is to show that you're one of the gang" (278). In the works that I examined I found many examples of slang use in the speech of the female characters.

Examples of slang use appear in both early and later works. For the sake of convenience, I've categorized them using the main parts of speech. Within each category, I've identified major subcategories when necessary.

Adjectives

Following is a small sample of slang expressions that use adjectives as part of the utterance. These examples are chosen primarily to give a sense of the style of use as well as to give some indication of how slang words representing certain concepts either change with time or remain the same. Slang is used by both Standard and Vernacular speakers. Occasionally, the two groups use the same slang term in very similar ways. In the first two examples, the slang word *mean* can be defined roughly as "done with great skill and knowledge." The speaker in the first example is a Standard speaker; the speaker in the second is a Vernacular speaker:

1. She may be sweet but she certainly can hand out a *mean* lesson. (Kelley-Hawkins 85)

2. You switches a *mean* fanny round in a kitchen. (Hurston, *Eyes* 15)

Both Standard and Vernacular speakers in early works produce slang expressions like the next four. The first one comes from a Vernacular speaker (an ex-slave); the others come from young, adult, Standard-speaking females who are speaking (or writing) to someone who is very close to them:

3. Well, de biscuits were *yum, yum, yum.* (Rose 436)

4. It feels *splendiferous.* (Kelley-Hawkins 50)

5. Now don't get *huffy.* (Kelley-Hawkins 88)

6. She's *all straight* on this race business. (Fauset, "Comedy" 73)

In later works, Standard speakers produce quite a few examples of slang terms. These speakers, like the early ones, are young adult females who are addressing intimate acquaintances. I found that a few words are used frequently by many females, and I've listed examples of two of the most common words.

Cool

In these examples, the slang term *cool* is used to mean roughly "all right, fine or okay, or very good/ pretty/ attractive":

1. That's *cool.* (Bambara, *Seabirds* 164)

2. In my mother's house pregnancy was just another word for doomed, and marriage was the same as failure. But sex was *cool.* (Sister Souljah 37)

3. because she thinks she's so *cool* and all. (Giovanni 264)

Sharp

In these examples, the word *sharp* is used to roughly mean "very attractively dressed or very good." Often the term is used to describe a male:

1. He's so handsome. He's so *sharp.* (Shange, *Betsey* 119)

2. These cooks and domestics were *sharp*! (Cooper, *Homemade* 36)

3. He was a *sharp* dancer. (Meriwether 177)

Other Adjectives

The next two adjectives are examples of the kinds of slang words that are used to describe how a person is dressed. The first example comes from a later work, and the young adult speaker is using an expression from an earlier time:

1. You're looking pretty *snazzy* yourself. (McMillan, *Waiting* 163)

In the next example, the young adult female is using an expression that was in use at the time the work was written:

2. Let's get *fly* [stylishly dressed]. (Sister Souljah 79)

In the following examples, some of the terms are more linked to a particular time period than are others. The first two could possibly be found in a wider range of time periods than the rest of the examples:

3. I hate to disappoint you, but it was *lousy*. (Briscoe 232)

4. You must be *pooped*. (Dove, *Ivory* 18)

5. I was *gone* for him. (Dove, *Fifth* 26)

6. Sixteen. What a *jazzy* age. (Meriwether 177)

7. Lord, but this hallway was *funky*. (Meriwether 12)

8. Oh they're trying to be hip. (Morrison, *Tar* 117)

9. Let me see what kind of *tired* music you have down here. (McMillan, *Waiting* 316)

Among the Vernacular speakers, I found fewer examples of adjectives used in slang expressions. All of the following examples come from later works; the first two come from older females, and the rest come from young adults:

10. Rena wasn't nothing but a *teetotal* mess. (S. E. Wright 118)

11. You *smokin'* [looking\doing good]. (Bambara, "Johnson" 173)

12. Oh, no sister, I ain't letting you pack this *draggy* number. (Bambara, "Johnson" 166)

13. It's a *hellafyin* thing. (Bambara, "Witchbird" 185)

14. I was having a *natural* ball! (Cooper, *Homemade* 35)

Verbs

Slang expressions using verbs are found in both early and later works. Most of the examples come from Standard speakers who are style-shifting. Generally, the slang expressions are made up of either single words or of some kind of verb phrase.

One example of a verb form appears to be used as a slang expression in both early and later works. The verb *crack* used with or without the particle *up* is used to mean roughly "to burst into laughter." The first example comes from an early work, and the speaker is an older Vernacular speaker (an ex-slave); the rest of the examples come from later works, and the speakers are young, adult Standard speakers:

1. Oh, honey, I war jis' ready to *crack my sides larffin.'* (Harper 11)

2. We all *crack up.* (Williams, "Tell Martha" 47)

3. Ethel is banging down boxes of Kotex *cracking up.* (Bambara, *Seabirds* 204)

4. Mama was *cracking up*, and I have to admit I found myself laughing too. (McMillan, *Waiting* 212)

5. He began to *crack up*, clearly amused by his own fat jokes. (Sister Souljah 76)

The next two sentences also make use of *crack* in connection with showing amusement. Both examples come from later works, and both the speakers are young, adult females:

6. they didn't even *crack* a smile. (Jones, *Corregidora* 35)

7. She had enough sense left to *crack* a joke or two. (Dove, *Fifth* 26)

There are a few examples of the verbs used as slang in early works. The first two examples come from Standard speakers; the last expression comes from a Vernacular speaker:

8. *Ain't* that something? (Fauset, "Comedy" 81)

9. For pity's sake, *don't begin to jaw.* (Kelley-Hawkins 36)

10. he *cuts up all kine ob shines and capers.* (Harper 11)

The pattern of using either single verbs or verbs in phrases continues into the later works. In the next set of examples, the young adult speakers all make use of one of the most frequently used slang expressions: *bug/bugging*. All of the speakers are Standard speakers who are style-shifting:

11. We started to *bug each* from the first day. (Briscoe 58)

12. walking out on a good-paying job where nobody *bugs* you. (Marshall, *Daughters* 45)

13. What's *bugging* you? (McMillan, *Waiting* 63)

14. Wow. And she's not *bugging* you anymore? (Morrison, *Tar* 280)

Other single-word verbs used in slang expressions include the following examples. The first two examples are in the form of mock directives or commands:

15. *Forget* you. (McMillan, *Wait* 17)

16. Go *cop* me some chocolate peanut butter in a sugar cone. (Tate 114)

17. Come on girl . . . let's *split*! (Tate 29)

Other slang expressions containing single verbs are listed next. With the exception of the first one, all of the expressions are used during a particular time period. The first expression comes from a Standard speaker. The next three expressions come from young, adult Vernacular speakers who regularly style-shifted; the last example comes from a young, Vernacular-speaking girl:

18. I think it *stinks* (Marshall, *Brown Girl* 227)

19. No use tryin' to *ig* [ignore] me, Honey. (Bambara,"Medley" 182)

20. We *tip* [style of walking] to 7th Avenue. (DeVeaux, "Remember" 112)

21. Mama puleeze. Have you completely *lost* it? (McMillan, *Disappearing Act* 162)

22. They *jammin* at the school yard. (Tate 29)

In the next set of examples, the speakers also use mock directives and command, but in this case, the expressions contain verb phrases. Many of the examples come from works that contain many characters who are young girls or young adults:

23. All right, let's *cool it* ladies. (McMillan, *Disappearing Act* 84)

24. Could you *chill out* a minute, Gloria? Please? (McMillan, *Waiting* 374)

25. Listen girl, *don't even play yourself.* (Sister Souljah 82)

Slang expressions containing verb phrases come in two forms—those that use intransitive verbs and those that use transitive verbs (see Adjectives and Nouns sections for copula and other linking verbs). All of these examples come from later works. The first three examples employ intransitive verbs and are produced by young adult Standard speakers. The first two examples use the expression *fell/fall out*, which roughly means "burst into laughter or to become weak with laughter"; the speakers are young adult females:

26. They *fell out* laughing. (Meriwether 59)

27. they *fall out.* (Bambara, "Johnson" 167)

In the next set of examples, the first expression may still be used in some segments of the community, but the others were popular only during a particular time period:

28. I *blew up*! (Marshall, *Brown Girl* 229)

29. In school Monday morning everybody who found out *was tripping on me.* (Sister Souljah 37)

30. My so-called girl friend *flaked out* on me. (McMillan, *Waiting* 111)

The next set of expressions uses transitive verbs. The examples come from later works, but each represents a particular time period. The first one comes from a young, Standard-speaking adult; the second one comes from a young Vernacular speaker, and the last one comes from a young Standard speaker. All of these speakers style-shift regularly:

31. It means *I could drop a dime on him* [call police/report him] and get his ass for fraud. (McMillan, *Waiting* 348)

32. *Copping an attitude.* (Tate 83)

33. all the girls around here *dig her the most.* (Guy, *Friends* 85)

Nouns

Nouns are used in many slang expressions. The speakers use both single words and phrases. One of the categories of use describes large amounts or large numbers of things or people. Many of the expressions use hyperbole. I found that Standard speakers in both early and later works use this type of slang most often. In the following examples only the first example comes from a Vernacular speaker (an ex-slave):

Amounts

1. Well, I'se got lots an' *gobs* ter tell you. (Harper 157)
2. And I bet there'll be *oodles* by the time we're all coming along. (Fauset, *Comedy* 51)
3. But he's *loads* better looking. (Fauset, *Plum* 101)
4. He's a *good bit of a* rotter. (Fauset, *Plum* 128)
5. she had *a gang of* white women here. (Fauset, *Comedy* 81)
6. Jim's wife had a way of collecting *mobs of* the most impossible people. (Larsen, "Passing" 156)

The next example comes from an adult Standard speaker in a later work:

7. I grew up in New York City all my life and I got *tons* of stories. (Sister Souljah 78)

One slang expression that is used by Vernacular speakers in both early and later works is *heap*. In the following examples the speakers are adult females, many of them older women. The last two examples come from later works:

8. and a *heap* ob news he gits dat way. (Harper 11)
9. Marse Sargeant he lose *heap* money. (Hopkins 47)
10. Come to think of it 'tis uh *heap* uh moufs in one meal barrel. (Hurston, *Jonah's* 6)
11. Ah shuah don' see nuffin' in you but a *heap* o' dirt. (Larsen, "Sanctuary" 321)
12. The Lord done put a *heap* of glory in the bodies of many a young man. (Shange, *Betsey* 123)
13. Well, that grin tells me he musta gotten a *heap* better. (Naylor, *Mama Day* 75)

A subcategory of the amounts category is slang expressions using nouns to describe amounts of money. I found examples in both early and later works and from both Standard and Vernacular speakers. In the following examples, the first one comes from an early work, and the character is a Standard speaker:

14. They've got *piles* of money. (Hopkins 224)

The next example comes from an adult, West Indian Vernacular speaker:

15. This looks like *a big set of* money don't it? (Marshall, *Daughters* 160)

The first two of the next examples come from adult Vernacular speakers; the last example, from an adult Standard speaker:

16. that man had *loads* of money. (Hunter 59)

17. they all got *lumps of* money. (Bolton 256)

18. paying some man *a bunch of* money to listen to your problems. (Ansa, *Baby* 241)

Big Deal

There are other noun slang expressions used by more than one group. One is *big deal*. All of the following examples come from later works. The first example comes from an older Standard speaker; the second example comes from an older female who style-shifts regularly; the third example comes from a young adult female who also style-shifts regularly; and the last example comes from a young girl who is a Vernacular speaker:

1. That was a *big deal*. (Delany et al. 140)

2. what's the *big deal* about that. (Naylor, *The Women* 81)

3. I mean it wasn't no *big deal*. (DeVeaux, "Tapestry" 172)

4. You think you such *a big deal* that everybody's round here trying to look like you or something? (Taylor, *Circle* 200)

Jiffy

The slang term *jiffy* is used in early works by a Standard speaker (first example) and by a female who speaks Standard but style-shifts regularly (second example):

1. Vera says she and Net will be down in a *jiffy*. (Kelley-Hawkins 133)

2. You be waitin' by the front door, an' I'll have 'm out in a jiffy. (Hopkins 240)

Freak

The slang expression *freak*, meaning roughly "out of control" or "out of the ordinary," is used by both Vernacular and Standard speakers. All of the examples come from later works; the first two come from Standard speakers who style-shift regularly. The first speaker is a young adult; the second, an older female:

1. She's a clothes freak. (McMillan, *Disappearing Act* 55)

2. You white *freak*. (Morrison, *Tar* 208)

The next two examples come from Vernacular speakers. The first is a young girl; the second, an adult:

3. Cause I'm a movie *freak* from way back. (Bambara, "Gorilla" 14)

4. We weren't no *freaks*. We went in for straight up-and-down fucking. (Guy, *Measure* 327)

Drag

The term, *drag,* meaning roughly, "something old fashioned or out of date," "boring," or "something that would slow a person down," is used by females in more than one work. The first three speakers are Standard speakers who style-shift regularly. The last female is a Vernacular speaker:

1. I'm still a lover girl, who thinks the rest of a marriage is a *drag*. (West 88)

2. Weight Watchers turned out to be a *drag*. (McMillan, *Disappearing Act* 14)

3. I know, I know, I'm being a *drag*. (Bambara, *Salt Eaters* 195)

4. You *a drag and a half.* (Bambara, "Witchbird" 184)

Other Nouns

I found other examples of noun slang expressions in both early and later works. Most of the expressions were popular for a particular time period and were used among members of a fairly limited group of people. For example, in the following expressions, which come from early works, all come from young, adult Standard speakers:

1. Oh he's a *scream* all right, a *regular scream*. (Larsen, "Passing" 169)

2. She found for her new friend "*a duck,—just a duck,*—no other word will describe it,—of an apartment." (Fauset, *Plum* 100)

3. I thought the eating *dodge* would quiet her. (Kelley-Hawkins 36)

4. Yes, you bet we do . . . if we do have to get seats in *nigger heaven*. (Kelley-Hawkins 81)

5. I don't think it's *quite the thing*. (Fauset, *Comedy* 73)

The following first slang expression comes from a book that is set in an earlier time but written in a later time; the speaker is a young adult. The second comes from a later work, and the speaker is an older, Standard-speaking female:

6. that style is *all the rage* now. (Morrison, *Jazz* 206)

7. I wouldn't put *bad mouth* on Addie Bannister. (West 54)

Young adult Standard speakers also produce the following examples. In both cases, they are engaging in style-shifting:

8. a brother I know once told me if he didn't have sex regular his *thang* would shrink. (DeVeaux, "Tapestry" 171)

9. Where is the little *sucker*. (McMillan, *Waiting* 163)

The last set of noun slang expressions comes from little girls. The next two examples come from young girls who are Standard speakers who style-shift regularly:

10. Ruby is such a *show-off.* (Guy, *Friends* 68)

11. Girl, I got some *hot stuff* to tell you. (Tate 164)

In some cases I found that the person using the slang expression has to explain the term. In the following exchange two young, adult, Standard speakers discuss the meaning of a slang term that one of them uses:

12. [About a new male friend] he's a *tenderoni*.
You mean he's younger than you are.
Very much so. (McMillian, *Waiting* 291)

Next, a teacher uses an old-fashioned term to tell her student what she thinks of her ability; she follows the term with a description to clarify it:

13. You're a *crackerjack*, smart. (Clair 9)

In the next example, two little girls are playing house, and one of them, who is playing the husband, is showing the other a rolled-up piece of newspaper that she has placed between her legs. The little girl who is speaking is a Vernacular speaker:

14. That's my thing. *My johnson*. I'm supposed to have it. (Ansa, *Baby* 94)

Prepositional Phrases

Prepositional phrases are sometimes used in slang expressions. The first example comes from a young, adult Standard speaker in an early work. The speaker wants to borrow an eraser because according to her:

1. All mine are *on the blink*. (Fauset, *Plum* 94)

In later works one of the most common expressions appears in the following first two examples. In the first example the female is a young adult Standard speaker; in the second example the women are young, adult Vernacular speakers:

2. Go on *with your bad self*. (McMillan, *Disappearing Act* 82)

3. Go on girl *with your bad self*! (Weems 128)

The last two example of prepositional phrases come from young people. The first is a Standard speaker; the second, a Vernacular speaker. Both regularly style-shift:

4. She and Big Boy are criminals *from way back*. (Tate 84)

5. Cause I'm a movie freak *from way back*. (Bambara, "Gorilla" 14)

Clauses

The female characters also produce slang expressions that contain clauses. All of the examples come from later works. The first two females are young adults; the third one is an older woman. They are all Standard speakers who style-shift regularly:

1. Anyway, *I'm out of here*. (Briscoe 232)

2. *She do not play*. (Bambara, "Gorilla" 15)

3. *Girl, you are something else*. (Wade-Gayles 223)

The last example comes from an adult Vernacular speaker who also style-shifts regularly:

4. Girl, *what are you trying to prove*? (White 39)

Answering Back

While collecting examples of slang expressions, I noticed that several of the expressions center around responses that are given to some question or comment. As with the other expressions examined, these slang responses are used in particular time periods. All of the speakers are Standard speakers. The first two examples come from early works:

1. *Right you are*, Al. (Kelley-Hawkins 30)
2. Come back to bed and run the risk of losing our train? *Not much.* (Kelley-Hawkins 9)
3. *Yeah. Whatever.* (Sister Souljah 79)

Strings

Often when slang is present, the characters are shown using more than one expression in a single utterance; I call these expressions strings. This way of using slang terms appears in later works, and both Standard and Vernacular speakers use these strings. The first set of examples comes from Standard speakers; the first slang expression comes from an early work: the rest of the examples come from Standard speakers who style-shift regularly. All of the females are young adults:

1. *Nothing doing, young-fellow-me-lad.* (Fauset, *Plum* 102)
2. And put on your *best shit.* Nothing glittery, but do *get clean.* (McMillan, *Waiting* 396)
3. So *what's up with him*? Is he tryna "*do*" Mommy? (Sister Souljah 47)
4. This artificial insemination *crap* gives me *the creeps.* (Briscoe 245)
5. to make your summer a *fly* and *funky* affair. (DeVeaux, "Tapestry" 168)

Vernacular speakers produce the following examples; both come from later works. The speaker in the first example is a young adult, and the second example comes from a young girl:

6. Just cause we from the country dont mean we ain't *hip* to niggas trying to be *big-time.* (Williams 45)
7. One thing though, you look *ba-a-ad*, since you started going to that school, *really gone.* (Guy, *Friends* 101)

I found an interesting use of strings of slang expressions in an exchange between two young girls. One little girl is a Standard speaker who style-shifts. She addresses another little girl (nicknamed "Bad Boy"), who is a Vernacular speaker. Big Boy has been described as a bully, and after she provokes the other girl, the girl being provoked answers her by supplying a series of comments, many of which contain slang expressions. I have modified the format slightly to keep the comments together:

8. Girl, *you ain't even fresh.* Always *woofing* about nothing.
   Just quit. You are so tired. You're not even fresh. (Tate 62)

SUMMARY

This section showed that there are many different ways that the female characters play with words. The examples come from both Standard and Vernacular speakers and from all age groups, and they cover many time periods. We looked at how females play with words, how some Standard speakers play with sounds (*dishabilly*), and how Vernacular speakers play with related concepts (*If you buys me for a fool, you loses your money sure*) and rhymes (*street feet)*. The section on comebacks supplied a range of possibilities from short a phrase (*Hey Baby yourself*), to an intricate interweaving of wordplay that might involve more than two people. Signifying was also discussed in this section (*Haven't seen you in ages*; *thought you were in jail*), as were euphemisms (*blamed, durn, daggone, rudeness)* and hyperbole (*too funny for words*; *Queen Ashy Mae*; *you'd think you were born in Switchblade Alley*). But more than anything else, this section focused on the various aspects of the use of slang.

The material on slang is not meant to be a comprehensive discussion; many fine books are available that already do that. The purpose of this section is to give a few examples of slang in various African American female speech communities to show how slang can be used to pinpoint a particular time period.

There seem to be two types of slang that are used regularly. The first type is a form that has lived past the normal span of time for slang expressions and has been adopted for general use. This type of expression is used across time and across age groups (*crack my sides/crack up*). The other type is much more tied to a particular time period and a particular group (*a duck/woof*).

Who uses slang? Generally, the speakers are children or young adults. Older females are more often shown resorting to platitudes, proverbs, and other forms of set expressions. Slang appears in both early and later works, but I found fewer examples of Vernacular speakers using slang in early works. There are probably a few reasons for the absence. First, the characters in the works containing Vernacular speakers are more diverse; there are many asymmetrical conversations between African American females and males, between older women and children, and between people who could not be considered friends. These types of interactions do not usually produce much slang. On the other hand, several of the early works featuring Standard speakers contain many instances of young females having long and animated conversations with intimate female friends. In later works I also found that more instances of slang occur between same-sex teenagers or young adults who have close ties. I also noted that slang, when used by young and old Standard speakers, often appears in utterances that contain mostly Standard forms.

Slang expressions come in many forms. I found instances of single word expressions (*cool, bugging, mobs*), phrases (*from way back*), clauses (*I'm out of here*), and strings (This artificial insemination *crap* is *giving me the creeps*). It seems that the speakers use slang expressions more in some areas than in others; for example, both Standard and Vernacular speakers use many different slang expressions to describe amounts (*oodles, a heap, loads, tons*).

10

Expressive Behavior

This chapter addresses various types of expressive behavior described in the works that I examined. In the following sections I discuss expressive language and non-verbal communication.

EXPRESSIVE LANGUAGE

One of the most persistent beliefs about the way that females use language is that their language use displays a high degree of emotionality. Some of the earliest folklinguistic descriptions of women talking claim that they use an excited tone of voice, even when talking about trivial things. In discussing these beliefs, Robin Lakoff (1975) wrote, "Women speak in italics, and the more ladylike and feminine you are, the more in italics you are supposed to speak" (56). In later years the picture of the female who spoke in italics was modified somewhat and generally recognized as a stereotype of the style of speech of a certain kind of middle-class female (usually white).

Members of the African American community are also often characterized as using highly expressive language in some situations. Many of the early works that investigated the language behavior of young African American men showed them using types of talk that called for a verbal performance of some type. Such activities as *rapping*, *woofing*, or *capping* often called for the males to display real or mock emotionality. Though I don't know of many studies that focus specifically on the African American female's use of expressive language, we have in the culture numerous stereotypes of the African American female who speaks her mind in a colorful and highly individualistic style. African American female writers also portray aspects of this kind of behavior in their works (e.g., see Cooper's [1993] discussion of language use in Morrison's novels). In the following sections I describe some of the forms of expressive language.

Exclamations

Exclamations are outbursts that reflect surprise, indignation, joy, and other strong emotions. Females in general as well as various ethnic groups are often described as using this type of excited language. In the works I that examined I found several types of exclamations that are used in different social contexts. The exclamations fit into a variety of categories, many of which are described in the following.

Religious References (*Lord, God, Jesus, Christ*)

Standard and Vernacular speakers produce a number of exclamations that include religious references. Females in early works tend to use the more euphemistic forms, while females in later works often make use of the more stigmatized forms.

Lord

Although no identical terms are used in common in the early works, both Standard and Vernacular speakers use some variant of the word *Lord* in their expressions. One example from a Standard speaker is, *Praise the Lordy!* Early Vernacular speakers produce the following examples: *Well, my Lord*; *My Lord; Lordy*; *Lor'*; *Lawd a' Mussy*.

In later works, both groups use the following terms containing the word *Lord*: *Oh, Lord*; *Lord, Lord, Lord*; *Lord Have Mercy!*

Standard speakers use the term in the following examples. In the first one, the speaker style-shifts: *Lordy, chile!*; *Lord in heaven*; *Thanks be to the Good Lord.*

The next set of examples comes from Vernacular speakers: *Lawd, Lawd, Lawd!*; *Lord, yes!*; *Lordy, yes!*; *Lord ham mercy*; *Thank you Lord, thank you.*

God

Both groups also have expressions that use the word *God.* A Standard speaker in an early work says, *Glory be to God*, and Vernacular speakers say, *My God* and *God help me!*

In later works Standard speakers produce the following examples of terms using *God*: *God!*; *God no!*; *Oh for God's sake*; *My God*; *Oh my God!*; *Oh Good God*; *Good God*; *God forbid*; *God help us*; *For God's sakes no*; *Oh God. Oh, God*; *Great God.*

Vernacular Speakers use the term in the following phrases: *God, Oh God*; *Oh my God!*; *for God's sake*; *God help you.*

Jesus/Christ and Jesus Christ

Early works show Vernacular speakers speaking of Jesus often, but they do not use his name in exclamations very often. A few early examples are: *Oh Jesus!*; *Do Jesus!*; *Thank yuh, Massa Jesus*. Vernacular speakers in later works follow a pattern similar to that used by speakers in early works. They talk about Jesus quite a lot but produce only a small number of expressions using his name: *Do Jesus. Do*; *Jesus, Mary and Joseph*; *Thank you Jesus*; *Great Jesus!*

I found no examples of this expression used among Standard speakers in early works. In later works Standard speakers use *Jesus* in the following ways: *Jesus!*; *So help me Jesus*; *For the love of Jesus*.

Later works show both Standard speakers and Vernacular speakers using *Christ* or a combination of both *Jesus* and *Christ*. Standard Speakers used *Christ* in the following expressions: *Christ!*; *Oh for Christ's sake*. Standard and Vernacular speakers use *Jesus* and *Christ* in the following examples. The first one comes from a Standard speaker, the second comes from a Vernacular speaker, and the last one comes from a speaker from the West Indies: *Jesus Christ*; *Oh Jesus Christ*; *But be-Jesus Christ!*

Some Standard speakers use the religious expressions in various combinations: *Lord Jesus!*; *Jesus-Christ-God*; *Yes Lord, thank you Jesus*; *Lord, Jesus, help me*; *O Lord, Lord, Lord.*

Other Terms for God

Some Vernacular Speakers produce other names for God. The second example comes from a speaker from the West Indies: *Merciful Father, no!*; *Bon Dieu.*

Other Religious Expressions

Both groups produce other forms of religious expressions, many of which are addressed directly to God. The first set of examples comes from early works and Standard speakers: *Amen!*; *Deliver me!*; *Great Goodness!*; *Thank heaven*; *Heaven forbid*; *for heaven's sake*; *Heaven help me.*

Vernacular speakers produce the following examples. Notice that with the exception of the first example, the words *soul* or *bless* appear in each of the expressions: *Fo mercy sake*; *My soul*; *Bless my soul*; *Bless yer soul*; *Bless yer heart.*

In later works both Standard and Vernacular speakers produce examples of these expressions. The Standard speakers produce the following examples. All of them are variants of the expression *Lord have mercy*: *Oooh Ha' mercy*; *Mercy!*; *Lord a mercy*; *Lord have mercy*; *Have mercy*. Vernacular speakers in later works produce the following examples: *Praise His name*; *Bless you*; *Mercy!*; *My soul.*

Interjections

According to *The Random House Dictionary*, an interjection is "a grammatically autonomous word or expression, esp. one conveying emotions, as *alas!*"

(Stein & Urdang 462). I found many examples of interjections used by female characters in the works that I examined.

Both groups of speakers make use of interjections. I've divided the interjections into two broad categories, mild and rough. Under the mild category I include general, female language, and softened expletives. Under rough interjections I include such categories as cursing, swearing, and the use of taboo language and obscenities. These categories reflect what may seem to be contradictory statements about how African American females use expressive language. But it appears that the mild interjections seem to mark those times when the speakers are talking "like ladies," and the rough interjections and expletives often reflect times when the speakers are displaying aspects of verbal creativity and wordplay often used in Vernacular speech communities. This chapter focuses on the mild interjections; the rough ones are discussed in the chapter on "Bad Language."

General Interjections

Standard and Vernacular speakers produce a number of general interjections in both early and later works. The first three examples come from early works and are used by both Standard and Vernacular speakers: *La me*; *my sakes*; *Oh no.*

The next set of examples also comes from early works; the females who produce these forms are Standard speakers: *Great Scott*; *Eureka!*; *Ugh!*; *Ow-w-w!*; *Oh honey*; *Caesar's host!*; *Hark!*; *Umph!*

Early Vernacular speakers also use interjections. Examples include: *Tut, tut*; *Humph!*; *Hallelujah.*

There are many interjections in the speech of females in later works also. Standard speakers use such expressions as: *Cool!*; *Gosh*; *Oh, swell!*; *Oh mama*; *I'll be*; *Yeah!*; *Right-o!*; *Wow!*; *Hah!*; *Hmph!*; *Tadah!* [imitating trumpet blast—calling attention to something]. Later Vernacular speakers use such expression as: *Good grief!*; *Hey-hey!*; *Hm!*; *Hmmmm!*; *Hmmmn-huh*; *Nigger puleez*; *Zing!*; *Ohhhhhhhhhh*; *Ooo-wee!*; *Whoa! Whoo-ee!*; *Whoo.*

Female Language

These are the forms that have been identified by Lakoff (1975), and others as being part of "women's language." In my research I found that the majority of these forms are used in the early works where there were very clear distinctions in the way that the higher-status and lower-status females speak. All of these early forms are produced by Standard-speaking females: *Dear me*; *Of all things!*; *Well, I never!*; *For shame!*; *My sakes!*; *Oh dear*; *Oh, me*; *Oh horrors*; *Gracious.*

I found only a few examples of these forms in later works. The first example was used by both Standard and Vernacular speakers; the rest were used by Standard speakers: *Oh me*; *Oh dear*; *Oh my*; *Oh my no.*

Softened Expletives

The Random House Dictionary defines an expletive as "an interjectory word or expression, frequently profane" (Stein & Urdang 305). I am calling softened expletives those expressions that are used the way that the other expletives are used, but the difference is that they display little, if any, profanity. Early Standard speakers use a variety of softened expletives. Some of them include: *Oh pshaw*!; *Oh piffle*; *Oh, pooh!*

In later works both groups also make use of forms that are milder variations of stronger expletives. Standard speakers say: *Sugar and Stuff!* [showing surprise]; and Vernacular speakers say: *Darn it!*; *Shucks!*; *Shoot!*

Forms Used Mostly by Standard Speakers

While examining the speech of some of the Standard speakers, I noticed that certain words appear again and again in their expressions. Some of these patterns are listed here. The examples come from both early and later works. *Oh* terms include: *Oh piffle!*; *Oh horrors!*; *Oh for Christ's sake!*; *Oh swell*; *Oh my*; *Oh Dear*; *Oh my no!*; *Oh God*; *Oh my my, my my*; *Oh boy*; *Oh hell*; *Oh baby*; *Oh me*. *My* terms include: *My goodness*; *Oh my*; *My sakes*; *Oh my my my my*; *Oh my Africa!* *Sakes* terms include: *My sakes*; *For pity's sake*; *For Christ's sakes*; *For God's sake*. *Goodness* terms include: *Goodness*; *my goodness*; *goodness gracious*; *goodness me*; *Great Goodness*.

Forms Used Mostly by Vernacular Speakers

Some of the Vernacular speakers use mock commands and forms of direct address as part of their expressive behavior. Mock commands, a way of showing surprise and astonishment, appears in the speech of early and later Vernacular speakers. The first two examples come from early works: *G'wan! G'wan!* [Go on]; *Hush yo' mouf'*. The next set comes from later works: *Get out of here!*; *G'long!*; *Go on, girl*; *Quit*.

Using a direct address form as a complete utterance is another form of expressive language used by the females in the works that I examined. The examples come from Vernacular speakers, the first from an early work featuring an old ex-slave and the other came from later works: *Oh honey, Chile!*; *Girl!*

Three or More Repetitions

One pattern of expressive behavior is used by both groups: the repetition of a word or phrase three or more times for emphasis or to express strong emotion. In fact, the number of repetitions is often an indication of the strength of the emphasis or emotion. This pattern shows up in early works as well as later works. The first example comes from a Standard speaker in an early work:

1. *My baby, my baby, my baby.* (Kelley-Hawkins 120)

The next two examples also come from early works; the females are Vernacular speakers:

2. *My my, my my.* (Hopkins, "Hagar's" 219)

3. *Jesus, Jesus, Jesus, Jesus, Jesus!* (Hurston, *Jonah's* 9)

Standard speakers in later works also use the pattern of threes or more:

4. *My, my, my.* (Morrison, *Tar*, 176)

5. *Umph, Umph, Umph.* (DeVeaux, "Tapestry" 171; Campbell 85)

6. *Girl, girl, girlgirlgirl.* (Morrison, *Sula* 174)

7. *Thank you, thank you, thank you.* (McMillan, *Waiting* 316)

8. *Oh God, Oh God, Oh oh oh oh oh Gooooood!* (Golden, *Migrations* 181)

All of the following examples come from Vernacular speakers in later works:

9. *Chile, chile, chile.* (Cooper, *Some Soul* 56)

10. *No, no, no!* (Naylor, *The Women* 103)

11. *bam, bam, bam.* (Bolton 239)

Expressive Language Use in Young Females

While investigating the use of expressive language, I noticed another group of characters that seem to have their own style of speaking—younger African American females.

Common Expressions

Young girls in both early and later works use a variant of the expression *Ooooo* to indicate that something that someone else has done is wrong or bad. The first example comes from an early work; the other two, from later works:

1. *Oooh.* (Hurston, *Jonah's* 32)

2. *Oooooo.* (McMillan, *Mama* 24)

3. *Ooooooh.* (DeVeaux, "Remember" 109)

Like the adults, young females also use exclamations to display strong emotion. The following three examples come from a young Vernacular speaker in a later work:

4. *Say what?*; *Bull's eye!*; *Go ahead!* (Tate 76, 101, 196)

Interjections

Both groups of young females use interjections. Standard speakers produce all of these examples. They come from later works by Tate that feature many young people:

1. *Oh wow! Whew! Shuh, Hunh, Whee! Phooey! Whoooeee, Bam! Zoom! Arrrgh!* (29–88, 115–118)

Young Vernacular speakers in later works produce the following:

2. *Wow.* (Bolton 22)

3. *Yippee!* (McMillan, *Waiting* 137)

Softened Expletives

Young girls' pattern of use of the softened expletives follows that of adult speakers. The forms are used in place of stronger ones. The first set of examples comes from Standard speakers in later works:

1. *My foot.* (Taylor, *Circle* 223)
2. *Gosh.* (Shange, *Betsey* 151)
3. *Shoot.* (Taylor, *Song* 2; Ansa, *Baby* 158)
4. *Darn.* (Taylor, *Song* 2)
5. *Dag; Daaag; Daaaaaaaaaag!* (Campbell 241, 200, 95)

The next set comes from Vernacular speakers; the first example comes from an early work:

6. *Ah shucks!* (Hurston, *Jonah's* 36)
7. *Dog!* (White 129)
8. *Shoot!* (Tate 72)

Three or More Repetitions

Young females also use the pattern of three or more repetitions. All but the last example come from Standard speakers:

1. *No, No, No!* (Ansa, *Baby* 73)
2. *Chocolate, Chocolate, Chocolate.* (Ansa, *Baby* 77)
3. *Bumpety, Bumpety, Bumpety.* (Campbell 32)
4. *Ugh! Ugh! Ugh!* (Campbell 48)
5. *Dumb, dumb, dumb.* (Tate 30)

Clichés and Commonplace Expressions

All of the female characters that I examined are English speakers, and many of the expressions that they produce are in the form of clichés and other commonplace expressions. The use of these expressions, like the use of the others discussed earlier, varies with social context. Both Standard and Vernacular speakers in early and later works use these expressions.

Standard speakers produce the following examples. The first two are from early works. All of the speakers are adults: *just like a man; can you tear yourselves away?; lo and behold; so be it!; rotten to the core; not really my cup of tea.*

The next set of examples comes from Vernacular speakers or from those who style-shift regularly: *acting ugly; over my dead body; biting the hand that feeds you; it ain't none of their business; I'm serious as a heart attack; give me the creeps; you justa putting nails in your coffin; don't have to kiss nobody's behind for nothing!; just going on down the line; but God don't like ugly; well don't let your mouth start nothing that your ass can't stand; to save my life; she do not play.*

The set of following examples includes more than one variant of a cliché or commonplace expression. I found the first expression, *you mean to tell me*, only in later works. The first example comes from an adult, Standard speaker who style-shifts regularly; the second example comes from an adult Vernacular speaker:

1. *You mean to tell me* you want me to cut off all your pretty long hair? (Ansa, *Baby* 134)

2. *You mean to tell me*, you on your death bed, and you still talking trash to me? (Bolton 238)

I found a variation of this expression in early works. The speakers are young, Standard-speaking females:

3. *You don't mean to tell me*, Allie Hunt, that you have come to say you are not going? (Kelley-Hawkins 11)

4. Yes I have . . . more than once! *You don't mean to tell me* you haven't, Tessa. (Fauset, "Comedy" 84)

In the next set of examples, the word *say* is substituted for the words *tell me*. The first speaker is an adult West Indian; the second is a young girl who style-shifts regularly:

5. *You mean to say* that after all you are really going to be the kind of woman who the baker won't let near the bread? (Kincaid, *At the Bottom* 5)

6. *You mean to say* we gotta stay with our heads high, knees locked, back straight, alla that just a get a date? (Shange, *Betsey* 195)

Although I have always believed that *I declare* was a very old expression, I was not able to find any examples in the early works that I examined. The first example comes from a work written in a later time but set in an earlier one:

7. *I declare* I don't know what to say. (Childress, "Wedding Band" 84)

The following examples come from older Vernacular speakers in later works:

8. Well, *I declare.* (Taylor, *Circle* 213)

9. *I declare*, some of these children haven't got no respect at all. (Birtha 58)

A slight variation of this expression comes from an older, Standard-speaking female:

10. *I do declare.* (Shange, *Betsey* 204)

The following examples using *pay . . . mind\attention* come from later works, and all of the speakers are adult females who are Vernacular speakers or those who style-shift regularly. Each example varies slightly from all of the others:

11. aw, don't *pay it no mind.* (Ansa, *Baby* 126)

12. Just don't *pay me no mind* and go back to sleep. (Birtha 59)

13. He don't *pay me the mind* you'd pay a dog. (Walker, *Third* 238)

14. But I don't *pay no attention* to that girl. (McMillan, *Waiting* 7)

Make(s) me sick was found only in later works. The next two examples come from Vernacular speakers:

15. You *make me sick.* (Morrison, *Jazz* 189)

16. You *make me sick* sometimes. (McMillan, *Disappearing Act* 56)

There are slight variations in some of the expressions. Note that in the following first two examples, the phrase *to my stomach* is added after *sick,* and in example 3, the word *ill* replaces the word *sick.* In example 4 the word *feel* is inserted before the word *sick.* The last example, which comes from an earlier work, uses the word *tired* instead of the word *sick.* All but the last example come from Standard speakers:

17. Oh, that *makes me sick to my stomach.* (Ansa, *Baby* 177)

18. *Makes me sick to my stomach.* (Morrison, *Jazz* 84)

19. *made me ill.* (Cooper, *Homemade* 56)

20. You *make me feel sick.* (West 54)

21. Y'all *makes me tired.* (Hurston, *Eyes* 13)

The expression *sick and tired* appears in later works, and the speakers are adult females. As with previous sets, the examples vary slightly from each other:

22. I'm *sick and tired* of it. I'm *sick and tired* of everything. (Brown 18)

23. She was *sick and tired and shamed* of being called U-ga-ly! (Cooper, *Homemade* 119)

The word *dog* appears in several phrases where an analogy is being made. It expresses the idea of treating a person badly. In most of the phrases, the comparison is made using the words *like* or *as.* The first example comes from an early work, and the female speaking is an older slave:

24. Oh my child! perhaps they will leave you in some cold cabin to die, and then throw you into a hole, *as if you were a dog.* (Brent 78)

Examples from later works follow a similar pattern. The first female in the following group is a Vernacular speaker. The other females are Standard speakers or those females who style-shift regularly:

25. My mama *sick as a dog.* (Monroe 507)

26. feeling as *sick as a dog.* (DeVeaux, "Tapestry" 173)

27. Girl, I'm *tired* as a *dog.* (McMillan, *Waiting* 372)

The following two passages show a variation on the pattern, but they don't use either *like* or *as* in the phrase. The speakers are adults:

28. he don't pay me the mind, you'd pay *a dog.* (Walker, *Third* 238)

29. You sound like you're talking about *some ole mangy dog* sleeping in the street instead of your own flesh-and-blood true sister. (Tate 120)

Summary

As one of the most common ways to express emotion, exclamations are used by females from both groups. There are some similarities across groups: both adult Vernacular and Standard speakers display instances of the use of religious references. Some of the expressions are used by both groups (*Lord, Lord have mercy*); some are used more by Standard speakers than by Vernacular speakers (*God, Christ*). Standard speakers also produce more combinations (*Jesus-Christ-God*). On the whole, Vernacular speakers use fewer religious expressions that use the name of God or Jesus (although they seem to talk *about* Jesus and God more than do the Standard speakers). They use other names for the deity, however (*Bon Dieu*; *Merciful Father*). This language behavior may stem from strong strictures in some churches that forbid their members from taking the name of God in vain. Vernacular speakers also use more terms containing words like *soul* and *bless*.

In their use of interjections, both groups show interesting patterns of use. Standard speakers used many forms identified as "women's language" (*Oh dear*); Vernacular speakers use mock commands (*Get out of here!*) and direct commands (*Chile*). Both groups use examples of terms that reflect certain time periods (*Shucks*; *oh piffle*), and they both use patterns using three or more of the same expression (*My baby, my baby, my baby, my baby*; *Jesus, Jesus, Jesus, Jesus, Jesus*).

Finally, young females use expressive language in ways similar to these of older females, but they show some differences in the lexicon. For example, some of the interjections appear in the speech of young girls (*Ooooo*) and some of the softened expletives reflect the age of the speakers (*daaag*).

The use of clichés and commonplace expressions further illustrates the conformity and creativity continuum discussed earlier. The female characters use traditional, well-recognized forms of expression. The set of clichés and commonplace expressions that have a variety of forms shows that these speakers were also making somewhat creative use of the language. But in this section, Standard speakers are not responsible for all of the traditional forms, nor do Vernacular speakers produce all of the variations. Both groups produce both types of expressions.

NONVERBAL COMMUNICATION

The female characters also describe nonverbal communication behaviors. Knapp (1981) defines nonverbal communication this way:

The term *nonverbal* is commonly used to describe all human communication events which transcend spoken or written words. At the same time we should realize that many of these nonverbal events and behaviors are interpreted through verb symbols. In this sense, then, they are not truly *non*verbal. The theoretical writings and research on nonverbal communication can be broken down into the following seven areas: (1) body motion or kinesics (emblems, illustrators affect displays, regulators and adaptors), (2) physical characteristics, (3) touching behavior, (4) paralanguage (vocal qualities and vocalizations),

(5) proxemics, (6) artifacts, (7) environment. . . . Nonverbal communication is important because of the role it plays in the total communication system, the tremendous quantity of informational cues it gives in any particular situation, and because of its use in fundamental areas of our daily life. Nonverbal behavior is partly taught, partly imitative, and partly instinctive. (622–623)

In this section I discuss some of the ways females describe their own nonverbal behaviors and those of others. The areas that are most relevant to my study are body motions (kinesics) and paralanguage.

Body Motions (Kinesics)

In describing the various aspects of body motion, Knapp (1981) writes:

Body motion, or kinesic behavior, typically includes gestures, movements of the body, limbs, hand, head, feet and legs, facial expressions (smiles), eyes behavior (blinking, direction and length of gaze, and pupil dilation) and posture. (611)

Eye Behavior

Several of the female characters describe the way that the eyes are used to convey various messages. Two types of behavior often associated with the African American community are *rolling eyes* and *cutting eyes*.

Rolling Eyes

The expression called *rolling eyes*, roughly meaning "showing defiance, disdain, displeasure, anger, or contempt" is used by Standard speakers in later works. The following example comes from an adult female:

1. She *rolled* her *eyes* at me as she handed me a tissue from my mother's drawer. (Campbell 164)

The next example comes from a young girl who style-shifts regularly:

2. I *rolled my eyes at Maizell* behind Hattie's back. (Tate 162)

Cutting Eyes

The expression *cutting eyes* roughly means "to flash the eyes quickly to convey some emotion, usually negative." I found examples in the speech of both young and old characters in later works. All of these females below style-shift.

1. *cut my eyes at him*, then sighed. (Taylor, "Friendship" 20)

2. I *cut my eyes* at Junebug. (Tate 143)

3. Nikki *cut her eyes* at me. (Sister Souljah 139)

The last example comes from an adult West Indian female who appears in a later work:

4. My mother would *cut her hawk-gray eyes* at me beneath their heavy black brows. (Lorde 73)

Wink

Wink, meaning "to be conspiratorial," is another term used by several of the female characters. All of the following examples come from adults in later works; the first example comes from a Standard speaker, the second speaker is a young female who style-shifts regularly, and the third example is from an older, Vernacular speaker whose language is being reported by a young, Standard-speaking female:

1. The old ladies would *wink* at me and ask me how I liked having a man in the house, and I'd smile. (Dove, *Fifth* 64)

2. Papa *winked* and Little Man smiled. (Taylor, *Circle* 36)

3. "Nicer for me than for you," said Mrs. Jeller, with a *wink.* (Lee 86)

Eyeball

In McMillan's *Disappearing Act,* one character is said to have *eyeballed* a beach, meaning that she looked at it speculatively to check it out. In a later book by Tate, a young girl uses variants of the term *eyeball* [*eyeballed, eyeballing*] to mean roughly "to look at someone directly, often in a challenging way." The girl style-shifts regularly:

1. giving Miss Aussie a strong *eyeballing.* (McMillan 37)

I found other examples of discussions of eye behavior. The first comes from an older woman who style-shifts regularly. She appears in a later work:

2. I declare if you had *batted them lashes* a little faster. . . . We'd of had a dust storm here. (Naylor, *The Women* 69)

In the last example in this section, a Standard-speaking adult describes two types of eye behavior that she recalls from a time when she was younger:

3. men passed me by on Philadelphia streets and *eyed me* with such open, common lust that instinctively I *lowered* my eyes at the violation. (Campbell 226)

Use of Mouth

The mouth was also used to convey nonverbal messages. The next section discusses "sucking teeth" and "popping/smacking gum."

Sucking Teeth

The expression to *suck teeth* is also used often in the African American speech community. When a person is described as using this paralinguistic feature, the implication is that the person is showing disapproval, disgust, disdain, or defiance. The first example comes from an adult, Vernacular speaker; the second, from a young, Standard-speaking female:

1. She *sucking her teeth.* (DeVeaux, "Adventures" 306)

2. "Damn!" Daddy said *sucking his teeth.* (Campbell 40)

The next three examples are interesting because they are descriptions of the sounds that the female characters make when they suck their teeth. The first comes from a West Indian adult, the second, from an African American adult, and the last one, from a West African woman:

3. "*Chu-Ps,*" I *sucked my back teeth.* (Guy, *Friends* 135)

4. Frieda *sucked her teeth* and made a *phttt* sound with her lips. (Morrison, *Bluest* 24)

5. She was looking at my mouth, and I laughed and *chipsed.* Sistah I *sucked my teeth* at that woman. (Angelou, *All God's* 192)

Popping/Smacking Gum

The second example of mouth behavior is the description of the noise that a person can make when chewing gum. In essence, the person makes tiny bubbles in the gum, then breaks them, making a sharp, cracking sound. Three young females describe this behavior:

1. *popping and smacking* her gum. (Tate 61)

2. as always chewing gum *to make sounds like a popping snare drum.* (Campbell 48)

3. *popping her bubble gum.* (Guy, *Friends* 43)

Shook Head

Several speakers use an expression that contains the words *shook head,* which could mean several things: resignation, dismay, disgust, or negation. The first example comes from an early work; the speaker is an adult Standard speaker and ex-slave, who describes the reaction of other slaves when they saw how badly she had been beaten:

1. The other slaves when they saw me, *shook their heads.* (M. Prince 8)

The next two examples came from later works; the first one comes from a Standard speaker; the second, from a Vernacular speaker:

2. I *shook my head no.* (McMillan, *Disappearing Act* 82)

3. Miss Billie *shook her head.* (Jones, *Eva* 84)

Other Gestures

Other gestures that females use to communicate with others are included next. All are from adult characters in later works. The first example comes from a Vernacular speaker who appears in a work set in an earlier time:

1. Shug say, uh-oh and *point with her chin.* (Walker, *Purple* 83)

The second example comes from a speaker who style-shifts regularly:

2. She *twisted her head from me so hard* that I had to think hard to remember if I had said something to insult her. (Guy, *Measure* 113)

The third example comes from a Standard speaker:

>   3. "I don't understand. How can you wonder if we'd still be friends?" I badgered her, standing up, *hands on hips*. (Golden, *Migrations* 156)

Strings of Gestures

In some cases, the speakers string together descriptions of more than one gesture. The first two examples come from adult speakers who appear in works written in the 1980s but set in an earlier time: Although both speakers are Vernacular speakers, only the first one style-shifts regularly:

>   1. *Hands on hips, foot patting the floor*, Bessie *throws her head around so that those feathers shake and tremble*. (Guy, *Measure* 88)
>   2. She say, Well take a good look. Even if I is just a bag of bones now. She have the nerve *to put one hand on her naked hip and bat her eyes at me*. Then *she suck her teef and roll her eyes at the ceiling*. (Walker, *Purple* 53).

The following four speakers are adults who appear in later works; the first two are Standard speakers; the next two examples are from a Standard speaker who occasionally style-shifts:

>   3. Marian *clicked her tongue* and *shook her head*. (Golden, *Migrations* 169)
>   4. I kind of *rolled my eyes and did a snake neck-grit* at her for about five seconds, first making sure there were no witnesses. (Campbell 92–93)
>   5. I *rolled my big brown eyes* at him and *sucked my teeth* like a New York girl with attitude would. (Sister Souljah 40)
>   6. She had *her hand on her hips* with *her neck working overtime* as she proceeded to put me in my place. (Sister Souljah 248)

The last three examples come from young girls; all appear in later works:

>   7. I *stare at Nigeria out of the corner of my eye*. She *sucking her teeth*. (DeVeaux, "Adventures" 306)
>   8. She *chewed hard on her gum, hands still on her hips, one foot patting the floor*. (Guy, *Friends* 37)
>   9. She *turned up one nostril at me and switched away*. (Taylor, *Circle* 30)

Paralanguage

Knapp (1981) writes, "Simply put, paralanguage deals with how something is said and not what is said. It deals with the range of nonverbal cues surrounding common speech behavior" (613). He refers to Trager, who in a 1958 article wrote that paralanguage had several components, one of which was vocal characterizers. These includes such things as:

laughing, crying, sighing, yawning, belching, swallowing, heavily marked inhaling or exhaling, coughing, clearing of the throat, hiccupping, moaning, groaning, whining, yelling, whispering, sneezing, snoring, stretching, etc. (613)

Next I discuss some of the paralanguage that I found in the works that I examined.

Crying

Discussions about *crying* appear in both early and later works and appear in works featuring both Standard and Vernacular adult speakers. In this set of examples from early works, all but the last two come from Standard speakers:

1. We all *cried* when she left us. (Albert 19)
2. At the same time he was kind a raising up out of the bed; then I began to *cry*. (Mattison 11)
3. our mother stood beside *crying* over us. (M. Prince 4)
4. Lors, chile! What you *crying* bout? (Brent 104)
5. Many a time has she set in my ole cabin an' *cried* 'bout yer wen you war fas' asleep. (Harper 176)

In later works, both Standard and Vernacular speakers discuss *crying*. In the first set of examples, adults are describing scenes from their childhoods. The first two examples are from Standard speakers:

6. After school I would sit in the basement *crying* and singing. (Campbell 227)
7. I started to *cry* and told him all about it. (Lee 84)

Example 8 comes from a Vernacular speaker, and example 9 comes from a West Indian speaker:

8. You making something inside me *cry*, son. (Hansberry 104)
9. Is *cry* you want to *cry*? I'll give you something hard to *cry* on! (Lorde 65)

The following examples also come from adults who discuss their own behavior and that of others:

10. I could have stayed right there kneeling in the mud and *cried*. (Dove, *Fifth* 65)
11. I just went right up to bed and *cried*. (Lee 84)
12. Around six I noticed I was still up and I was really tired and I started *crying* and saying, "If I just understand what's wrong I would feel better!" (Giovanni 267)
13. I can hear my mother *crying* and pleading with me, as I massaged her chest to leave her alone. (Weems 124)
14. Efua put her hand on my cheek and repeated, "Sister you have need of a Sister friend because you need to weep . . . I began to *cry*. (Angelou, *All God's* 12)

The last example comes from a Vernacular speaker:

15. I don't want them *cryin'* all over the place. (Taylor, *Thunder* 78)

Gasping

In the following examples, the females, adult Standard speakers, describe their own behavior:

1. I let out a *gasp*. (Taylor, *Circle* 205)

2. I *gasped* for air. (Campbell 73)

Groaning

In these examples, all but the last one come from adult Standard speakers. The last example comes from a female who regularly style-shifts:

1. Crystal would *groan* if she heard me say that. (Golden, *Woman's* 16)

2. Nana *groaned*. (Campbell 164)

3. "Oh, Lord," Mama *groaned*. (Taylor, *Thunder* 94)

4. I *groaned*. Matthew threw down his fork. (Lee 64)

5. When the squeaking and *groaning* ended I crawled past the window to the ladder. (Meriwether 183)

Laughing

Standard and Vernacular female speakers in both early and later works describe *laughing*. In these examples, which are taken from early works, the first two are from Standard speakers, and the third one comes from an old ex-slave who style-shifts regularly:

1. I *laughed* and said, "That one has the stain on it." (Mattison 41)

2. I'd never in this world would have known you if you hadn't *laughed*. (Larsen, "Passing" 152)

3. I was too drunk to *laugh*. (Larison 63)

The next four examples come from later works. All of the speakers are adult Standard speakers; Example 7 comes from a West Indian speaker:

4. I was *laughing* and being witty like a fool. (Cooper, *Homemade* 36)

5. When I first met Serena, I couldn't resist her *laugh*. (Golden, *Woman's* 6)

6. *Laughing* I said, "Not my dee-but." Mama *laughed* too. (Wade-Gayles 219)

7. How you make me *laugh*. (Kincaid, *At the Bottom* 26)

The last examples come from Vernacular speakers:

8. Oh, a whole lotta folks was busy *laughin'* at me. (Shange, *Betsey* 85)

9. She *laughed*, "Aw I call my man Sweet Man." (Jones, *Eva's* 84)

Moaning

Females in both early and later works describe *moaning*. The first example comes from an adult Standard speaker in an early work:

1. Some of her hearers *moaned*, others rocked to an fro. (Harper 181)

The next example comes from an adult Standard speaker in a later work:

2. Mr. Abe *moaned* hymns so old and handed-down, so syncopated by human rhythms that there was a clink of chains in each verse. (Campbell 55)

The final example comes from a speaker from a later work who style-shifts regularly:

3. I *moaned* my back luck. (Meriwether 96)

Screaming

With the exception of the first example, all of the examples that describe *screaming* come from later works:

1. When I was coming up the hill I heard a great *screaming*. (M. Prince 13)

The next three examples come from young girls; the first two are Standard speakers, and the third style-shifts regularly:

2. "I want my daddy," I *screamed*. (Campbell 73)

3. "What did you bring me? What did you bring me?" I *screamed*. (Dove, *Fifth* 60)

4. "Thirti-five dollars and ninety-five cents!" I *screamed*, "Just for an ole gun?" (Taylor, *Thunder* 92)

The last example comes from an adult Standard speaker recounting an incident from her childhood:

5. "Tap, tap, slap!" Tap, tap, slap!" Toni would be *screaming*. (Cleage 71)

Sighing

The first example that discusses *sighing* comes from an early work; the speaker is a Standard-speaking adult:

1. Without a struggle or *sigh*, she passed away beyond the bower of oppression and prejudice. (Harper 108)

Adult speakers from later works produce the next set. The first two females are Standard speakers. The third example comes from a West Indian female, and the last one comes from someone who style-shifts regularly.

2. and a *sigh* barely audible, issued from her lips. (Dove, *Fifth* 62)

3. I *sighed*, then objectively tried to assess my good points. (Taylor, *Circle* 199)

4. To make sure she believed in my frailness, I *sighed* occasionally, long soft *sighs*, the kind of *sigh* she long ago taught me could evoke sympathy. (Kincaid, *At the Bottom* 55–56)

5. "Yeah I know," I *sighed*. (Meriwether 177)

Whispering

There are discussions of *whispering* in both early and later works. The first example comes from an adult Standard-speaking female who appears in an early work:

1. I saw Miss Packer *whisper* something to the other girl. (Fauset, "Comedy" 237)

The next two examples come from adults in later works. Both speakers style-shift, and the second female is an older woman:

2. I said in a *whisper*, "Die, DIE!" (Cooper, *Some* 84)

3. Leaned over and *whispered* that I could fix it so the only thing he'd be able to whip out of his pants for the rest of his life would be pocket change. (Naylor, *Mama Day* 68)

Several adults describe how *whispering* was used when they were young. The next two examples come from Standard speakers.

4. "Look at her!" Mary Alice might *whisper* loudly at her cronies as I passed by. (Brown 34)

5. My grandmother would *whisper* her thanks. (Angelou, *All God's* 103)

Yelling

The two examples that discuss *yelling* come from later works; both females are adult Standard speakers:

1. they *yelled* before they actually burst into view. (Taylor, *Circle* 181)

2. One woman would *yell* across the room to another. (Weems 128)

Other Paralinguistic Behaviors

The females in the next set of examples are Standard speakers who discuss other paralinguistic forms from their childhood:

1. "I have to go now!" I *whined*. *Whining* got on Nana's last nerve. (Campbell 192)

2. "Enhenhenhehnenh," I *hiccuped* out my response. (Campbell 64)

3. "Enhenhenh," I *twittered*. (Campbell 64)

4. I could get more mileage out of a mere *whimper* than a loud wail at any other time. (Coleman 23)

5. I hear Maggie go "Uhnnnh" again. (Walker, "Everyday Use" 2369)

Strings of Paralinguistic Behaviors

The females from both early and later works often string together more than one of the paralinguistic descriptions. The first two examples come from early works, the third example comes from a work set in earlier times but written in the 1980s. All of the females are adult Vernacular speakers:

1. An' when she war done she jis' set down and *sniffled* an' *cried*. (Harper 11)

2. They was all *cheerin'* and *cryin'* and *shoutin'* for de men dat was ridin' off. (Hurston, *Eyes* 32)

3. She die *screaming* and *cussing*. (Walker, *Purple* 12)

The next three examples come from later works. The first female is an adult Vernacular speaker who appears in a work set in an earlier time; the next two speakers are adult females recounting incidents from their childhood:

4. When I'm *laughin'*, I'm *laughin'* to keep from *cryin'*. (Childress, "Wedding Band" 93)

5. On some occasions that first flap of the comb brought not my usual obedient response but a *sniffle*. On the second flap I escalated to a *whimper* and the third was almost anticipated by a full-scale *yell*. Always an overly dramatic child, I played the *sniffle*, *whimper*, *yell*, routine for a full three minutes to my one-woman audience. (Coleman 23)

6. I let out a horrible *roar*, then a self pitying *whine*. (Kincaid, *At the Bottom* 56)

SUMMARY

Females in the works that I examined describe a number of paralinguistic and kinesic behaviors. In the subsection on paralinguistic and kinesic behaviors, Standard speakers appear in most of the categories that I describe. Standard speakers, Vernacular speakers, and West Indian speakers describe *crying* and *laughing*. Standard speakers, West Indian speakers, and those who style-shift regularly describe *sighing*. Standard speakers and those who style-shifted regularly describe *groaning*, *whispering*, and *screaming*. Standard speakers alone also describe *gasping*, *moaning*, *yelling*, *whining*, *hiccuping*, *twittering*, and *whimpering*. Vernacular speakers alone described a few paralinguistic behaviors; most appear in combinations: *sniffled and cried*; *cheerin', cryin' and shoutin'*; *screaming and cussing*. In some examples, the speaker describes a sound (I hear Maggie go *"Uhnnnh"* again; *"Enhenhenhehnenh,"* I hiccuped). The subsection on kinesic behavior examined descriptions by females who appear in various works. Most of the examples come from later works or works set in earlier times but written in later times. The descriptions are supplied by all age groups, though the majority of them come from adult speakers. Both Standard and Vernacular speakers use these descriptions, though Standard speakers supply most of the examples. An explanation for the larger number of adult Standard speakers using these forms may stem from the fact that most of the descriptions come from the Standard lexicon. It is quite likely that younger speakers and Vernacular speakers might employ other means to describe kinesic behavior. One possibility is that younger speakers and perhaps some of the Vernacular speakers might use such nonverbal means as mimicking or mocking (some researchers call this activity "marking"; see Mitchell-Kernan [1972]).

I discovered many interesting patterns. For example, in the area of eye behavior, I found that both Standard and Vernacular speakers are described as using phrases employing such terms as *roll eyes*; *cut eye*; *bat eyes*; *wink*. Expressions containing terms like *lowered eyes* and *eyed* are used only by Standard speakers, and Vernacular speakers use the description of looking at someone *out of the corner of . . . eye* to mean something similar to *cut eye* (I stare at Nigeria *out of the corner of my eye*).

In the area of *using the mouth*, all of the groups of females supply at least one example. A Standard speaker describes someone who *clicked her tongue*; a West Indian speaker and two speakers who style-shift regularly describe a method of gum chewing that is used to partly convey a message (*chewed hard on her gum*; *popping her bubble gum*; *popping and smacking her gum*).

One of the most prevalent patterns that I found is the use of the term *suck teeth*. This is used not only by Standard- and Vernacular-speaking adults but also by an adult West Indian and an adult West African. This finding is especially interesting since it demonstrates what many language researchers have suggested: that the verbal and nonverbal behavior of those who are part of the African diaspora still contains links to some African languages.

Two other gestures that are described with some regularity are *hand on . . . hips*, which is used by both Standard and Vernacular adults, and *shook . . . head*, which is used in both early and later works and by Standard, Vernacular, and West Indian speakers. A particular movement of the neck often associated with the African American Vernacular-speaking style is described by young adult females who style-shift (*with her neck working overtime*; *did a snake neck-grit at her for about five seconds*). Other descriptions of behaviors that are less likely to turn up in a Standard speaker's speech include the following examples, which are used by Vernacular speakers and those who style-shift regularly: *twisted her head so hard*; *pointed with her chin*; *turned up one nostril and switched away*.

11

Bad Language

"Women are now talking seriously dirty," says Coward in an 1989 article. Coward is quoted by Hughes (1998, 211) in his book *Swearing*. In his chapter on "Sexuality and Swearing" Hughes notes that, although a traditional view of females has said that they should avoid all forms of bad language, some of those views are changing. He writes, "One consequence of the feminist movement, notably in modern America, has certainly been the growth of a more 'liberated' attitude toward swearing." (211)

Andersson and Trudgill (1992) write, "Swearing is 'bad language.' There is no question about it. If ordinary people are asked, 'What do you think of when you hear the phrase *bad language*?' most of them will certainly say 'swearing' " (53). This chapter discusses the various types of bad language used by some of the female characters in the works that I examined. I focus on some of the major aspects of swearing. The definition that I'm using for swearing comes from Andersson and Trudgill:

Swearing can be defined as a type of language use in which the expression
a) refers to something that is taboo and/or stigmatized in the culture;
b) should not be interpreted literally;
c) can be used to express strong emotions and attitudes. (53)

They supply a model that includes the following five levels:

1. Taboo behaviors

2. Taboo words

3. Swearwords

4. Grammar of swearing

5. Social restrictions on swearing

In this chapter I am concerned with discussing three of these levels: (1) taboo words, (2) swearwords, and (3) grammar of swearing. I collapse levels 2 and 3 to talk about swearwords in the context of how they appear in grammatical constructions.

TABOO WORDS

According to Andersson and Trudgill (1992), in Western societies we have taboos relating to sex, religion, and bodily functions (55). The female characters in the works that I examined use most of their taboo words to refer to bodily functions or sex. I found no obvious taboo words referring to bodily functions in the speech of either Vernacular speakers or Standard speakers who appear in early works. I did find some examples of the use of *shit* and *piss* in some of the later works.

Shit

Although both Standard and Vernacular speakers use this term, most of the examples come from young, adult Vernacular speakers who regularly style-shift. The last example comes from a young girl:

1. goes through his money like a maggot going through a pile of *shit*. (Guy, *Measure* 328)

2. slapped the living *shit* out of the man. (Cooper, *Homemade* 129)

3. If I yes ma'am her she slap the *shit* out of me. (Jones, *Corregidora* 41)

4. What you and Michael making anyhow? A better grade of horse *shit*? (Meriwether 169)

Piss

The first example comes from an older female; the second, from a young girl. They are Vernacular speakers who style-shift regularly:

1. If I recollect, you *pissed* right in my hand when you got here. (Naylor, *Mama Day* 74)

2. We *didn't* [emphasis in original] have a pot to *piss* in or a window to throw it out of. (Meriwether 187)

The sexual taboo words used most often in these later works include *fuck*, *pussy*, and *dick*.

Fuck

Fuck is used in a number of different contexts, but the only examples I include here are those that actually refer to sexual relations:

1. Lord, could he do the wild thing. That's all we did was *fucked*. (McMillan, *Waiting* 320)

2. I didn't kill him, I just *fucked* him. (Morrison, *Sula* 145)

3. i waz dreamin bout cuba & you wanna *fuck*. (Shange, "Comin" 251)

4. Sukie said that everybody did it. *Fucked*. (Meriwether 15)

Pussy

This word is used most often by two sets of speakers—very young females and young adult females, both Standard and Vernacular speakers—to refer to female genitalia. Examples from young girls are listed. In the first example a little Vernacular speaker is introducing her Standard-speaking friend to a new game:

1. That'll be your thing, you a grown 'oman, so that'll be your *pussy*. (Ansa, *Baby* 94)

The second example also comes from a young Vernacular speaker:

2. I heard Mama talking bout women like that. Mess up their minds and then fuck up their *pussy*. (Jones, *Corregidora* 42)

The rest of the examples come from adult females; the first is a Standard speaker, and the others are Vernacular speakers:

3. you haven't filled us in on a single detail, like can he eat *pussy*—or if he's even willing. (McMillan, *Disappearing Act* 83)

4. Then he push his thing inside my *pussy*. (Walker, *Purple* 11)

5. he pulled this big black rubbery thing look like a snake out of my *pussy*. [Mad woman describing an examination.] (Jones, "Asylum" 131)

Dick

Both Standard and Vernacular speakers use the word *dick* to refer to a man's penis. The first example comes from a Standard speaker; the second is a Vernacular speaker.

1. He had the biggest *dick* in the universe. (McMillan, *Waiting* 320)

2. when you been out all Saturday night swinging your *dick*. (Walker, *Third* 138)

The last example is from the perspective of a Standard speaking young female who uses two of the taboo words:

3. That's where everybody practiced writing nasty words like "*pussy*" and "*dick*." (Shange, *Betsey* 60)

Summary

Although this section discusses the use of taboo words, it should be noted that there are relatively few instances of their use by all groups, and most of the examples come from a small number of females.

GRAMMAR OF SWEARING

Females use swearing in a number of contexts. For this section of the chapter, I rely on the patterns proposed by Andersson and Trudgill (1992), since they write, "The ordinary rules of the grammar taken together with the vocabulary of swearing give us grammatical swearing in that language" (61). They further note, "Swear words may intrude into grammatical patterns" (62). I discuss how the use of swearwords by females fits into three patterns: as separate utterances, as adsentences, and as major constituents in a sentence.

As Separate Utterances

Expletives

Andersson and Trudgill note that expletives are used to express emotions; they are not directed toward others (61). I found examples of expletive use in both Standard and Vernacular speakers, mostly in later works. The expletives most often used are *shit* and *damn*.

Shit

The first three examples come from Vernacular speakers; the fourth is from a Standard speaker who style-shifts regularly:

1. *Shit!* . . . Oh, *shit!* (Morrison, *Jazz* 113)
2. Aw *shit!* (Naylor, *The Women* 118)
3. Oh, horse*shit*! (Morrison, *Tar* 127)
4. *Shit*! (Walker, *Third* 131)

In the following example, the speaker uses a series of threes as well as strings of expletives to express strong emotion: "*Shit,* Gloria thought. *Shit shit shit.* She forgot just that fast that she hadn't told the boy [that his father was gay]. *Shit. Shit shit shit. Well, shit.* It was done now. So to hell with it" (McMillan, *Waiting* 192).

Damn

This expletive is used by both Standard and Vernacular speakers. The first example is one of the rare instances of a Standard speaker from an early work using an expletive. The rest come from later works and feature Standard speakers and those females who regularly style-shift. All of the speakers are young adults:

1. *Damn*! (Larsen, "Passing" 165)
2. *Damn.* (Dove, *Ivory* 15)
3. Aw *dammit*! (Naylor, *The Women* 119)
4. *Damn, damn, damn.* Why me? (Giovanni 267)

In the next example, the speaker uses both *shit* and *damn:*

5. *Damm* it! Hurry up! *Shit!* (Cooper, *Some* 110)

The final expletive comes from a later work and is used by another young adult female:

6. Well, *fuck* it! (McMillan, *Waiting* 325)

Abusives

According to Andersson and Trudgill, abusive swearing is directed toward others; it's derogatory, and it includes name-calling and different types of curses (60). I found many examples of abusive swearing. Most of the examples come from name-calling; a few come from curses.

Name-Calling

Investigators of females' use of language tell us that, on the whole, women prefer the softer expletives when expressing anger or annoyance. In my investigations, I found that when it comes to name-calling, females generally tend to use descriptive phrases rather than obscenity, curse words, and profanity. If there is any difference here in terms of groups, it is in the fact that the Vernacular speakers use more taboo words and more colorful names than do the Standard speakers.

A few names appear in both groups; the first example, *motherfucker*, is used by Standard speakers who appear in later works and who are generally young adult females who regularly style-shift: *motherfucker*; *bitch*; *son-of-a-bitch*; *liar*; *devil*; *poor white trash.*

Often the names that Standard speakers use center around body type, clothing, and hair and skin color; all of the examples come from later works, and the last two examples come from young females:

1. *Fatso.* (Bambara, "Raymond" 27)

2. *machete-hair* [a woman's haircut]. (Morrison, *Tar* 108)

3. *Bow-tie* [man who always wears a bow-tie]. (Morrison, *Tar* 108)

4. *ya ugly yellow lemons.* (Campbell 113)

5. *ya black tar-babies.* (Campbell 113)

Most of the examples from the Vernacular speakers are creative descriptions that cannot be taken literally. The first two examples come from early works. The last two examples come from young females:

6. He look like some *old skullhead in de grave yard.* (Hurston, *Eyes* 28)

7. *ole springy-leg husband.* (Hurston, *Jonah's* 77)

8. *U-ga-ly* [ugly]. (Cooper, *Homemade* 119)

9. you *ugly varmint.* (McMillan, *Mama* 96)

10. *old wet-eyed white man.* (White 36)

11. you *black bastards.* (Meriwether 40)

12. *ole Blackie.* (Guy, *Measure* 114)

13. the *Gold Dust Twins* [comparing two people to two very dark figures that once appeared on a commercial product]. (Walker, *Third* 283)

14. *Pus mouth!* (Morrison, *Sula* 93)

15. That *beat-up looking chick?* (Guy, *Friends* 139)

16. The *scroungy bastard.* (McMillan, *Waiting* 333)

17. *Thunder buns.* (Bambara, "Gorilla" 15)

18. *old big-tittied Beulah.* (Guy, *Friends* 35)

Both Standard and Vernacular speakers supply a number of names that describe the mental or psychological state of the person whom they are describing. They both use these names: *fool, ignorant, silly, simple, stupid.*

Standard speakers also use the following names. The first example comes from an early work:

1. we are two big *simpletons.*(Kelley-Hawkins 164)

2. *damn fool woman.* (Guy, *Measure* 149)

3. *ignorant motherfucker* [author writes that the speaker said this "with the accent on the syllable *ig*"]. (Morrison, *Tar* 120)

4. She's *crazy* like her brother! (Lee 66)

5. *Simple bitch.* (McMillan, *Disappearing Act* 274)

Vernacular speakers use the same type of names; the first example comes from an early work and examples 7 through 12 come from later works. The last two speakers are young females:

6. *silly chile.* (Hopkins, "Hagar's" 171)

7. You *simple-minded* or something? (Naylor, *The Women* 30)

8. *Dumb bastard.* (Naylor, *The Women* 187)

9. *simple jokers.* (Guy, *Measure* 214)

10. Your mama is a *Bible-thumping idiot* (Naylor, *Mama Day* 72)

11. you *mean old fool*! (Walker, *Third* 136)

12. Y'all *so dumb.* (Shange, *Betsey* 4)

Many Standard speakers call names based on what they perceived to be improper, questionable, or bad behavior or attitudes. The first set of examples comes from early works:

1. Oh, Vera, you *wretch*! (Kelley-Hawkins 38)

2. You are the *queerest girl.* (Kelley-Hawkins 88)

3. That *great lummax* of a man. (Kelley-Hawkins 13)

4. that *old drunkard.* (Larsen, "Passing" 159)

5. the *good-for-nothing hussy*! (Brent 105)

6. *mother of harlots.* (N. Prince *14)*

7. A *black alley-cat*, if ever there was one. (Fauset, *Comedy* 306)

8. you *murderer!* (Fauset, *Comedy* 306)

9. *Horrid, little pushing thing* [mother's thoughts about her daughter's lower-class friend]. (Fauset, *Comedy* 34)

The following examples come from later works; examples 10 through 26 came from adults. The last two are from young females:

10. *Contrary.* (Morrison, *Tar* 33)

11. *Hincty* [stuck up]. (Morrison, *Jazz* 19)

12. *uppity darkies.* (Delany et al. 109)

13. *rebby boys* [older term for some Southern white males]. (Delany et al. 109)

14. Miss Lass is a *Jew-u.* (Guy, *Friends* 43)

15. you *freak.* You *crazy white freak.* (Morrison, *Tar* 208)

16. *chippy.* (Morrison, *Beloved* 246)

17. *Hussy.* (Guy, *Measure* 279)

18. *whore.* (Bolton 127)

19. the husband is nothing but *a he-whore?* (Marshall, *Brown Girl* 73)

20. *slut.* (Bolton 127)

21. *cocksucker.* (Meriwether 39)

22. *Queers!* (Marshall, *Brown Girl* 226)

23. *Mr. Yes, Ma'am–No Ma'am* [old lady's name for granddaughter's suitor]. (Naylor, *Linden* 220)

24. *Poor-great* [acting grand despite being poor]. (Marshall, *Brown Girl* 304)

25. You *baby killer!* (Morrison, *Tar* 208)

26. You *sneaky little cunt,* you . . . *little whore?* (McMillan, *Mama* 186)

27. *Mary Louise Williams of Raggedy Town, Baltimore.* (Bambara, "Raymond" 27)

28. *Countre-e-e-e-e!* [young girls about older woman]. (Holloway 30)

Vernacular Speakers in early works produce the following names:

1. *lim' o' de debbil* [devil]. (Hopkins, "Hagar's" 256)

2. *dat villyun* [villain]. (Hopkins, "Hagar's" 255)

3. *dat debbil* [devil]. (Hopkins, "Hagar's" 257)

4. *breath-and-britches.* (Hurston, *Eyes* 27)

5. *scoundrels.* (Larison 53)

6. you *yaller rascal.* (Hurston, *Jonah's* 19)

7. *Mouth-Almighty.* (Hurston, *Eyes* 16)

8. *zigaboos.* (Hurston, *Eyes* 17)

Later examples from Vernacular speakers include:

9. You *goddamn bastard.* (Jones, *Corregidora* 100)

10. The *slick bastard!* (Cooper, *Some* 54)

11. they were just *hellions*. (Shange, *Betsey* 201)

12. *a mama's girl.* (Guy, *Friends* 35)

13. that *little rascal.* (Taylor, *Circle* 92)

14. The *big LIAR!* (Cooper, *Some* 62)

15. You *a drag and a half.* (Bambara, "Witchbird" 184)

16. those *slack-mouth gossips* on Brewster. (Naylor, *The Women* 70)

17. that *ole devil.* (Taylor, *Circle* 93)

18. *scoundrel.* (Shange, *Betsey* 115)

19. you *no-good bum*, you. (Naylor, *Linden* 30)

20. he thinks he's cute but he's an *asshole.* (Meriwether 178)

Quite a number of names include animal imagery. Both Standard and Vernancular speakers employ this type of imagery. These examples come from later works. Standard Speakers use the following names:

1. you're an *animal.* (Morrison, *Tar* 121)

2. you, *ape.* (Morrison, *Tar* 121)

3. You . . . you . . . you . . . *black cow!* [one old woman to another]. (Jackson 385)

4. *Dirty dog.* (Wade-Gayles 218)

5. *jackass.* (Guy, *Friends* 134)

6. *Young jackass* (Lee 65)

7. You *crazy roach!* (Morrison, *Sula* 93)

8. That is nothing but a *toothless rat.* (Hansberry 105)

Vernacular speakers use a similar set of names; the last two examples come from young girls:

1. that *little cripple-looking colt* you been fuckin'. (McMillan, *Mama* 90)

2. *dirty dog.* (Wade-Gayles 218)

3. a *stuttering jackass.* (Bolton 56)

4. *you old hen's ass.* (Naylor, *The Women* 144)

5. *monkey* [referring to a young West Indian female]. (Guy, *Friends* 5)

6. you so *chicken!* (Tate 105)

Many of the names appear in combination with other words and phrases. The following words, *heifer*, *bitch*, and *nigger*, appear in four or more such combinations.

All of the following examples using the word *heifer* come from later works, and all of the females are Vernacular speakers or females who style-shift regularly. The last example comes from a young girl:

1. this *lil ol' heifer.* (Shange, *Betsey* 186)

2. you *fresh heifer.* (Naylor, *Mama Day* 49)

3. You *stinkin' li'l' heifer* you! (Hurston, *Jonah's* 77)

4. De *two-faced heifer!* (Hurston, *Mules* 149)

5. You *red-headed heifer.* (Jones, *Corregidora* 82)

6. *rhiney* [color] *heifer.* (Shange, *Betsey* 35)

With the exception of the first example, the following examples using the word *bitch* come from later works, and all of the speakers are adult Vernacular speakers or females who style-shift regularly:

1. you *rich son of a bitch.* (Hurston, *Mules* 148)

2. you *son of a bitch*, (Morrison, *Tar* 125)

3. Mrs. Mackey was a *black bitch.* (Meriwether 182)

4. *bitch.* (Giovanni 269)

5. *nappy-head bitch.* (Bambara, "Lesson" 88)

6. *daughters of bitches.* (Jones, *Corregidora* 32)

7. *first class bitch.* (Bambara, "Witchbird" 171)

In the next passage, Walker describes how a little girl is so angry with her father that she calls him a name (sonofabitch), but she is unable to pronounce it properly:

8. "You know what," . . . "Hey, I say do you know what," she said again loudly, in her best fearless voice, though the pit of her stomach quivered. . . . "You nothing but a *sonnabit.*" (Walker, *Third* 153)

Although the word *nigger* is strongly stigmatized both in and outside the African American speech community, characters in early and later works use it extensively. Many of the early works show female speakers using this word as a general term of reference for African Americans. Often the term is used to express disapproval, and it is usually used by Vernacular speakers. For one example of how this word is used in name-calling, refer to the following passage. An old ex-slave is admonished for using the word *nigger* to describe a group of African American men who sold their votes. She replies:

1. I jis' calls em *niggers*, an' *niggers* I means; an' de bigges' kine ob *niggers*. An' if my John war sich a *nigger* I'd whip him an' leave him. (Harper 176)

With the exception of the following first example, Hurston supplies the rest the other examples from early works:

2. you *fool nigger?* (Rose 436)

3. *some low-lifed nigger.* (Hurston, *Eyes* 53)

4. *trashy nigger.* (Hurston, *Eyes* 27)

5. dis *big yaller bee-stung nigger.* (Hurston, *Jonah's* 13)

6. *uppity yaller niggers.* (Hurston, *Jonah's* 19)

The term *nigger* is also used extensively in later works. The speakers are generally Vernacular speakers or those females who regularly style-shifted. The first two works were set in earlier times:

7. *biggity niggers.* (Guy, *Measure* 114)

8. *trifling nigger.* (Walker, *Purple* 29)

9. you *just a nigger.* (Jones, "Asylum" 139)

10. *swamp nigger.* (Morrison, *Tar* 100)

11. *little spoiled nigger* of yours. (Naylor, *The Women* 39)

12. You *goddamned black niggah!* (Shange, *Betsey* 144)

13. You *nasty lil niggah.* (Shange, *Betsey* 35)

Name-calling is usually perceived as an aggressive act, perhaps an act of courage if there is any danger of retaliation. It can also be used in the African American female speech community as a form of performance. Many of the characters in the works that I examined string together two or more descriptions, using apt phrases, colorful language, and creative juxtapositions. With the exception of the first two, all of the following examples come from later works: The female in the next two examples is a Vernacular speaker.

1. *grass-gut, liver-lipted nigger.* (Hurston, *Eyes* 40)

2. Dat *li'l narrer contracted piece of uh meatkin. . . . De two-faced heifer*! (Hurston, *Mules* 149)

Guy's work *A Measure of Time* is set in an earlier time, though it was written in 1983. Dorinne, a Vernacular speaker, produces all of these examples:

3. that *high yeller, smoochy-eyed bitch.* (110)

4. that *two-faced, tit-sucking mother's child.* (105)

5. [to the rhythm of a train] *master, master childfucker, pussysucker, childfucker, pussysucker, childfucker, pussysucker.* (128)

In the next two examples the first speaker is an adult; the second, an older woman. Both are Vernacular speakers who style-shift regularly.

6. You *sneaky little cunt,* you . . . *little whore.* (McMillan, *Mama* 186)

7. you *addle-brained, slew-footed son-of-a-crow.* (Naylor, *Mama Day* 46)

In Standard speakers there is very little use of taboo words, although the strings are used extensively by all age groups. In this first set of examples, the females are adults:

1. you *ugly barefoot baboon!* (Morrison, *Tar* 121)

2. *some lowly sick acting-the-fool stinking niggahs* so dumb they can't find the goddam clinic! (Shange, *Betsey* 48)

3. That *middle-of-the-road, Uncle Tom dumping ground for black Republicans*! [describing the National Association for the Advancement of Colored People (NAACP)]. (Naylor, *The Women* 85)

4. You *goddamned black niggah!* . . . *African!* . . . *Heathen! Low-down colored jackass!* (Shange, *Betsey* 144)

5. He flew to marry a *cheap city girl* from a *family of ignorant flashy people.* (Walker, "Everyday Use" 2369)

The next set of examples comes from children:

6. *old stupid smelly ugly Rufus?* (McMillan, *Mama* 72)

7. He sure was *one evil black West Indian.* (Meriwether 50)

8. That *ole scrawny, chicken-legged, snaggle-toothed, cross. . .* (Taylor, *Roll* 95)

In the next two examples, the young females are calling their teachers names. In the Guy example, the teacher is a Jewish female; in the Walker example, the teacher is a middle-class, African American female:

9. *Whitey, dirty cracker, Jew.* (Guy, *Friends* 45)

10. *You goddam mean evil stupid motherfucker*! (Walker, *Third* 262)

The majority of names come from middle-aged or older females, many of whom style-shift regularly:

11. The *chippy.* The *fast-ass.* (Morrison, *Tar* 107)

12. you *snake-eyed ungrateful hussy.* (Morrison, *Sula* 69)

13. *ungrateful, conniving, wuthless whelp!* (Marshall, *Brown Girl* 304)

14. Why, you *evil, narrow-tailed heifer.* (Naylor, *The Women* 36)

15. The most *contentious, cantankerous old witch* that ever lived. (Walker, *Temple* 101)

16. you're a *tired, weak, snivelling, old . . . Old . . . 'fraidy cat!* (Jackson 396)

Sometimes the strings are incorporated into narratives. Older Vernacular speakers from works by Cooper produce the following examples:

1. I looked, by accident, in the mirror one day . . . and I cried! I was a fat, *sloppy-dressed, house-shoe wearin, gray-haired, old-lookin woman*! I was forty-three and looked fifty-five! (Cooper, *Some* 48)

2. My daughter ran off with *one of them card-playin double-dealin suckers* that hang around the Buzzards Nest nightclub. (Cooper, *Homemade* 96)

3. You don't think I love *that ole fat-bellied, bald-headed man of mine* cause he's a sex king, do you? (Cooper, *Homemade* 152)

Standard speakers produce the following examples; the second example comes from an older speaker:

4. Cause the super and his cronies is *a nasty bunch of low life, filthy bad, jive ass.* (Bambara, "Basement" 143)

5. That *lil ol' twitch of a gal* callt me out my name. Trying to say that I didn't came from a upstanding Christian God-fearing home and *was a kind a evil mess.* (Shange, *Betsey* 186)

As is true of other areas that I've discussed, name-calling has some distinct differences in the way it is used. For example, in almost all of the preceding categories, both Standard and Vernacular speakers are likely to use conventional forms of name-calling, but the Vernacular speakers and those females who regularly style-shift also produce a set of more fanciful, colorful names. In the section on set terms, it appears that the Vernacular speakers are displaying both conformity and creativity. On one hand, they often use the same three words again and again in their name-calling (*heifer*, *bitch*, and *nigger*). On the other hand, they combine them with other words and phrases in ways that show individualistic style. Strings of names are used by both groups, but those strings that contain some of the most unusual descriptions are those produced by Vernacular speakers and those that style-shift regularly. Name-calling is used by all groups that I studied. Older women in both early and later works use them; so do young girls. I found examples from adult West Indian females and ones from young West Indian girls. Though some examples are taken from early works, most come from later works.

Curses

The second type of abusive language is curses. I found several curses in which the speaker, according to *The Random House Dictionary*, wishes "that misfortune, evil, etc. befall another" (216). All of the examples come from later works, and all of the speakers are adult, Standard speaking females or females who style-shift regularly.

In the following set of examples all of the curses come from later works:

1. *Fuck you.* (Jones, *Corregidora* 3)

2. *Go to hell*, nigger. (Bambara, *Seabirds* 162)

3. Now, I do not curse, but . . . *fuck the landlady*! (Cooper, *Some* 199)

4. *Goddamn you, nigger.* (Marshall, *Praisesong* 106)

As Adsentences

Andersson and Trudgill (1992) describe adsentences as "loosely tied to a sentence before or after" (62). In the examples, the swearwords appear as attachments either before or after full sentences. I found many examples of this form of swearing. All of the examples here come from adult females who appear in later works. Most of the speakers are Standard speakers or females who regularly style-shift. The speaker in the first example is a Vernacular speaker. The swearwords used most often in this pattern are *shit*, *damn/goddam(n) it*, *hell*, and *my ass*.

Shit

1. *Shit*, married or single they still doing the same thing when they goes to bed. (Williams 49)

2. Help me play Santa Claus. *Shit*, help me cook. (McMillan, *Waiting* 396)

3. *Shit.* It's enough to make you crazy. (Bambara, "Witchbird" 174)

4. *Shit*, I'd cut it off myself if I didn't think they'd all kill me. (Ansa, *Baby* 135)

5. *Shit*, yeah. (Briscoe 58)

6. *Holy shit*, the ground's moving. (Bambara, *Salt Eaters* 291)

Damn/Goddam(n)

1. Portia, . . . I haven't had one in four years, *damn*. (McMillan, *Disappearing Act* 60)

2. God *dammit*, Greer! Do you understand anything I ever say to you? (Shange, *Betsey* 48)

Hell

1. *Hell*, it's an emergency situation. (Bambara, *Salt Eaters* 243)

2. *Hell*! I was tired! (Cooper, *Some* 104)

3. *hell* yeah girl! (DeVeaux, "Tapestry" 169)

My Ass

1. White man *my ass*. (Williams 54)

2. Integrity, *my ass!* (Shange, *Betsey* 158)

As Major Constituents of a Sentence

Subject

Swearwords appear as subjects of sentences in both early and later works. The first two examples come from an early work featuring the ex-slave Silvia Dubois; the third example comes from an adult in a later work. All of the females are Vernacular speakers.

1. they're the *damnedest* that ever lived. (Larison 51)

2. You think I don't know what that apple pie *shit* is for? (Morrison, *Tar* 208)

3. this old-fashioned potion *shit*. (Ansa, *Baby* 33)

Verb

Swear words are used as verbs in both early and later works. Example 1 is the only examples from early works. The rest of the examples come from later works, and the speakers are adult females:

1. Mama, yuh *been hell-hackin'* me eve' since us tole yuh us wuz gointer git married. (Hurston, *Jonah's* 77)

2. He'll want to get our license plates to maybe *fuck* with us later. (Bambara, *Seabirds* 26)

3. We weren't no freaks. We went in for straight up-and-down *fucking*. (Guy, *Measure* 327)

4. she had already *shitted* up her clothes. (Bolton 17)

Object

Swearwords are used as objects in both early and later works. In this section on Standard speakers, example 1 comes from Silvia Dubois, the ex-slave; it is the only example from an early work. The second example comes from an older woman, and the rest of the examples come from adult females:

1. if only you knew what I am doing, you'd throw that fan away and give me *hell*. (Larison 63)

2. pulling that black-woman-white-woman *shit* on me. (Morrison, *Tar* 121)

3. But I was gettin really sick of all this *shit*! (Cooper, *Some* 87)

4. all kinds of weird *shit*. (Golden, *Woman's* 22)

5. Nobody ever give a *shit* about you but me, you mean old fool! (Walker, *Third* 136)

6. You still dranking that *shit*? (McMillan, *Mama* 187)

7. I was an intellectual. I thought things through. I didn't know *shit* about action. (Giovanni 267)

8. If you got any God in your heart, you will not put your mama through this *shit* tonight. (Ansa, *Baby* 256)

9. you don't want no *bullshit*. (Jones et al. 182)

10. That is *bullshit* of a non-biogradable sort. (Bambara, *Salt Eaters* 244)

11. And she was black as *hell*. (Bambara, "Lesson" 87)

12. you can take a flying leap and go straight to *hell*. (Angelou, *All God's* 34)

13. I wouldn't *care a damn*! (Cooper, *Some* 149)

Vernacular speakers supply the following examples. All come from later works. The first two speakers are adult; the next two are young girls:

14. Ethel and Fur Coat don't give a *shit*. (Bambara, *Seabirds* 204–205)

15. Well. She can catch pneumonia of the *asshole* for all I care. (Jones, *Corregidora* 44)

16. and the first time I catch ya I'm gonna beat the *shit* out of ya. (Meriwether 14)

17. my pinafore scratching the *shit* outta me. (Bambara, "Lesson" 88)

Occasionally, the speaker attaches a short phrase consisting of *and shit* to signal a meaning something like, "and so forth." The two next examples come from later works:

18. You mean you foam at the mouth and fall out *and shit*? (McMillan, *Disappearing Act* 59)

19. All that damn finagling *and shit* going on back there. (Guy, *Measure* 313)

Adjective

Swearwords used as adjectives appear extensively in some of the works that I examined. The swearwords that appear most often in this position are *damn/goddam(n)*, *fucking*, and *shit*.

Damn/Goddam(n)

The following two examples come from early works; the first one is from an ex-slave; the second one is from a middle-class, educated female:

1. They're a set of *damned* turtles: they carry all they've got on their backs. (Larison 51)
2. But you don't have the *damned* stairs when you came in late at night. (Fauset, *Plum* 103)

The following examples come from later works, and most of the speakers are Standard-speaking adults or adults who style-shift regularly:

3. Yes, *damned* nonsense! (Naylor, *The Women* 52)
4. I ain't never seen you have no *damn* fits. (McMillan, *Disappearing Act* 60)
5. Mary got this *damn* dryer on KILL. (Bambara, "Witchbird" 186)
6. don't squeeze his *goddamn* blackheads. (Bambara, "Medley" 114)
7. if you ever use a cuss word in my new house I'm going to cut out your *goddam* tongue. (Walker, *Third* 138)

The last two examples come from Vernacular speakers; both are adults:

8. Spending *damn* near your whole paycheck on some barfly and a bunch of good-timing niggers. (Marshall, *Praisesong* 107)
9. You ain't gon no *damn* New York City and it ain't the white man what gon keep you. (Williams, "Martha" 54)

In McMillan, speakers often insert adjectives between words or constituents of an utterance:

10. The first time ever I saw your *goddamn* face. (McMillan, *Waiting* 321)

Fuck

I was not surprised to find no examples of this swearword in early works. I did find a few examples in later works; the speakers are Standard speaking females or females who regularly style-shift:

1. *Fucking* earthquake. (Bambara, *Salt Eaters* 291)
2. I'm gonna start from the top of your head and split you down like a *fucking* string bean. (Guy, *Measure* 56)

As above, a character in McMillan inserts the adjective between words:

3. Earth, Wind and *Fucking* Fire! (McMillan, *Waiting* 321)

Shit

I didn't find examples of this swearword used as an adjective in any of the early works. In the later works I found the following two examples. Both come from adult speakers; the first one comes from a Vernacular speaker:

1. She got the cow by the tail and gon on down *shit* creek. (Williams 55)

2. Ain't no better way to get them than when you ain't got to change *shitty* drawers. (Guy, *Measure* 328)

Adverb

I did not not find any examples of swearwords used as adverbs in early works. The pattern that most of these examples follow is that of a speaker's inserting a phrase consisting of the word *the* + a swearword in between words or constituents in an utterance. The phrases used most often are *the hell* and *the fuck*:

The Hell

Most of the following examples come from later works that feature adult Standard speakers or speakers who style-shift regularly. The last example comes from a young Vernacular speaker:

1. Tell 'em you my brown-skin Carolina daddy, that's who *the hell* you are. (Childress, "Wedding Band" 90)
2. LET'S GET *THE HELL* OUT OF HERE! (Hansberry 109)
3. Right this minute I can't tell you what *the hell* it means! (Shange, *Betsey* 158)
4. how in *the hell* do it taste? (Bolton 32)

As is the case with some of the adjective examples, the following three examples show a somewhat unusual placement of the inserted swearword. This time the positioning serves the purpose of simultaneously calling attention to the action while commenting favorably on it:

5. And somebody had made *the hell* out of the potato salad, too. (Guy, *Measure* 117)
6. She acted like she was on something. But she could do *the hell* out of some weaves. (McMillan, *Waiting* 375)
7. I raise *the hell* outta that veil, transforming myself into Mother with a capital M. (Bambara, "Witchbird" 172)

The Fuck

Three examples come from later works, and the females are adult Standard speakers or those who style-shift regularly:

1. Leave me *the fuck* alone. (McMillan, *Waiting* 386)
2. I just want you to get *the fuck* out of my house. (Naylor, *Linden* 246)
3. Where *the fuck* is the right one? (Sister Souljah 79)

Damn

The next example shows *damn* used in an unusual position to stress the duration of the stay in the tub. The speaker is a young woman: "She stayed in that tub all *damn* night long." (Bolton 18)

Fixed Expressions

Some of the swearwords previously discussed often appear in fixed expressions. The words used most often are *damn* and *hell*.

Damn

These examples come from adult Vernacular speakers who style-shift regularly:

1. *Damn* if I hadn't known. (Guy, *Measure* 238)
2. I'll be *damned* if I was coming into this city on a raggedy old Greyhound. (Naylor, *The Women* 58)
3. And you and the rest of those slack-mouthed gossips on Brewster be *damned*! (Naylor, *The Women* 70)

Hell

Example 1 comes from an adult Vernacular speaker; example 2 comes from a Standard speaker. Both females style-shift regularly:

1. Got so we spent a *helluva* lotta time in the shower. (Bambara, "Medley" 106)
2. So to *hell* with it. (McMillan, *Waiting* 192)

Strings of Swearwords

As in other sections, the speakers string together series of swearwords using the words previously discussed. All of the examples come from later works. The first one comes from a young girl. The others come from adult, Standard-speaking females or from females who style-shift regularly:

1. And if you touch me just one more *damn* time, my granddaddy and me will pull this piece of junk right down on your head and cram planks and bricks down your lying dumb *motherfucking* throat! [young girl to a teacher]. (Walker, *Third* 262)
2. Naw, *bitch*, you get the *hell* out of here, . . . You take that *goddamn* blanket and get the *goddamn hell* out of here. (Jones, *Corregidora* 43)
3. I told ya to stop them *goddamned* children from jumping over my *goddamned* head all the *goddamn* day! Now I'm gonna call the police—do you hear me? The *goddamned* police! (Naylor, *The Women* 109)

In a conversation between mother and daughter in McMillan's *Waiting to Exhale*, the mother of Savannah, one of the main characters, asks her daughter to "try not to swear." The daughter answers: "I won't, Mama. And give me *some* credit. I don't use the same kind of language around men that I do when I'm with my girlfriends—at least not until I get to know him better" (8). Savannah's description of how she uses swearing represents the behavior of many of the female characters whose language behavior I've described in this section. Most of the passages that contain swearwords are produced in settings where females are either talking to those younger than they are, their female friends, or men whom they know very well. There are a few occasions where the female uses swearwords to strangers, and in most of those cases they are using the words to express anger. Much of the swearing that occurs in these passages, however, is not produced in anger. It is often used in casual and intimate conversation.

SUMMARY

There are several striking findings. First, there is very little evidence of swear-words used in the early works and no evidence of the use of the most highly stigmatized forms such as *fuck, pussy*, and *cunt*. Also, these forms are rarely used by older females, although some of these females do speak quite openly and frankly about sexual matters and bodily functions. Young girls do use these forms, but the use is limited to occasionally including one or two words in an utterance (how in *the hell* do it taste?). A second finding is that the vast majority of swearwords are used by Standard-speaking females or females who regularly style-shift.

When I looked for evidence of conformity or creativity, I found that both Standard and Vernacular speakers show use of traditional forms. They use the swear-words in conventional ways in both early and later works (They're a set of *damned* turtles; Yes, *damned* nonsense!). In later works I found that the Vernacular speakers pepper their phrases with occasional swearwords (She got the cow by the tail and gon on down *shit* creek). The Standard speakers and those who style-shift regularly use the swearwords as part of a stylistic technique, inserting the words for casual emphasis (*fucking* earthquake), using them to express strong emotions (Look at this little piece of *shit* Nellie bought to put on my child's feet), and inserting them into sentences and phrases to form unusual juxtapositions (That is *bullshit* of a non-biogradable sort; Earth, Wind and *Fucking* Fire).

I also found that the word *shit* is used most often and in most of the categories that were discussed in the section on the "Grammar of Swearing." It is used as a verb (And when we looked, she had already *shitted up* her clothes); as an object (You still drinking that *shit*?) and adjective (She got the cow by the tail and gon on down *shit creek*); it is as also used as a filler in some utterances, taking the place of such expressions as "and so on" (All that damn finagling and *shit* going back there).

Some people will be surprised to see that women use this much swearing in the works that I examined. But many will agree with Kramer, who wrote that "there seems to be a conflict between what women's speech really is like and what people think women's speech really is like" (quoted in S. Hughes 293). Finally, this chapter on bad language points out one of the features of women's language use that has been alluded to before, the use of expressive language to show strong emotions. It also points out a feature of Vernacular use that has been noted—the use of a creative, individualistic style of expression.

12

Language Use

In the first chapter of *Attitudes towards Language Variation*, Ryan, Giles, and Sebastian (1982) write: "Whether speaking one or five languages, all individuals belong to at least one speech community, a community all of whose members share at least a single speech variety and the norms for appropriate use" (1). In this section I discuss the way female characters express their opinions about their own language use as well as the language use of others.

TALKING ABOUT LANGUAGE USE

The first section is divided into two subsections. The first subsection focuses on teaching about proper language use. The second subsection focuses on commenting about language use.

Teaching about Language Use

John R. Edwards, a psychology professor, notes that "language varieties which diverge from standard English are likely to be viewed, even by speakers of those varieties, less favorably than Standard" (Ryan and Giles 30). In the following passages, females correct the language use of others. In most cases, the female is older, and in many cases the caregiver. The two types of corrections are those that involve grammatical errors and those that have to do with communicative competence; that is, they describe or explain the appropriate use of language for a particular context.

Correcting Grammatical Errors

The first set of examples shows young people being corrected for making grammatical errors. All but the first example come from later works. The first example shows two young ladies discussing the use of the word *mighty*. One tells the other that the word is not an appropriate choice:

1. "Jessie, will you *please* stop using that word?" asked Garnet.
   "What word?"
   "Mighty, you know it is not only unladylike but actually wrong." (Kelley 80)

In the next passage a female Vernacular speaker who style-shifts regularly addresses her son:

2. What did I tell you about sayin' ain't boy? You'd thank [*sic*] they didn't teach you how to speak English in school. (McMillan, *Mama* 53)

In the three examples that follow, Standard-speaking mothers correct their children's grammatical errors:

3. "Kathleen taked us shopping yesterday. She picketed this one out."
   "And Onika, you know how to talk. It's took not taked and picked not pickted." (McMillan, *Waiting* 333)

4. "And that lady said that it was a crime for colored to live like this, and after that the man spit in the street."
   "Spat," corrected my mother automatically. (Lee 44)

Sometimes the young are the teachers. In the following passage, a young female tells her mother how to pronounce a word:

5. "My debut," I answered, giving the French pronunciation. Laughing I said, "Not dee-but." Mama laughed, too. (Wade-Gayles 219)

Teaching Appropriate Language Use

Sometimes the females are concerned with teaching appropriate language behavior. Ansa has an example of an older, Standard-speaking female correcting the language use of a younger person. In this case, the woman is coaching a little, Vernacular-speaking girl in the proper way to respond to an older person:

1. "So you're our baby's new friend?" Grandmama said out loud.
   "Yeah," Sarah answered, her voice gravelly from getting up so early but so respectful that her short answer didn't imply rudeness, even to Grandmama.
   "Say, 'yes, ma'am,' " Grandmama instructed Sarah gently.
   "Yes, ma'am," Sarah said carefully, repeating Grandmama's gentle inflection. (Ansa, *Baby* 85)

In contrast to the preceding passage, two young girls from a Childress play had the following exchange:

2. PRINCESS: You wanta jump?
   TEETA: Yes.

PRINCESS: Say "Yes M'am."
TEETA: No.
PRINCESS: Why?
TEETA: You too little. ("Wedding Band" 93)

The preceding passage is interesting because the young girl Teeta is able to clearly articulate a rule covering the proper use of the term *M'am*, which many say is to be used to address those who are approximately fifteen years older.

Meriwether supplies examples of a Vernacular-speaking mother's instructing her children in the way that they should use language. In the first example, the brother and sister are arguing, and the brother has threatened to "slap the pee" out of his sister:

3. "What's gotten into both of you," Mother cried, "that you use such language in front of me? And if I ever hear you talk to your sister like that again, Sterling, I'm gonna break your neck. You understand me?" (117)

In the second example her daughter uses the word "horseshit" when she talks to her brother. The mother angrily instructs her daughter to substitute a refined word:

4. "Francie!" Mother aimed a backhanded slap at me but I ducked. "Stop using such language. You don't have to be so coarse. Say horse manure." (169)

In her book *Sweet Summer*, Bebe Moore Campbell gives several examples of how her older relatives correct her use of language. Bebe's mother corrects a grammatical error when a young Bebe asks, "Can I walk to the corner?" Her mother says, "Do you mean *may*?" Bebe answers, "May I walk to the corner?," and her mother answers, "Yes" (32). Bebe's grandmother, Nana, prompts her to supply an appropriate answer to a question in another exchange. Nana offers her some cake by saying, "you want some of this?" Bebe answers "Uh huh." Nana then says, "What do you say?," " and Bebe answers, "Thank you Nana," and the grandmother answers, "You're welcome." Finally, in the following passage, Campbell gives further information about how she was schooled in using both correct grammar and appropriate language. She describes what would happen to her after she returned from a yearly visit with southern relatives:

5. My mosquito bites healed and as September wore on I faded from brown to yellow again, the darkness peeling away under the dimmer Philadelphia sun. I returned to a household where capable and loving women made sure I had enough culture and Christianity, that I greased my legs and learned the difference between nice and riff-raff, that I was proper. My southern speech evaporated in a swirl of corrections.

   Bebe, don't say, "He be," my mother said frowning.
   "Don't talk flat," Nana admonished me.
   "Open your mouth when you speak and don't call me ma'am. I hate that. It's so country," Aunt Ruth said irritably.

   My North Carolina words need a softer setting, corn standing tall in the background, roosters, chickens, pigs, people who wore shoes only on Sunday, folks who cure their own headaches by humming them away. Nana and Ruth hated the South. "Atlantic City. That's as far south as I go," Nana said flatly. (72)

The preceding passage shows several interesting ways to look at attitudes about language use. In the story, Campbell writes about her love for her father, who is living in North Carolina. Her use of, and love for, the language of the South seem to be tied to her love for her father and the life that she experiences when she visits him. Her mother, who is described as an educated, professional woman, focuses on correcting Bebe's grammatical errors, and her Aunt Ruth and Nana, both of whom hated the South, seem to be concerned about Bebe's sounding as if she were from the country. In addition, Bebe suggests that all of the corrections of the language may be tied into the older females' plan to see to it that she becomes one of the "nice" children who display "proper" behavior.

Commenting about Language Use

Longman Dictionary of Applied Linguistics (1985) says of language attitudes:

Expressions of positive or negative feelings towards a language may reflect impressions of linguistic difficulty or simplicity, ease or difficulty of learning, degree of importance, elegance, social status, etc. Attitudes towards a language may also show what people feel about the speakers of that language. (Richards, Platt, & Weber 154)

This section is concerned with the way that female characters express themselves on the topic of language use. As with the previous examples, the comments can be divided into those that focus on the grammatical aspects and those that focus on language use that is appropriate for a particular situation or context.

Grammatical Use

The first set of examples shows older females commenting on the language use of someone younger. All of the examples in this set come from later works, and most of the speakers are Standard speakers. In the first example an adult, middle-class female complains about her son's deliberate use of non-Standard Vernacular:

1. Did you hear that English? "I can't find no coaster." And he knows better, Willie. He just does that to plague me. He's decided to be nothing and do nothing with his life, and he never lets a day go by without reminding me of it in some way. (Naylor, *Linden* 51)

In the next passage, a mother complains about the way that the neighborhood children pronounce the name of her daughter, Teresa:

2. Treesa! Why can't they pronounce your name right? (Fauset, *Comedy* 3)

Many of the characters comment on the kind of language that is used by others or on their own language use. Both of the following examples come from *Some Soul to Keep* by Cooper:

3. She spoke very proper, dressed very discreet, and like that, but she laid very loose. Very properly discreet, of course. (105)

4. laughed too loud and talked that ole bad English, worser than mine! (150)

Sometimes it is not clear what language behavior is being condemned:

5. What a way to talk. (Naylor, *The Women* 114)

6. Seemed like not a child in there could talk decent. All of them screaming and hollering like they were out on the farm. (Shange, *Betsey* 56)

In the next passage, a young Standard speaker tells her new West Indian friend that the way she speaks prevented their becoming friends sooner:

7. I wanted to meet you last term but my girl friend was so funny. She said you talk too bad. I don't think you talk that bad anyway, I'll get used to it. (Guy, *Friends* 84)

The young, Vernacular-speaking girl in the next example tells the lengths to which she is willing to go to try to "talk right":

8. I was scared to open my mouth. . . . I told them I couldn't see, but I was lying. I wanted cat-eye glasses. Somehow, I thought if I had those cat-eye glasses, I would be able to talk right. (Bolton 56)

Sometimes the characters comment on the way that someone uses "good English":

9. Gennie saying her mother had once been a school teacher down South and prided herself on her proper speech. (Lorde 102)

At other times a character might choose a particular aspect of language use to talk about. In the following example, a female describes the way that her mother talked:

10. She would speak to me matter-of-factly, in run-on sentences, while ironing a pretty dress for me or fixing my hair or washing out my undies. (Brown 34)

In another passage, the same speaker describes how she learned to speak a particular type of English:

11. I learned to speak exactly like white people, learned to enunciate their language, to say "these" and not "dese" and "he'll be going" rather than "he be goin'." (Brown 31)

Appropriate Use

In this section I discuss the way that female characters comment on the sometimes unstated rules of language behavior. In the following example, Maya Angelou describes some rules followed by some members of the African American speech community, especially those who are Vernacular speakers:

1. Blacks concede that hurrawing, jibing, jiving, signifying, disrespecting, cursing, even outright insults might be acceptable under particular conditions, but aspersions cast against one's family call for immediate attack. (Angelou, *All God's* 10–11)

Bessie Delany, an older Standard speaker, compares the way that she talks with the way that her sister talks, noting that her sister's manner is more pleasant. But she defiantly notes that she is over 100, so she can do as she pleases. In other words, she doesn't have to follow the rules:

> 2. Ain't nobody going to censor me, no, sir! I'm a hundred-and-one years old and at my age, honey, I can say what I want! (Delany et al. 16)

In a work written in an earlier time, a young, Standard-speaking adult describes to a young male friend what she feels are the proper rules of address for their relationship:

> 3. And dont call me Miss Angela. Call me Angela as you've done all our lives or else call me Miss Murray. (Fauset, "Passing" 53)

Sometimes the speakers condemn others for using inappropriate language. In one example, a Vernacular speaker comments on people who are "talking all vulgar" (McMillan, *Waiting* 240); in another, a Vernacular-speaking female criticizes a man for saying "Jesus" by saying:

> 4. You blaspheme too much. . . . You ain't supposed to use Lord's name in vain. (Naylor, *The Women* 15)

In example 5 a teacher comments on the language used by her student; in example 6, a tenant comments on the language used by her landlord. Example 7 comes from a young, adult female who is visiting a bad neighborhood:

> 5. What's the problem Elizabeth? You never use language like that. (Brown 35)
>
> 6. but I can tell one complaint was about foulmouthed language on the premises. Yours. (Hunter 71)
>
> 7. Although it was late at night, there were plenty kids outside. Hair uncombed, shoes dirty, language foul. (Sister Souljah 131)

Several Vernacular speakers, both young and old, comment on cursing. In example 8, the speaker makes a very strong (and funny) statement about the rules of "cussing" in her new house:

> 8. If you ever use a cuss word in my new house I'm going to cut out your goddamn tongue. (Walker, *Third* 138)

In the next three examples, speakers comment on the fact that adults usually don't or shouldn't curse in front of children. The first female is an adult; the other two are children:

> 9. Don't you think Mildred curses too much in front of those kids? (McMillan, *Mama* 92)
>
> 10. Daddy didn't usually cuss around me. (Campbell 40)
>
> 11. It was the first time I ever heard her curse [about her mother]. (Meriwether 191)

Sometimes young people comment on the language used by older people. In example 12, a young, Standard-speaking girl tells her grandmother that she hopes she wasn't too hard on her young friend, and the grandmother answers her, defending the way she talks:

12. I just hope you didn't hurt his feelings, that's all. You know how you can talk sometimes, and everybody might not understand you like I do.
    Now, I like that. . . . I talk the way I've talked all my life, miss—plain and clear. And the folks around here don't have no trouble understanding me. (Naylor, *Linden* 219)

A young, Standard-speaking girl comments on the language used by some older, Vernacular-speaking females:

13. They didn't talk like us—me, or Shirl or Mama. They sounded like M'dear, our grandmama back in Sedalia. (Holloway 28)

In an early work featuring several young Standard speakers, the following exchange takes place between two of the young ladies:

14. "An' phwere did yez get the news?" asked Vera.
    "I advise you to stop practicing that dialect, Jess" said Garnett, "You'll use it some time when you don't mean to." (Kelley-Hawkins 114)

In a later work, another young girl comments on the language used by her friend:

15. Lord have mercy, listen to you. You sound like an old woman (Tate 85)

Female characters also occasionally comment on the way that others use or don't use the English language. In the next example, the speaker describes the language used by the Jewish grandmother of one of her friends:

16. She would proclaim, in her broken English, that I had such a shayne punim and how much I looked just like a little Sabra. (Brown 28)

In the next passage, a Vernacular speaker comments on the language used by the mother of a Native American friend:

17. How come your mama don't talk American?
    She does talk American, we're speaking the first American language!
    Maybe if you spoke that white man's talk you wouda known better when one of em was lyin' to you! (Cooper, *Homemade* 27)

Finally, the last two examples show females commenting on paralinguistic behavior. The first speaker comments on the loudness of speech; the second speaker, a young female, comments on the style of delivery:

18. "No use trying to ig me honey," Bertha says real loud. (Bambara, "Medley" 187)

19. mad at him for being so smart-mouth. (Tate 121)

Summary

This section focused on the way that females teach others to use the language and on the way females comment on their own language use or the language use of others. In both areas, the comments are divided into comments about grammar or about appropriateness. Language attitudes are displayed by both Standard and Vernacular speakers. Most of the teaching is done by older females, but old and young comment on language use. Most, but not all, of the comments focus on mistakes, errors, or inappropriate use of language. Often, information about the speakers' social status or condition is included.

METALANGUAGE—TERM FOR TYPES OF TALK

In this section, I use the term metalanguage, which I define as the way that members of a speech community talk about types of talk and other communicative behavior. Many of the descriptive terms about language use are supplied by the authors of the works examined, but occasionally a character describes her own language behavior or the language behavior of others. I discuss the latter type of description.

Prattle and *Fib*

The following examples come from Standard speakers in early works. The first two terms mentioned are *prattle* and *fib:*

1. When she repeated their *prattle* and told me how they wanted to see their ma, my tears would flow. (Brent 104)
2. Don't *fib*, Jasmine. (Kelley-Hawkins 129)

Babble

Standard speakers in both early and later works use the term *babble*. The first example comes from an early work; the second, from a work written in the 1950s; the last, from the 1970s:

1. Darling infant she is *babbling* about taking a place for the summer. (Fauset, *Comedy* 130)
2. I could hear voices, but the Oval was beginning to *babble*. (West 85)
3. Here I've been *babbling* like a brook, Abbie, and I never once thought to ask you about Deacon Lord's funeral. (Petry, *Narrows* 236)

Loud Talk, Holler, and *Shout*

Vernacular speakers in both early and later works use expressions such as *loud talk*, *holler*, and *shout*. Both of the following examples of *loud talk* come from adult females. Example 1 comes from an early work, example 2 comes from a work set in an earlier time.

1. Look at her puttin' out her brags. . . . *Loud-talkin* de place. (Hurston, *Mule* 150)
2. I knew what they wanted . . . to have me talk to them so they could *loud-talk* me. (Guy, *Measure* 113)

The term *holler* is used by Vernacular speakers and those who style-shift regularly. It appears in both early and late works. The next two examples come from early works:

3. He didn't like too much *hollerin'*. (Harper 63)

4. an' you *hollerin'* down these stairs to me that you can't go holp her 'cause you's got a teaseus [thesis]. (Hopkins, "Hagar's" 169)

This example comes from a later work, but the speaker is the apparition of an old slave:

5. He was just slow and the white folk *hollers* at him for it. (Ansa, *Baby* 164)

The rest of the examples come from later works:

6. What's the Principal Beauty *hollering* about. (Morrison, *Tar* 34)

7. Mama in the kitchen
Papa in jail
Baby 'round the corner
Hollerin' "pussy for sale." [children's rhyme] (Brown 34)

Hollerin(g) is also used in combination with other terms. All of the following examples come from later works; the first two females are Vernacular speakers; the last is a young, Standard-speaking girl who style-shifts regularly:

8. She started *hollering and screaming and hollering and screaming*.

9. Gone be bloody and I don't want you getting scared and *hoopin' and hollerin'* and having nightmares and all. (Campbell 46)

10. and *scream and holler* on account of some white man coming to the door. (Shange, *Betsey* 110)

The term *shout* roughly meaning an outburst reflecting religious fervor, is used by Vernacular speakers in both early and later works. In the following examples, the first one comes from an early work; all of the speakers are adults:

11. Well, you had better look out, and not *shout* too much, and pray and sing too loud, because, 'fore you know, the patrollers will be on your track and break up your meetin' in a mighty big Jack Robinson. (Harper 13)

12. Just like when I'm in church and the spirit of God touches me and I get happy and *shout*. (Walker, "Everyday Use" 2373)

13. Mother start to *shout*. "Jesus, help O Lord, Lord, Lord." She stiffened in her seat, flinging her arms up over her head, crying out loud for God's mercy. (Meriwether 184)

Several expressions and terms are used by both Standard and Vernacular speakers in early and later works.

Playing the Dozens

The expression *playing the dozens*, meaning to intentionally insult another's relatives, especially the mother, is used by a Vernacular speaker in an early work and by a Standard speaker in a later work. The first speaker is a child; the second speaker is a young adult:

> 1. Git back out mah face, Phrony, Ah don't *play de dozens.* (Hurston, *Jonah's* 24)
> 2. It's like *playing the dozens* with your own self. It's counter revolutionary, in fact. (Weems 122)

An indirect reference to the dozens appears in a comment made by an adult Standard speaker in a later work:

> 3. Lester, *I'm not trying to talk about your mother.* (Naylor, *Linden* 39)

Elaine Brown, another Standard speaker, supplies an example of a childhood rhyme that demonstrates one of the ways to play the dozens:

> 4. I ain't gon' *talk about your mama*
>   She's a sweet ole soul
>   She got a ten-ton pussy
>   And a rubber asshole. (Brown 34)

Several other terms are used in both early and later works by both Standard and Vernacular speakers; these include *laughing and . . . /and laughing*; *curse/cuss*; and *chastise.*

Laughing and . . . / . . . and Laughing

Expressions using the word *laughing* + at least one other word are used to characterize activities where people are having a good time. The expressions appear in both early and later works and are used by both Standard and Vernacular speakers. Example 1 comes from a Vernacular speaker in an early work. Examples 2 through 4 are from later works. All of the speakers are young females who style-shift.

> 1. *whoopin' and hollering' and laughin'* over nothing. (Hurston, *Eyes* 210)
> 2. It had once been Louisa's daybed the one where Gennie and I lay *laughing and talking and smoking.* (Lorde 102)
> 3. She was forever in the kitchen *laughing and talking* with Big Ma. (Taylor, *Circle* 185)
> 4. They were *laughing and joking* on the stoop. (Meriwether 178)

Curse/Cuss

The term *curse* appears in a number of expressions in both early and later works; it is used by both Standard and Vernacular speakers. The first example comes from an early work; the female is a Standard speaker:

1. They made a dreadful uproar, and from that day they constantly kept *cursing* and abusing me. (M. Prince 19)

The next two examples come from later works; both the females are young girls:

2. She was just fussing and *cussing*. (Tate 122)

3. Betsey thought on those thoughts and bout what she'd do if a crowd of crackers came *cursing* her and throwing eggs on her pressed clothes. (Shange, *Betsey* 43)

The speaker in the next passage is a West Indian adult; she appears in a later work and also uses similar terms like *damn* and *blast*:

4. The hair like it *curse* comb, *damn* oil and *blast* the hairdresser. (Marshall, *Brown Girl* 14)

The rest of the examples come from later works; all of the speakers are adult females who either style-shift regularly or are Vernacular speakers. Note the examples 5 and 6 use *cuss/curse* in combination with other terms:

5. *Holler and cuss* at you at the same time as he'd be trying to deceive you. (S. E. Wright 22)

6. What would they do if parent and child came on the show only to *curse out and insult* each other? (Walker, "Everyday Use" 2367)

7. Yeah, so how come he tip his hat to Sula? How come he don't *curse* her? (Morrison, *Sula* 117)

Chastise

The next two examples come from early works; the first female is a Standard speaker; the second, a Vernacular speaker:

1. And my master, having no pity for my sufferings from this cause, rendered them far more intolerable, by *chastising* me for not being able to move so fast as he wished me. (M. Prince 10)

2. Naw, you ain't tried tuh *chesstize* [chastise] 'im nothing uh de kind. (Hurston, *Jonah's* 3)

The next example comes from a work written in the 1980s but set in an earlier time; the female style-shifts regularly:

3. I'll *chastise* her. You leave her alone. (Morrison, *Beloved* 45)

The last example in this set comes from a later work, and the female is a young, adult Standard speaker:

4. Her gaze was severe, as if she were about to *chastise* me for something. (Lee 84)

Both Standard and Vernacular speakers in later works use terms such as *remarks*, *fuss*, *signify*, and *testify*.

Remarks

The first two examples come from early works. The first female is an older Vernacular speaker; the second, an adult Standard speaker:

1. Them *remarks* o' yourn is suttingly curious. (Hopkins, "Hagar's" 178)
2. so frank and unreserved were her *remarks* that "confidences" was hardly the name to apply to them. (Fauset, *Plum* 107)

The rest of the examples came from later works; example 3 comes from a young girl; example 5 comes from an older female. All style-shift occasionally:

3. I kept my *remarks* to myself. (Taylor, *Circle* 184)
4. Leafing through all of the bittersweet, acidly polite, smart *remarks* I had stored up for just such an occasion, I stared at her. (Guy, *Friends* 43)
5. they made some nasty *remarks* about this little colored girl and her underpants. (Delany et al. 15)

Fuss

The term *fuss*, meaning "to complain or fret" (Stein & Urdang 358), is used in later works by both Standard and Vernacular speakers. In the following examples, the first example comes from a Vernacular speaker in a work set in an earlier time but written in the 1980s. The other two examples come from later works. The female in example 2 is a young Vernacular speaker, and the third female is a Standard speaker; both style-shift regularly:

1. My mama, she *fuss*. (Walker, *Purple* 11)
2. My first impression was to toss the dress in a chair, but knowing the *fussing* that was sure to come, I was about to hang it up. (Taylor, *Circle* 26)
3. It would only start an argument and she already had enough to *fuss* about. (Briscoe 38)

Signify

In the following two examples, the terms *signifying* and *signified* are used to imply that one speaker is employing indirection to make a negative comment about another person. Both of the females are young girls. The first speaker is a Vernacular speaker:

1. Sukie's face turned red. "You *signifying* something bad about me?" (Meriwether 175)
2. So much of life was white, except when I returned to York Street and somebody like Mary Alice, who lived down the street, snidely "*signified*" at me coming home from school or a ballet lesson.
   "Look at her!" Mary Alice might whisper loudly at her cronies as I passed by. "She must think she cute. She ain't poot." (Brown 33)

Testify

The term *testify,* meaning "to serve as evidence or proof" (Stein & Urdang 896), is used by Standard speakers and those who style shift-regularly. All of the following speakers are adults:

1. I can *testify* to that. (Naylor, *The Women* 68)

2. You right bout that, Betsey. I could *testify* on that one. (Shange, *Betsey* 83)

3. Over the click of steaming curlers, they *testified*, embellishing the fabric of their lives. (Golden, *Migrations* 24)

Other Examples

Other examples of terms used by Vernacular speakers in later works include *bad talk, rap, straighten out, talking back, mealy-moufin', talking trash,* and *lip*:

1. Ain't never heard no *bad talk* 'bout her. (Taylor, *Circle* 180)

2. Heff. No *raps* from the roots today. I need the present. (Sanchez, "Just Don't" 284)

3. remember having to *straighten out* some no good with a terrible mouth. (Shange, *Betsey* 86)

4. Hush your mouth gal. Don't *talk back* to me. (S. E. Wright 80)

5. You *mealy-moufin'* round cause you skeered tuh *talk back tuh* Rush Beasley. (Hurston, *Jonah's* 6)

6. You mean to tell me, you on your death bed, and you still *talking trash* to me? (Bolton 238)

7. So the matron come trottin down the aisle with her chunky self flashin that flashlight dead in your eye so you can give her some *lip*. (Bambara, "Gorilla" 14)

Standard speakers used terms such as: *confess, chatter, comment, confide,* and *quibble*. All but the first example of the following come from later works. The last female is an older woman:

8. I must *confess* that this wind is a little too much for me. (Kelley-Hawkins 23)

9. She should be humble at all costs, listen to Mrs. Woods *chatter* about the exalted realm of education. (Dove, *Ivory* 109)

10. I made no *comment* just kept on walking. (Taylor, *Circle* 94)

11. He didn't *comment*; he just smiled. (Morrison, *Jazz* 207)

12. Anything that happens, you can *confide* in Mama. (Delany et al. 70)

The last example occurrs in a conversation between two older female friends:

13. Who's going to *quibble* with you over a few years one way or the other. (Jackson 398)

Summary

The preceding examples represent a very small sample of the metalanguage that appears in the works of African American female writers. One reason that there are so few is that I restricted my discussion to only those forms used by the female characters or by first-person narrators. Another reason is that these forms appear only in very restricted contexts—usually in conversations between females who know each other well or in passages taken from first-person narratives in which the writer adopts a conversational tone. Still, within this set there are some interesting patterns. One pattern that I find is the persistence of the older term *chastise*; both Standard and Vernacular speakers use this term, which appears in both early and later works. I also noted that some Standard speakers use terms that are normally associated with Vernacular speakers (*playing the dozens*; *signifying*; *laughing*; *talking*). Finally, the female characters use metalanguage in ways consistent with patterns that I've discussed in other chapters: the Standard speakers use more of the Standard or dictionary definition terms (*testify, chatter, comment, confide, quibble*), while the Vernacular speakers and those who style-shift regularly use more regional, ethnic, and informal terms (*loud talk*; *bad talk*; *talking back*; *talking trash*; *mealy-moufin'*; *shout*; *lip*; *rap*; *straighten out*).

USING LANGUAGE

Many sociolinguists believe that descriptions of most language use can be placed along a continuum between language used to show solidarity or intimacy, on one end, and language used to reflect power or status, on the other. In the passages that follow, I describe how female characters in the works that I examined demonstrate language use at both ends of the continuum.

In the following sections, I'll reverse the usual order of discussion and describe language used to reflect power or status first.

Language Used to Show Power or Status

African American female characters in the works that I examined often use language in ways that indicate feelings and opinions about themselves or others. In some cases they use this language in conversational interactions; in other cases they use monologues or narratives to express themselves.

Showing Off

The following example below comes from an early work by Hurston and shows young children engaged in conversation. The main speakers are little girls who are showing off to impress a young male whom they have just met; all are Vernacular speakers. Features include teasing, boasting, name-calling, and smart talk:

One little girl with bright black eyes came and stood before him, arms akimbo. She must have been a leader, for several more came and stood back of her. She looked him over boldly from his tousled brown head to his bare white feet. Then she said, "Well, folks! Where you reckon dis big yaller bee-stung nigger come from?" . . .

"Ah think he musta come from over de Big Creek. 'Tain't nothin' lak dat on dis side," the little tormenter went on. Then she looked right into his eyes and laughed. All the others laughed. John laughed too.
"Dat's whar Ah come from sho 'nuff," he admitted.
"Whut you doin' over heah, then?"
"Come tuh see iffen Ah could git uh job uh work.". . .

"Kin yuh tell whar Marse Alf Peason live at?"
The little girl snorted, "Marse Alf! Don't y'all folkses over de creek know slavery time is over? 'Tain't no mo' Marse Alf, no Marse Charlie, nor Marse Tom neither. Folks whut wuz borned in slavery time go 'round callin' dese white folks Marse but we been born since freedom. We calls 'em Mister. Dey don't own nobody no mo'."
"Sho don't," the budding girl behind the little talker chimed in. She threw herself akimbo also and came walking out hippily from behind the other, challenging John to another appraisal of her person.
"Ah calls 'em anything Ah please," said another girl and pulled her apron a little tight across the body as she advanced towards the fence.
"Aw, naw, yuh don't, Clary," the little black-eyed girl disputed, "youse talkin' at de big gate now. You jus' want somebody tuh notice yuh." (Hurston, *Jonah's* 13–15)

Gossiping

There are many different examples of gossiping, including the classic sequences produced by Hurston's porch sitters in her novel *Their Eyes Were Watching God*. The following example comes from Standard-speaking females in an early work by Larsen. Two females are engaged in conversation; one of them is condemning the behavior of a third female. Features include female adjectives and adverbs, expressive language, name-calling, and indirection:

Anne had rage in her eyes. Her voice trembled as she took Helga aside to whisper: "There's your Dr. Anderson over there, with Audrey Denney."
"Yes, I saw him. She's lovely. Who is she?"
"She's Audrey Denney, as I said, and she lives downtown. West Twenty-second Street. Hasn't much use for Harlem any more. It's a wonder she hasn't some white man hanging about. The disgusting creature! I wonder how she inveigled Anderson? But that's Audrey! If there is any desirable man about, trust her to attach him. She ought to be ostracized."
"Why?" asked Helga curiously, noting at the same time that three of the men in their own party had deserted and were now congregated about the offending Miss Denney.
"Because she goes about with white people," came Anne's indignant answer, "and they know she's colored."
"I'm afraid I don't quite see, Anne. Would it be all right if they didn't know she was colored?"
"Now, don't be nasty, Helga. You know very well what I mean." Anne's voice was shaking. . . .

"Why, she gives parties for white and colored people together. And she goes to white people's parties. It's worse than disgusting, it's positively obscene."

"Oh, come, Anne, you haven't been to any of the parties, I know, so how can you be so positive about the matter?"

"No, but I've heard about them. I know people who've been."

"Friends of yours, Anne?"

Anne admitted that they were, some of them.

"Well, then, they can't be so bad. I mean, if your friends sometimes go, can they? Just what goes on that's so terrible?"

"Why, they drink, for one thing. Quantities, they say."

"So do we, at the parties here in Harlem," Helga responded. An idiotic impulse seized her to leave the place, Anne's presence, then, forever. But of course she couldn't. It would be foolish, and so ugly.

"And the white men dance with the colored women. Now you know, Helga Crane, that can mean only one thing." Anne's voice was trembling with cold hatred. As she ended, she made a little clicking noise with her tongue, indicating an abhorrence too great for words.

"Don't the colored men dance with the white women, or do they sit about, impolitely, while the other men dance with their women?" inquired Helga very softly, and with a slowness approaching almost to insolence. Anne's insinuations were too revolting. She had a slightly sickish feeling, and a flash of anger touched her. She mastered it and ignored Anne's inadequate answer.

"It's the principle of the thing that I object to. You can't get round the fact that her behavior is outrageous, treacherous, in fact. That's what's the matter with the Negro race. They won't stick together. She certainly ought to be ostracized. I've nothing but contempt for her, as has every other self-respecting Negro." ("Quicksand" 60–61)

Advising

In the next example from a later work by Kincaid, a young West Indian female shows her mother's style of advising. The passage in italics represents the speakers comments and questions to her mother. Features include directives, instructions, suggestions, warnings, insults, threats, and teasing:

Wash the white clothes on Monday and put them on the stone heap; wash the color clothes on Tuesday and put them on the clothesline to dry; . . . always eat your food in such a way that it won't turn someone else's stomach; on Sundays try to walk like a lady and not like the slut you are so bent on becoming; . . . you mustn't speak to wharf-rat boys, not even to give directions; . . . this is how you sweep a whole house; this is how you sweep a yard; this is how you smile to someone you don't like too much; this is how you smile to someone you don't like at all; this is how you smile to someone you like completely; . . . be sure to wash every day, even if it is with your own spit; don't squat down to play marbles—you are not a boy, you know; . . . this is how to love a man, and if this doesn't work there are other ways, and if they don't work don't feel too bad about giving up; this is how to spit up in the air if you feel like it, and this is how to move quick so that it doesn't fall on you; . . . always squeeze bread to make sure it's fresh; *but what if the baker won't let me feel the bread?*; you mean to say that after all you are really going to be the kind of woman who the baker won't let near the bread? (Kincaid, *At the Bottom* 2–5)

Fussing

In a later work by Morrison, a young girl named Pecola has been placed in the home of one of the "good" women of the community while some of her turbulent family life is being straightened out. Pecola likes a special mug with Shirley Temple on it, and she continually drinks milk from it so that she can look at the star's face. In the following passage the woman's daughter reports her mother's fussing. The woman is a Vernacular speaker who style-shifts regularly. Features include indirection, word play, hyperbole, expressive language, softened expletives, repetition, and rhetorical questions:

Three quarts of milk. That's what was *in* that icebox yesterday. Three whole quarts. Now they ain't none. Not a drop. I don't mind folks coming in and getting what they want, but three quarts of milk! What the devil does anybody need with three quarts of milk? . . .

I don't know what I'm suppose to be running here, a charity ward, I guess. Time for me to get out of the *giving* line and get in the *getting* line. I guess I ain't sup*posed* to have nothing. I'm sup*posed* to end up in the poorhouse. Look like nothing I do is going to keep me out of there. Folks just spend all their time trying to figure out ways to send *me* to the poorhouse. I got about as much business with another mouth to feed as a cat has with side pockets. As if I don't have trouble enough trying to feed my own and keep out the poorhouse, now I got something else in here that's just going to *drink* me on in there. Well, naw, she ain't. Not long as I got strength in my body and a tongue in my head. There's a limit to everything. I ain't got nothing to just throw *away*. Don't *no*body need *three* quarts of milk. (*Bluest* 22–24)

Getting Acquainted

In the next passage in this section, Virginia, an art teacher, arrives at her new school and is greeted by her principal, Mrs. Peck. These Standard-speaking females are meeting for the first time, and they spend the first few minutes in light, pleasant conversation. Features: female adjectives and adverbs, expressive language, informal language, questions, laughter, and politeness routines:

Mrs. Peck was a vigorous pepper-haired woman who had somehow managed to retain a casual manner without losing an ounce of efficiency. "Miss King, you're early!" she said, and held out a hand. "The entire school is delighted you could join us. I understand this is your hometown."
Virginia nodded. "Yes. We moved to Arizona when I was in fourth grade."
"We never forget those early moves, do we? When I was coming out of anesthesia after my second child was born, my husband claims I begged not to leave my friends in Pittsburgh. We had moved from Pittsburgh to Akron when I was twelve." She chuckled. "Well, enough of my past. Now, *yours* has been busy: Dean's List, Thespian Society, Puppets & People Repertory Theater—that must have been exciting!"
"Yes," Virginia replied, stifling a yawn. They both laughed.
"You must be pooped," said Mrs. Peck.

"I'm not as pooped as I am contrite. I should have called when I knew I might arrive early." (Dove, *Ivory* 18)

Language Used to Reflect Solidarity

The majority of the female characters in the following passages are adults. I found examples in both early and later works of females interacting in an intimate, informal manner when talking to other females who were either close friends or relatives. Following are a few representative examples of how these females use language when engaged in conversational interactions variously called talking/chatting/running mouth/laughing and talking.

Language features that these passages have in common are affectionate teasing, informal language, compliments, jokes, word play, slang, verbal dueling, signifying, endearments, hyperbole, regionalisms, and laughter.

The first passage comes from an early work by Hurston. Pheoby Watson is visiting her friend Janie, who has returned to the town after a long absence; both of the females are Vernacular speakers:

When she arrived at the place, Pheoby Watson didn't go in by the front gate and down the palm walk to the front door. She walked around the fence corner and went in the intimate gate with her heaping plate of mulatto rice. Janie must be round that side.

She found her sitting on the steps of the back porch with the lamps all filled and the chimneys cleaned.

"Hello Janie, how you comin'?"

"Aw, pretty good, Ah'm tryin' to soak some uh de tiredness and de dirt outa mah feet." She laughed a little.

"Ah see you is. Gal, you sho looks *good*. You looks like youse yo' own daughter." They both laughed. "Even wid dem overhalls on, you shows yo' womanhood."

"G'wan! G'wan! You must think Ah brought yuh some thin'. When Ah ain't brought home a thing but mahself."

"Dat's a gracious plenty. Yo' friends wouldn't want nothin' better."

"Ah takes dat flattery offa you, Pheoby, 'cause Ah know it's from de heart." Janie extended her hand.

"Good Lawd, Pheoby! ain't you never goin' tuh gimme dat lil rations you brought me? Ah ain't had a thing on mah stomach today exceptin' mah hand." They both laughed easily. "Give it here and have a seat."

"Ah knowed you'd be hongry. No time to be huntin' stove wood after dark. Mah mulatto rice ain't so good dis time. Not enough bacon grease, but Ah reckon it'll kill hongry."

"Ah'll tell you in a minute," Janie said lifting the cover. "Gal, it's too good! you switches a mean fanny round in a kitchen."

"Aw, dat ain't much to eat, Janie. But Ah'm liable to have something sho nuff good tomorrow, 'cause you done come."

Janie ate heartily and said nothing. The vari-colored loud dust that the sun had stirred up in the sky was settling by slow degrees.

"Here, Pheoby, take yo' ole plate. Ah ain't got a bit of use for a empty dish. Dat grub sho come in handy."

Pheoby laughed at her friend's rough joke. "Youse just as crazy as you ever was."

"Hand me dat wash-rag on dat chair by you, honey. Lemme scrub mah feet." She took the cloth and rubbed vigorously. Laughter came to her from the big road.

"Well, Ah see Mouth-Almighty is still sittin' in de same place. And Ah reckon they got *me* up in they mouth now." (Hurston, *Eyes* 14–16)

The next passage comes from an early work by Kelley-Hawkins and shows the friendly, informal banter of Standard-speaking females who are good friends. The conversation takes place on a train as they begin a vacation together:

"Dear me, Vera, do tell me if there is a smooch on my face," exclaimed Jessie, impatiently, as the four girls entered the car and stopped at two seats near the door. "That great lummax of a man brushed his dirty old gossamer right against my cheek."

Vera turned with her hand on the half-turned seat. "Nothing there but roses, Jess," she said, and over went the seat.

"You'll spoil the child Vera," said Garnet, settling her plump little form comfortable upon the seat facing Allie and Jessie, and making room for Vera beside her.

"Child!" pouted Jessie. "What do you call yourself, Granny?"

"I am three years your senior," replied Garnet, calmly. "And therefore feel responsible for your behavior while away from home."

"H'm. You be responsible for your own behavior and I'll look out for mine. Hey, Allie?"

Vera laughed outright. Allie smiled her sweet, pretty smile and threw Jessie's gossamer up into the rack with her own.

"My sakes!" exclaimed Jessie. "I have just this moment thought of it, Allie! We are going off with two sedate school-marms. We'll have to behave or we'll have curtain-lectures read to us every night."

"Girls who are seniors in the High School should never OBLIGE any one to deliver curtain-lectures to them." . . .

"Now look her, girls," said Garnet, in her matter-of-fact voice. "Suppose we give our tickets up to one, and let her keep them until we need them. What do you say?"

"Depends upon whom that one will be. If it is my sister Garnet Maria, Jessie, says 'No thanks'; but if it is Vera—" said Jessie.

"Yes, let Vera keep them," said Allie, passing her's [*sic*] over.

"I didn't have the least idea of offering myself as banker for the party," said Garnet. "I'm careless about such things and know it. Others are careless and don't know it; or if they know it, wont acknowledge it." ("That's me," murmured Jessie, making up a face.) "Besides my reticule is about full and I've no outside pocket." ("Have you an inside one with fifteen cents in it?" asked Jessie innocently.) Garnet passed over this slangy question as being unworthy of notice. "Vera, yours has a nice long pocket with a clasp. Do you dare to take the responsibility?" "Yes, and I'll add to the responsibility by keeping your purses for you if you would like to have me. We'll call it the bank," said Vera, opening her reticule to show how much room there was in it.

In flew Jessie's dainty little purse before the words were hardly spoken. The silver clasp struck against a bottle.

"Got a 'shothecary pop' in there?" asked Jessie, bending over and peering in.

Vera dashed a fine spray of violet water into the pretty, laughing face. Jessie sprang back, a little startled, then leaned forward again, shut her eyes and puckered up her rosy little mouth.

"What you might call a 'mute appeal,' " said Vera, with a laugh, and dashed a second spray into Jessie's face. Then she put the bottle back into her reticule and closed it with a decided little snap. "No more this time, Jasmine. Perhaps you'll need a shower of it before we get to Cottage City. It looks as if it might be decidedly rough on the water."

Jessie pushed her white tennis cap on the back of her dark head, and nestled down in the corner of the seat. "I hope I shan't be sick," she murmured. Then she commenced to laugh. "But I bet a cookie Net will. She ate the biggest breakfast you ever saw. I kept telling her to stop, but she seemed to think she must either eat or die—one of the two." (*Four Girls* 12–16)

A later work by Briscoe contains the following passage. It shows a conversation between sisters who are at a gathering at their parents' house; the females are Standard speakers who style-shift:

"This house has a way of making *me* feel old," Beverly said, looking around. "Seems like eons ago that we all lived here."

"It was eons ago," Evelyn said. "Do you even remember when we moved here from D.C.?"

"Of course I do. I remember you two carrying on like the end of the world was coming."

"It was," Charmaine said. "Moving out to Maryland with all those white people."

"It was like moving to a foreign country," Evelyn said. "There were a lot fewer black people out here then. You remember the first day of school?" she asked Charmaine. "It was awful. We were the only black people in most of our classes."

"What about gym class?" Charmaine said. "Those white chicks couldn't understand why we didn't wash our hair every time we showered after gym. Or why we put so much lotion all over our arms and legs after wards. Evelyn started waiting until she got out of class to sneak into the girls room and put the lotion on."

"I did not."

"Yes, you did. Me, I got that big old bottle of Jergen's out and slapped that stuff all over my ashy body right in front of their faces."

Charmaine and Evelyn giggled. "She made a spectacle of herself just so they'd have something to gossip about after class," Evelyn said.

"It was harder for me" Charmaine said. "You just became a bookworm, Evelyn. Me, I went from getting B's and C's to C's and D's."

"You wouldn't apply yourself," Evelyn said. "Too busy chasing boys. The few you could find, anyway." Beverly giggled. (*Sisters* 66–68)

The next passage comes from a later work by Bambara. The females are in a beauty parlor, and they discuss a variety of topics. They are adult Vernacular speakers who style-shift:

"No use you trying to ig [ignore] me, Honey," Bertha says real loud. "Cause I'm Mary's last customer. We got all night."

"Saw Frieda coming out of the drugstore," somebody is saying. "Package looked mighty interesting."

Everybody cracking up, Bertha too. I ease my head back and under the comb scratching up dandruff.

"Obviously Ted is going on the road again and Frieda gonna pack one of her famous box snacks."

"Got the recipe for the oatmeal cookies richeah [right here]," someone saying. "One part rolled oats, one long drip of sorghum, fistful of raisins, and a laaaarge dose of saltpeter."

"Salt pete-er salt pete-er," somebody sing through the nose, outdoing Dizzy.

"Whatchu say!"

"Betcha there'll be plenty straaange mashed potatoes on the table tonight."

The young girl's rubbin is too hard in the part and the oil too hot. But she so busy cracking up, she don't notice my ouchin.

"Saltpetertaters, what better dish to serve a man going on the road for three days. Beats calling him every hour on the half-hour telling him to take a cold shower."

"Best serve him with a summons for being so downright ugly. Can't no woman be really serious about messin' with Ted, he too ugly."

"Some that looks ugly . . ." Couldn't catch the rest of it, but followed the giggling well enough after what sounded like a second of silence.

"Mary"—someone was breathless with laughter—"when you and the sisters gonna give another one of them balls?"

"Giiiirl," howls Bertha. "Wasn't that ball a natural ball?" ("Witchbird" 182)

The last passage comes from a later work by Naylor. The speakers are two older females who are sisters. They discuss various things as they prepare for the visit of a niece. They are Vernacular speakers who style-shift:

"Baby Girl is coming in today."

"Well, Lord. It's gonna be good to see my child. I better get her room dusted out and ready. And she thought she was catching the train up there tomorrow night—even wrote and said to meet her at the station Tuesday morning."

"It's the airplane though, at that field beyond the bridge."

"Oh, no. Now what put it in her mind to do that? I never did trust them things—they ain't natural. If I can get my hands on Buzzard, I'll have him go pick her up."

"If I get *my* hands on him. I'm gonna wring his scrawny neck. Ain't seen a speck of that honey he's supposed to bring me. Having the last in my tea this minute."

"Sister, waiting on Buzzard is like waiting on Judgment Day. How Old Arthur [arthritis] doing you this morning?"

"Now, he's dependable as ever. Only man I been able to roll out of bed with since I passed my seventies."

"Stop your badness. I got another poultice for you, found some black cohosh growing down by Ruby's. Soon as it's dry good, I'll make you up a nice plaster."

"Hope it ain't like that other mess that burns so."

"Miranda, you gotta feel it if it's gonna help."

"Felt Old Arthur this morning, and he sure don't help. Just a poking me in my back, poking in my left hip. You think he gonna get it right one day and start poking in my—"

"Uh, uh—let me get off this line before I lose my religion. Listen, bring me over a batch of that dried rosemary you got out at the other place to season this pork shoulder—Baby girl loves herself some roast pork. And a good half-dozen eggs—I'll do up one jelly and one coconut cake. We only got two weeks to fatten her up—know she gonna come dragging in here puny as the law allows—'less you wanna make the jelly and I'll do two coconuts. Your jelly cakes always turn out better than mine."

"I ain't making her nothing, 'cause she's too fresh. You go spend all day over a hot stove in this heat—and all my eggs is for setting now."

"A good half dozen now, Miranda. And did you know it's almost nine o'clock?"

"Dear Lord, let me get off this phone. See you in the by-and-by." (*Mama Day* 36–37)

SUMMARY

In this final section we see how some of the features discussed in other chapters are used in longer passages. The speakers come from early and later works; they are very young and very old; they come from a variety of social class backgrounds, and they engage in a variety of interactions. This section represents only a very small part of the language use appearing in the speech communities described by African American female writers. But the passages serve the purpose of showing the richness and variety of talk that can be found in African American speech communities.

Bibliography

Abrahams, R. D. (1975). Negotiating respect: Patterns of presentation among black women. In Clair R. Farrar (Ed.), *Women and folklore* (pp. 58–80). Austin: University of Texas Press.

Albert, O.V.R. (1988). *The house of bondage or Charlotte Brooks and other slaves.* New York: Oxford University Press.

Anderson, C., et al. (1983). Black talk on television: A constructivist approach to viewers' perceptions of "BEV" in "Roots II." *Journal of Multilingual and Multicultural Development 6* (23), 181–195.

Andersson, L., & Trudgill, P. (1992). *Bad language.* New York: Penguin.

Angelou, M. (1986). *All God's children need traveling shoes.* New York: Random House.

Angelou, M. (1993). Foreword. In P. Bell-Scott et al. (Eds.), *Double stitch: Black women write about mothers & daughters* (pp. xi–xii). New York: HarperCollins.

Ansa, T. M. (1989). *Baby of the family.* New York: Harcourt Brace.

Ansa, T. M. (1995). Willie Bea and Jaybird. In C. H. Rowell (Ed.), *Ancestral house: The black short story in the Americas and Europe.* Boulder, CO: Westview Press.

Arkin, M., & Shollar, B. (Eds.). (1989). *Longman anthology of world literature by women: 1875–1975.* New York: Longman.

Bambara, T. C. (1981). Basement. In *Gorilla, my love* (pp. 139–147). New York: Random House.

Bambara, T. C. (1981). Gorilla my love. In *Gorilla, my love* (pp. 13–20). New York: Random House.

Bambara, T. C. (1981). *Gorilla, my love.* New York: Random House.

Bambara, T. C. (1981). Happy birthday. In *Gorilla, my love* (pp. 61–65). New York: Random House.

Bambara, T. C. (1981). The Johnson girls. In *Gorilla, my love* (pp. 163–177). New York: Random House.

Bambara, T. C. (1981). The lesson. In *Gorilla, my love* (pp. 85–95). New York: Random House.

Bambara, T. C. (1981). Mississippi ham rider. In *Gorilla, my love*. (pp. 47–57). New York: Random House.

Bambara, T. C. (1981). Playin with Punjab. In *Gorilla, my love* (pp. 69–75). New York: Random House.

Bambara, T. C. (1981). Raymond's run. In *Gorilla, my love* (pp. 23–32). New York: Random House.

Bambara, T. C. (1981). *The salt eaters*. New York: Vintage Books.

Bambara, T. C. (1982). Christmas eve at Johnson's drugs n goods. In *The seabirds are still alive* (pp. 187–208). New York: Vintage Books.

Bambara, T. C. (1982). Medley. In *The seabirds are still alive* (pp. 103–124). New York: Vintage Books.

Bambara, T. C. (1982). *The seabirds are still alive*. New York: Vintage Books.

Bambara, T. C. (1982). Witchbird. In *The seabirds are still alive* (pp. 166–186). New York: Vintage Books.

Baugh, J. (1983). *Black street speech: Its history, structure, and survival*. Austin: University of Texas Press.

Bell-Scott, P., Guy-Sheftall, B., Royster, J. J., Sims-Wood, J., Decosta-Willis, M., & Fultz, L. P. (Eds.). (1991). *Double stitch: Black women write about mothers & daughters*. New York: HarperCollins.

Birtha, B. (1990). In the life. In J. Nestle & N. Holoch (Eds.), *Women on women: An anthology of American lesbian short fiction* (pp. 51–65). New York: Penguin.

Bland, E. T. (1994). *Gone quiet*. New York: Penguin Group.

Bolton, R. (1994). *Gal: A true life*. New York: Harcourt Brace.

Brent, L. (1973). *Incidents in the life of a slave girl*. New York: Harcourt Brace Jovanovich.

Briscoe, C. (1994). *Sisters & lovers*. New York: Ballantine.

Brown, E. (1992). *A taste of power: A black woman's story*. New York: Doubleday.

Brown-Guillory, E. (Ed.). (1990). *Wines in the wilderness: Plays by African-American women from the Harlem Renaissance to the present*. New York: Praeger.

Brown, R., & Ford, M. (1961). Address in American English. In D. Hymes, *Language in culture and society: A reader in linguistics and anthropology* (pp. 234–244). New York: Harper & Row.

Brown, R., & Gilman, A. (1960). The pronouns of power and solidarity. In P. P. Giglioli (Ed.), *Language and social context* (pp. 252–282). Baltimore: Penguin.

Cade, T. (1970). *The black woman: An anthology*. New York: Penguin Group.

Campbell, B. M. (1989). *Sweet summer: Growing up with and without my dad*. New York: Ballantine. Reprinted 1990 by arrangement with G. P. Putnam's Sons, New York.

Chaika, E. (1982). *Language: The social mirror*. Rowley, MA: Newbury House.

Chapman, A. (1968). *Black voices*. New York: New American Library.

Childress, A. (Ed.). (1971). *Black scenes*. New York: Zenith.

Childress, A. (1986). Wedding band: A love/hate story in black and white. In M. B. Wilkerson (Ed.), *9 plays by black women* (pp. 75–133). New York: New American Library.

Clair, M. (1994). *Rattlebone*. New York: Penguin.

Clark, V. P., Eschholz, P. A., & Rosa, A. F. (Eds.), *Language: Introductory readings*. New York: St. Martin's.

Clarke, J. H. (Ed.). (1966). *American Negro short stories*. New York: Hill & Wang.

Cleage, P. (1991). Lessons. In P. Bell-Scott et al. (Eds.), *Double stitch: Black women write about mothers & daughters* (pp. 71–73). New York: HarperCollins.

Coates, J. (1986). *Women, men, and language: A sociolinguistic account of sex differences in language*. New York: Longman.

Cohane, M.-E. (1985). Style in the novels of William Carleton. *Dissertation Abstracts International, 46* 230A.

Coleman, W. (1991). Closets and keepsakes. In P. Bell-Scott et al. (Eds.), *Double stitch: Black women write about mothers & daughters* (pp. 21–23). New York: HarperCollins.

Collins, K. (1986). The brothers. In M. B. Wilkerson (Ed.), *9 plays by black women* (pp. 299–346). New York: New American Library.

Cooper, G. C. (1993). Language in Morrison's novels. *MAWA Review 8* (1), 27–31.

Cooper, J. C. (1986). *Homemade love*. New York: St. Martin's.

Cooper, J. C. (1987). *Some soul to keep*. New York: St. Martins.

Cooper, J. C. (1992). *Family*. New York: Anchor.

Courtney, A. E., & Lockeretz, S. W. (1971, February). Women's place: An analysis of roles portrayed by women in magazine advertisements. *Journal of Marketing Research 8*, 92–95.

Courtney, A. E., and T. W. Whipple. (1974). Women in t.v. commercials. *Journal of Communication 25* (2), 110–118.

Dandridge, R. B. (1992). *Black women's blues: A literary anthology*. New York: Maxwell McMillan International.

Daniel, J. L. (Ed.). (1974). *Black communication: Dimensions of research and instruction*. New York: Speech Communication Association.

DeCosta-Willis, M. (1991). Smoothing the tucks in father's linen: The women of Cedar Hill. In P. Bell-Scott et al. (Eds.), *Double stitch: Black women write about mothers and daughters* (pp. 131–138). New York: HarperCollins.

Dee, R. (1989). Aunt Zurletha. In L. Goss & M. E. Barnes (Eds.), *Talk that talk: An anthology of African-American storytelling* (pp. 278–283). New York: Simon & Schuster.

De Klerk, V. (1992). How taboo are taboo words for girls?" *Language in society (21)*, 291–303.

Delany, S. L., Delany, A. E., & Hearth, A. H. (1993). *Having our say: The Delany sisters' first 100 years*. New York: Dell.

DeVeaux, A. (1980). Remember him a outlaw. In M. H. Washington (Ed.), *Midnight birds: Stories of contemporary black women writers* (pp. 109–120). New York: Anchor Press/Doubleday.

DeVeaux, A. (1986). The tapestry. In M. B. Wilkerson (Ed.), *9 plays by black women* (pp. 141–195). New York: New American Library.

DeVeaux, A. (1991). Adventures of the dread sisters. In M. H. Washington (Ed.), *Memory of kin: Stories about family by black writers* (pp. 305–312). New York: Doubleday.

Dillard, J. L. (1972). *Black English: Its history and usage in the United States*. New York: Random House.

Doty, K. L. (1984). Fiction into drama: A pragmatic analysis of dramatic dialogue in adaptations. *Dissertation Abstracts International (45:5)* 1383A.

Dove, R. (1985). *Fifth Sunday*. Lexington: University of Kentucky Press.

Dove, R. (1992). *Through the ivory gate: A novel*. New York: Random House.

Eble, C. C. (1975). Etiquette books as linguistic authority. Papers from the Linguistic Association of Canada and United States Forum. University of Toronto, Aug. 3–7.

Erlich, H. (1973). *The Social Psychology of Predjudice.* Summarized in Barrie Thorne and Nancy Henley (Eds.), *Language and Sex: Difference and Dominance.* Rowley, MA: Newbury House, 1975.

Farb, P. (1973). *Word play: What happens when people talk.* New York: Knopf.

Fasold, R. (1984). *The sociolinguistics of society.* New York: Basil Blackwell.

Fasold, R. (1990). *The sociolinguistics of language.* Cambridge: Basil Blackwell.

Fauset, J. (1969). *Comedy: American style.* College Park, MD: McGrath.

Fauset, J. R. (1990). *Plum bun: A novel without a moral.* Boston: Beacon.

Fischer, J. L. (1964). Social influences on choice of linguistic variant. In D. Hymes (Ed.), *Language in culture and society* (pp. 483–488). New York: Harper & Row.

Francis, W. N. (1983). *Dialectology: An introduction.* New York: Longman.

Gaines, P. (1994). *Laughing in the dark: From colored girl to woman of color—a journey from prison to power.* New York: Doubleday.

Gates, H. L., Jr. (Ed.). (1988). *Collected black women's narratives.* New York: Oxford University Press.

Gates, H. L., Jr. (Ed.). (1988). *The magazine novels of Pauline Hopkins.* New York: Oxford University Press.

Gates, H. L., Jr. (Ed.). (1988). *Six women's slave narratives.* New York: Oxford University Press.

Gates, H. L., Jr. (Ed.). (1988). *Spiritual narratives.* New York: Oxford University Press.

Giglioli, P. P. (1972). *Language and social context: Selected readings.* Baltimore: Penguin.

Gilbert, S. M., & Gubar, J. (1985). *The Norton anthology of literature by women.* New York: W. W. Norton.

Giles, H., & Powesland, P. F. (1975). *Speech style and social evaluation.* London: Academic Press.

Giovanni, N. (1989). Don't have a baby till you read this. In L. Goss & M. E. Barnes (Eds.), *Talk that talk: An anthology of African-American storytelling* (pp. 263–277). New York: Simon & Schuster.

Glowka, A. W., & Lance, D. M. (1993). *Language variation in North American English: Research and teaching.* New York: Modern Language Association.

Golden, M. (1983). *Migrations of the heart.* New York: Ballantine.

Golden, M. (1986). *A woman's place.* New York: Ballantine.

Goss, L., & Barnes, M. E. (Eds.). (1989). *Talk that talk: An anthology of African-American storytelling.* New York: Simon & Schuster.

Graddol, D., & Swann, J. (1989). *Gender voices.* New York: Language & Ethnic Group.

Guy, R. (1973). *The friends.* New York: Bantam.

Guy, R. (1983). *A measure of time.* New York: Bantam.

Hacker, D. (1995). *A writer's reference.* Boston: Bedford.

Hall, E. T. (1959). *The silent language.* Garden City, NY: Anchor Press/Doubleday.

Hansberry, L. (1971). A raisin in the sun. In A. Childress (Ed.), *Black scenes* (pp. 99–110). Garden City, NY: Doubleday.

Harper, F. E. W. (1988). *Iola Leroy, or shadows uplifted.* New York: Oxford University Press.

Heath, S. B. (1983). *Ways with words: Language, life, and work in communities and classrooms.* New York: Cambridge University Press.

Hill, D. (1990). *Rooms of the heart.* Silver Spring, MD: Odyssey.

Holloway, K.F.C. (1991). The Thursday ladies. In P. Bell-Scott et al. (Eds.), *Double stitch: Black women write about mothers & daughters* (pp. 27–31). New York: HarperCollins.

Holmes, J. (1992). *An introduction to sociolinguistics*. New York: Longman.

Hopkins, P. (1988). Hagar's daughter: A story of southern caste prejudice. In H. L. Gates Jr. (Ed.), *The magazine novels of Pauline Hopkins* (pp. 1–284). New York: Oxford University Press.

Hopkins, P. (1988). Of one blood or, the hidden self. In H. L. Gates Jr., (Ed.), *The magazine novels of Pauline Hopkins* (pp. 441–621). New York: Oxford University Press.

Huddleston, R. (1988). *English grammar: An outline*. New York: Cambridge University Press.

Hudson, B. H. (1984). A descriptive study of male and female speech stereotypes on selected television shows with predominantly black characters. *Dissertation Abstracts International 44* 309A. University Microfilms No. DA8404047.

Hudson, B. H. (1986). A sociolinguistic approach to examining literature. Paper presented at the Annual Meeting of the Language Arts Conference, Montreal, Quebec, Canada, May.

Hudson, B. H. (1993). Sociolinguistic analysis of dialogues and first-person narratives in fiction. In A. W. Glowka & D. M. Lance (Eds.), *Language variation in North American English: Research and teaching* (pp. 28–36). New York: Modern Language Association.

Hughes, G. (1998). *Swearing: A social history of foul language, oaths and profanity in English*. Oxford: Blackwell.

Hughes, S. E. (1992). Expletives of lower working-class women. *Language in society (21)*, 291–303.

Hunter, K. (1966). *The landlord*. New York: Charles Scribner's Sons.

Hurston, Z. N. (1935). *Mules and men*. New York: Harper & Row.

Hurston, Z. N. (1938). *Tell my horses: Voodoo and life in Haiti and Jamaica*. New York: Harper and Row.

Hurston, Z. N. (1978 [1937]). *Their eyes were watching God*. Chicago: University of Illinois Press.

Hurston, Z. N. (1990 [1934]). *Jonah's gourd vine*. New York: Harper & Row.

Hurston, Z. N., & Hughes, L. (1931). *Mule bone: A comedy of Negro life*. New York: HarperCollins.

Hymes, D. (1964). *Culture and society: A reader in linguistics and anthropology*. New York: Harper & Row.

Jackson, E. (1986). Paper dolls. In M. B. Wilkerson (Ed.), *9 plays by black women* (pp. 347–423). New York: New American Library.

Jacobs, J. B. (1990, September). Names, naming, and name calling in practice with families. *Families in Society: The Journal of Contemporary Human Services*, (pp. 415–421).

Jones, A., et al. (1970). Ebony minds, black voices. In T. Cade (Ed.), *The black woman: An anthology* (pp. 180–188). New York: Penguin Group.

Jones, G. (1975). *Corregidora*. New York: Bantam.

Jones, G. (1976). *Eva's man*. Boston: Beacon.

Jones, G. (1977). Jevata. In M. H. Washington (Ed.), *Midnight birds: Stories of contemporary black women writers* (pp. 132–149). Garden City, NY: Anchor Press/Doubleday.

Jones, G. (1980). Asylum. In M. H. Washington (Ed.), *Midnight birds: Stories of contemporary black women writers* (pp. 128–131). Garden City, NY: Anchor Press/Doubleday.

Jones, L., & Neal, L. (Eds.). (1968). *Black fire*. New York: William Morrow.

Kelley, E. D. (1988). *Megda*. New York: Oxford University Press.

Kelley-Hawkins, E. D. (1988). *Four girls at Cottage City*. New York: Oxford University Press.

Key, M. R. (1975). *Male/female language*. Metuchen, NJ: Scarecrow Press.

Kincaid, J. (1978). *At the bottom of the river*. New York: Penguin.

Kincaid, J. (1991). The circling hand. In M. H. Washington (Ed.), *Memory of kin: Stories about family by black writers* (pp. 111–125). New York: Doubleday.

King, Y. D. (1989). Daddy. In L. Goss & M. E. Barnes (Eds.), *Talk that talk: An anthology of African-American storytelling* (pp. 227–229). New York: Simon & Schuster.

Knapp, M. L. (1981). A structure for the analysis of nonverbal communication. In V. P. Clark, P. A. Escholz, & A. F. Rosa (Eds.), *Language: Introductory readings* (pp. 611–623). New York: St. Martin's Press.

Kochman, T. (1972). *Rappin' and stylin' out: Communication in urban black America*. Chicago: University of Illinois Press.

Kramarae, C. (1981). *Women and men speaking: Frameworks for analysis*. Rowley, MA: Newbury House.

Kramer, C. (1974, June). Folklinguistics. *Psychology Today*, 82–85.

Kramer, C. (1976, May). Excessive loquacity: Women's speech as represented in American etiquette books. Unpublished paper summarized in *Women and Language News 2*.

Labov, W. (1972). *Sociolinguistic patterns*. Philadelphia: University of Pennsylvania Press.

Labov, W. (1973). *Language in the inner city*. Philadelphia: University of Pennsylvania Press.

Labov, W. (1981). The study of nonstandard English. In V. P. Clark, A. Escholz, and A. F. Rosa (Eds.), *Language: Introductory readings* (pp. 512–520). New York: St. Martin's Press.

Lakoff, R. (1975). *Language and woman's place*. New York: Harper & Row.

Larison, C. W. (1988). *Silvia Dubois, a biograpfy of the slav who whipt her mistres and gand her fredom*. New York: Oxford University Press.

Larsen, N. (1986). Passing. In D. E. McDowell (Ed.), *Quicksand and passing* (pp. 143–242). New Brunswick, NJ: Rutgers University Press.

Larsen, N. (1986). Quicksand. In D. E. McDowell (Ed.), *Quicksand and passing* (pp. 1–135). New Brunswick, NJ: Rutgers University Press.

Larsen, N. (1989). Sanctuary. In M. Arkin & B. Shollar (Eds.), *Longman anthology of world literature by women* (pp. 320–323). New York: Longman.

Lee, A. (1984). *Sarah Phillips*. New York: Penguin.

Lorde, A. (1982). *Zami: A new spelling of my name*. Freedom, CA: Crossing Press.

Macaulay, R. (1994). *The social art: Language and its uses*. New York: Oxford University Press.

Major, C. (Ed) (1994). *Juba to Jive*. New York: Penguin.

Malmkjaer, K. (1991). *The linguistics encyclopedia*. New York: Routledge.

Marshall, P. (1961). Brooklyn. In W. Martin (Ed.), *We are the stories we tell: The best stories by North American women since 1945* (pp. 77–97). New York: Random House.

Marshall, P. (1981). *Brown girl, brownstones*. New York: Feminist Press.

Marshall, P. (1983). *Praisesong for the widow*. New York: E. P. Dutton.

Marshall, P. (1991). To da-duh, in memoriam. In M. H. Washington (Ed.), *Memory of kin: Stories about family by black writers* (pp. 385–396). New York: Doubleday.

Marshall, P. (1992). *Daughters*. New York: Plume.

Martin, W. (Ed.). (1990). *We are the stories we tell: The best stories by North American women since 1945*. New York: Random House.

Matthews, B. (1977). Voice of Africa in the diaspora. *New Directions 4* (2), 16–19.

Mattison, H. (1988). Louisa Piquet, the octoroon: Or inside views of Southern domestic Life. In H. L. Gates Jr. (Ed.), *Collected black women's narratives* (pp. 1–60). New York: Oxford University Press.

McMillan, T. (1987). *Mama*. New York: Washington Square.

McMillan, T. (1989). *Disappearing acts*. New York: Washington Square.

McMillan, T. (Ed.). (1990). *Breaking ice: An anthology of contemporary African-American fiction*. New York: Penguin Group.

McMillan, T. (1992). *Waiting to exhale*. New York: Simon & Schuster.

Meriwether, L. (1986). *Daddy was a numbers runner*. New York: The Feminist Press.

Meyer, K., et al. (1980, Winter). Women in July Fourth cartoons: A 100-year look. *Journal of Communication 30 (1)*, 21–29.

Meyers, W. E. (1980). Aliens and linguists. *Language study and science fiction*. Athens: University of Georgia.

Mitchell-Kernan C. (1972). *Signifying and marking two Afro-American speech acts*. In T. Kochman (Ed.), *Rappin' and stylin' out: Communication in urban black America* (pp. 315–335). Chicago: University of Illinois Press.

Monroe, M. (1990). The upper room. In T. McMillan (Ed.), *Breaking ice: An anthology of contemporary African-American fiction* (pp. 504–519). New York: Penguin Group.

Morrison, T. (1970). *The bluest eye*. New York: Washington Square.

Morrison, T. (1973). *Sula*. New York: Plume.

Morrison, T. (1977). *Song of Solomon*. New York: Penguin.

Morrison, T. (1981). *Tar baby*. New York: New American Library.

Morrison, T. (1988). *Beloved*. New York: Knopf.

Morrison, T. (1992). *Jazz*. New York: Penguin.

Munson, C. P. (1988). *Cousin Mattie's daddy's sister's people*. [greeting card catalog]. San Francisco: Love, Auntie Cheryl Greetings.

Murray, P. (1987). *Song in a weary throat: An American pilgrimage*. New York: Harper & Row.

Naylor, G. (1980). *The women of Brewster Place*. New York: Penguin.

Naylor, G. (1985). *Linden Hills*. New York: Ticknor & Fields.

Naylor, G. (1988). *Mama day*. New York: Random House.

Nestle, J., & Holoch, N. (Eds.). (1990). *Women on women: An anthology of American lesbian short fiction*. New York: Penguin.

Nilsen, A. P. (1977). Sexism in children's books and elementary teaching materials. In A. P. Nilsen et al. (Eds.), *Sexism and language*. Urbana, IL: National Council of Teachers of English.

Penfield, J. (Ed.). (1987). *Women and language in transition*. New York: State University of New York Press.

Petry, A. (1947). *Country place*. Cambridge, MA: Riverside Press.

Petry, A. (1953). *The narrows*. Boston: Beacon Press.

Prince, M. (1988). The History of Mary Prince. In H. L. Gates Jr. (Ed.), *Six women's slave narratives* (pp. 1–44) New York: Oxford University Press.

Prince, N. (1988). A narrative of the life and travels of Mrs. Nancy Prince. In H. L. Gates Jr. (Ed.), *Collected black women's narratives* (pp. 1–89). New York: Oxford University Press.

Rahman, A. (1986). Unfinished women cry in no man's land while a bird dies in a gilded cage. In M. B. Wilkerson (Ed.), *9 plays by black women* (pp. 201–237). New York: New American Library.

Richards, J., Platt, J., & Weber, H. (1985). *Longman dictionary of applied linguistics.* Harlow, Essex, England: Longman.

Robins, K. N., & Adenika, T. J. (1987). Informal conversation topics among urban Afro-American women. In J. Penfield (Ed.), *Women and language in transition.* (pp. 180–195). New York: State University of New York Press.

Romaine, S. (1994). *Language in society: An introduction to sociolinguistics.* New York: Oxford University Press.

Rooks, B. (1991). Precious memories. In P. Bell-Scott et al. (Ed.), *Double stitch: Black women write about mothers and daughters* (pp. 119–122). New York: HarperCollins.

Rose, W. L. (Ed.). (1976). *A documentary history of slavery in North America.* New York: Oxford University Press.

Ryan, E. B., & Giles, H. (1982). *Attitudes towards language variation.* London: Edward Arnold.

Ryan, E. B., H. Giles, & R. J. Sebastian (1982). An integrative perspective for the study of attitudes toward language variation. In E. B. Ryan and H. Giles (1982). *Attitudes towards language variation.* (pp. 1–19). London: Edward Arnold.

Sanchez, S. (1989). Just don't never give up on love. In L. Goss and M. E. Barnes (Eds.), *Talk that talk: An anthology of African-American storytelling* (pp. 284–287). New York: Simon & Schuster.

Sanchez, S. (1991). Dear mama. In P. Bell-Scott et al. (Eds.), *Double stitch: Black women write about mothers & daughters* (pp. 24–26). New York: HarperCollins.

Schneider, D. M. (1980). *American kinship: A cultural account* (2nd ed.). Chicago: University of Chicago Press.

Schneider, D. M., & Smith, R. T. (1973). *Class differences and sex roles in American kinship and family structure.* Englewood Cliffs, NJ: Prentice-Hall.

Sewell, D. R. (1985). Varieties of language in the writings of Mark Twain. *Dissertation Abstract International 46:2,* 426A.

Shange, N. (1980). Aw babee, you so pretty. In M. H. Washington (Ed.), *Midnight birds: Stories of contemporary black women writers* (pp. 87–92). Garden City, NY: Anchor Press/Doubleday.

Shange, N. (1980). Comin to terms. In M. H. Washington (Ed.), *Midnight birds: Stories of contemporary black women writers* (pp. 251–254). Garden City, NY: Anchor Press/Doubleday.

Shange, N. (1985). *Betsey Brown: A novel.* New York: St. Martin's.

Sister Souljah. (1994). *No disrespect.* New York: Random House.

Smith, P. M. (1985). *Language, the sexes and society.* New York: Basil Blackwell.

Smitherman, G. (1994). *Black talk: Words and phrases from the hood to the amen corner.* Boston: Houghton Mifflin.

Stein, J., & Urdang, L. (1981). *The Random House dictionary of the English language.* New York: Random House.

Stevenson, B. (Ed.). (1988). *The journals of Charlotte Forten Grimke.* New York: Oxford University Press.

Stoelje, B. J. (1973). Bowlegged bastard: "A manner of speaking" speech behavior of black women. *Folklore Annual 4* (5), 152–178.

Tannen, D. (1984). *Conversational style: Analyzing talk among friends.* Norwood, NJ: Ablex.

Tate, E. E. (1987). *The secret of Gumbo Grove.* New York: Bantam.

Taylor, M. (1976). *Roll of thunder, hear my cry.* New York: Bantam.

Taylor, M. D. (1975). *Song of the trees.* New York: Bantam.

Taylor, M. D. (1981). *Let the circle be unbroken.* New York: Bantam.

Taylor, M. D. (1987). The friendship. In *The friendship and the gold Cadillac* (pp. 1–47). New York: Bantam Skylark.

Taylor, M. D. (1987). The gold Cadillac. In *The friendship and the gold Cadillac* (pp. 48–87). New York: Bantam Skylark.

Taylor, O. L. (1974). Black language: The research dimension. In J. L. Daniel (Ed.), *Black communication: Dimensions of research and instructions* (pp. 145–159). New York: Speech Communication Association.

Taylor, S. K. (1988). Reminiscences of my life in camp: With the 33d United States colored troops late 1st S.C. volunteers. In H. L. Gates Jr. (Ed.), *Collected black women's narratives* (pp. 1–75). New York: Oxford University Press.

Thorne, B., & Henley, N. (Eds.). (1975). *Language and sex: Difference and dominance.* Rowley MA: Newbury House.

Thorne, B., Kramarae, C., & Henley, N. (Eds.). (1983). *Language, gender, and society.* Rowley, MA: Newbury House.

Trudgill, P. (1983). *Sociolinguistics: An introduction to language and society.* New York: Penguin.

Veit, R. (1986). *Discovering English grammar.* Boston: Houghton Mifflin.

Veney, B. (1988). The narrative of Bethany Veney a slave woman (pp. 1–47). In H. L. Gates Jr. (Ed.), *Collected black women's narratives* (pp. 1–47). New York: Oxford University Press.

Wade-Gayles, G. (1991). Connected to mama's spirit. In P. Bell-Scott et al. (Eds.), *Double stitch: Black women write about mothers & daughters* (pp. 214–238). New York: HarperCollins.

Walker, A. (1970). *The third life of Grange Copeland.* New York: Simon & Schuster.

Walker, A. (1982). *The color purple.* New York: Simon & Schuster.

Walker, A. (1985). Everyday use. In *The Norton anthology of literature by women* (pp. 2366–2374). New York : W. W. Norton.

Walker, A. (1989). *The temple of my familiar.* New York: Simon & Schuster.

Wallace, M. (1991). Baby faith. In P. Bell-Scott et al. (Eds.), *Double stitch: Black women write about mothers & daughters* (pp. 12–20). New York: HarperCollins.

Wardhaugh, R. (1986). *An introduction to sociolinguistics.* Oxford: Basil Blackwell.

Washington, M. H. (Ed.). (1980). *Midnight birds: Stories of contemporary Black women writers.* New York: Anchor Press/Doubleday.

Washington, M. H. (Ed.). (1991). *Memory of kin: Stories about family by black writers.* New York: Doubleday.

Weems, R. (1991). Hush. Mama's gotta go bye-bye. In P. Bell-Scott et al. (Eds.), *Double stitch: Black women write about mothers & daughters* (pp. 123–130). New York: HarperCollins.

West, D. (1995). *The wedding.* New York: Doubleday.

White, P. C. (1978). The bird cage. In M. H. Washington (Ed.), *Midnight birds: Stories of contemporary black women writers* (pp. 33–41). New York: Anchor Press/Doubleday.

Wilkerson, M. B. (Ed.). (1986). *9 plays by black women.* New York: New American Library.

Williams, S. (1970). Tell Martha not to moan. In T. Cade (Ed.), *The Black woman: An anthology* (pp. 42–55). New York: Penguin.

Williams, S. (1980). Meditations on history. In M. H. Washington (Ed.), *Midnight birds: Stories of contemporary black women writers* (pp. 200–248). New York: Anchor Press/Doubleday.

Wilson, H. E. (1983). *Our NIG; Or, sketches from the life of a free black, in a two-story white house, north. Showing that slavery's shadows fall even there.* New York: Random House.

Wolfram, W. (1991). *Dialects and American English.* Englewood Cliffs, NJ: Prentice-Hall.

Wolfram, W., & Christian, D. (1989). *Dialects and education: Issues and answers.* Englewood Cliffs, NJ: Simon & Schuster.

Woodson, J. (1990). Causes. In J. Nestle and N. Holoch (Eds.), *Women on women: An anthology of American lesbian short fiction* (pp. 171–175). New York: Penguin.

Wright, R. (1977). Black language research from a black perspective: Some new data to consider. Unpublished manuscript. Howard University.

Wright, S. E. (1969). *This child's gonna live.* New York: The City University of New York.

Index

234

Index

D, AAVE consonants, 23–24
Daddy Was a Numbers Runner, 120
Damn/damned,184, 193–195, 197, 209; adverb, 90, 196
Dare [to], female verbs, 58–59
De Klerk, Vivian, 150
De, NSE structures, 56
Dee, Ruby: adjectives, 75; adverbs, 85, 94, 96; forms of address, 126
Delaney sisters (Bessie and Sadie): AAVE structures, 36; abusive swearing, 187; adjectives, 69, 73, 74; adverbs, 85, 86, 88, 90, 92, 95–96, 102, 105, 113; language use, 204; metalanguage, 210–211; NSE structures, 49; Standard structures, 62; word choice, 135, 138–139; wordplay, 143, 156
Demonstrative, adjective type, 67
DeVeaux, Alexis: adjectives, 71, 78–79; adverbs, 90–91, 102, 105; expressive behavior, 172, 174; expressive language, 166, 169; forms of address, 122; NSE structures, 48, 53; NSE vowels, 22; swearwords, 193; world play, 144, 154, 156–157
Dialects and American English, 18, 39
Dialogue, African American writings, 2
Dick, taboo word, 183
Dillard, J. L.: AAVE consonants, 23, 26; AAVE structures, 27, 30–31, 37
Disappearing Act, 172
Distressed, use of adjectives, 73
Do: AAVE structures, 6; absence of auxiliary, 47–48, 56; Standard structures, 57
Documentary History of Slavery in North America, 80
Does, NSE structures, 46
Done: completive, 27–29, 36–37; past participle, 42
Dove, Rita: abusive swearing, 184; adjectives, 72; adverbs, 90, 99, 102, 107–110, 112; expressive behavior, 172, 175, 177; language use, 211, 215–216; NSE structures, 50; Standard structures, 60; wordplay, 152–153, 159
"Down by the Riverside," 133

Downright, adverb, 100
Drag, slang expressions, 156–157
Dubois, Silvie, 62, 193, 194

E, NSE vowel patterns, 19, 20, 21
Edwards, John R., 199
Endearment terms, 6, 129–130, 216
English (British), influence of, 15, 79–80
English: non-Standard and Standard form, 3
Enough, adverb, 99–100
Entirely, adverb, 95
Erlich, H., 2
Ethnic groups: adjectives, 67, 74, 82; language usage, 1, 3, 4; word choice, 133
"Ethnic" adjectives, 78–80
Euphemisms, wordplay, 147–148, 160
Evil, AAVE adjective, 76
Exasperation, tag question, 61
Exclamations, expressive language, 6–7, 162, 170
Expletives: expressive language, 6–7, 164–165; swearing, 184–185
Expressive behavior, 170–180
Expressive language, patters of use, 6–7, 161–170, 215
Eyeball, expressive behavior, 172, 179
Eyes, expressive behavior, 171–172, 179

F: AAVE consonants, 24–25; NSE consonants, 11
"Family," 126
Fasold, R., 117
Fauset, Jessie: adjectives, 71–72, 82; adverbs, 89–90, 94, 102, 107–108; bad language, 186–187, 195; expressive behavior, 178; expressive language, 168; forms of address, 118, 130; language use, 202, 204, 206, 210; northern dialect, 2–3; NSE structures, 53; Standard structures, 58–60, 63–64; word choice, 136; wordplay, 148, 151, 153, 155, 157–159
Female language: adjectives, 6, 67, 70–74, 82, 215; adverbs, 98, 106–110, 215; forms, 164–165; speech stereotypes, 5, 161; Standard structures, 57–58, 60–61

About the Author

BARBARA HILL HUDSON is Professor of English at Indiana University of Pennsylvania.